S0-ATI-556

THE BRITISH NEW TOWNS POLICY

Harvard City Planning Studies | XVI

THE BRITISH NEW TOWNS POLICY

Problems and Implications

Lloyd Rodwin

HARVARD UNIVERSITY PRESS · CAMBRIDGE · 1956

HT
164
.G5R6

© Copyright 1956 by the President and Fellows of Harvard College

Distributed in Great Britain by
Geoffrey Cumberlege, Oxford University Press, London

Library of Congress Catalog Card Number 56–6512
Printed in the United States of America

TO MY MOTHER AND FATHER

Foreword

The good fortune of my friendship with Lloyd Rodwin has enabled me to be in some touch with that part of his work over the past decade which is reflected in this book. We met at the University of Wisconsin in 1945. His work in land economics at that center of pioneering in the subject, and mine in public administration gave us common ground for discussions, from which I derived much pleasure and profit. A particular topic of interest to us then was Ebenezer Howard's ideas on the garden city and their possible significance for the modern metropolis. We could hardly have guessed, flattering as it may be to think otherwise, that the main ideas would be adopted by the Labour government under Prime Minister Attlee and developed in subsequent legislation and administration as the British policy of "new towns." Mr. Rodwin prepared at that time an examination of Ebenezer Howard's proposals, relating them to other aspects of land use, to the "journey to work," ideas of industrial location, public finance, and similar considerations. Something of that paper of ten years ago has its place in the present volume.

So many of us were enthusiastic at the challenge of the new towns policy, based as it was on considerable British experience and on a series of committee reports on land use, distribution of population, and related questions, that I was struck with the objectivity of Mr. Rodwin's informed analysis, which was also reflective of his human sympathy with the aims of its sponsors. As the policy has unfolded in subsequent applications, difficulties and frustrations, in part the product of the larger catastrophic forces affecting British life after the war, have been experienced. Many former enthusiasts have become disillusioned or lukewarm. But here again I have been impressed by the way in which Mr. Rodwin has retained his even temper and intellectual integrity in his further studies of the new towns program. He used opportunities that came with travel abroad and with a faculty appointment at the Department of Civic Design at the University of Liverpool to obtain direct acquaintance with the evolution of the program. He has traced its interrelations with many agencies of the national and local governments, with professional and civic associations, and with the participants in the planning and development of the new towns thus far authorized and constructed. And he has demonstrated so clearly that a scholar in the social studies may unite a sharing of social responsibility with the forwarding of scientific method that he is entitled to include in this volume an appendix on the education and training of personnel for city and regional planning.

The substantive issues in the new towns program are important to everyone. We live in a period of rapid urban growth. But it is the suburban and metropolitan aspects of this growth which create some of the most difficult problems. These include problems not only of physical design but also of social design — the relation of population to area, and the design of appropriate legal, administrative, and fiscal units and procedures of government. Even if one rejects the idea of change through the device of new towns, or Mr. Rodwin's conception of the new town as one of a kit of tools available to the city planners for use under certain conditions, there is still much to be learned from this careful account of the British experience that is relevant to the physical and social development of cities. That development continues relentlessly. It causes alarm and criticism because of the costs, wastes, hazards to life, inefficiencies, ugliness, and the complex and resented tasks of citizenship which accompany it. Yet there are also achievements here and there which should be known to us. Mr. Rodwin has sought to learn from the decade of experience with this particular device, the new town, and gives us this interim report with data and references which enable us to explore particular phases further.

I have been reading his manuscript after completing a journey of six thousand miles by automobile, which extended from New England to Texas, the Upper Mississippi Valley, and Ontario. I have been trying to assimilate that wonderful experience with its total sense of the power and range of resources and variety of cultures of this less than half of the United States and Canada, and that not the most dramatic sample. Everywhere there is the expansion of cities and villages into open country. Some of the results are sobering and depressing at first and fleeting view. There is the increase in traffic hazards and frustrations, the ugliness of main-traveled ways that seem to be an almost endless street of shoddy and confused building and neon lights winding about the continent of North America. Yet there are the balancing particular features of well-designed roads, schools, playgrounds, industrial plants, and bridges. One recalls gratefully a recreational area evolved from a TVA dam-created lake in North Carolina; a superb camping area incorporating an old submarginal land project in Georgia, where some county health centers also impress even the hurried motorist; the embanked and engardened river in the heart of San Antonio; and the Blue Ridge Parkway. The depressing features come partly from the fact that the myriad of individual decisions to have a neon light or a particular structure seem to be taken without regard for the concealed costs to others, to everybody else. The cost accounting is incomplete, the consequences unexamined, because "the public," as John Dewey has pointed out, has not yet recognized itself and organized through genuine agents so that it might be consulted when the decisions that are to affect it are being made. But we have discovered that even air and water, traditionally ample and free, are not easy to have in proper quantity and quality, and that human life itself is cheap when automobile ownership mounts with horsepower.

And when we do organize to make decisions relevant to our safety and welfare, the need for experience and skill in policy making, administration, and the selection of devices is great. Similarly there is the need for experience and skill in physical design, which here and there does give promise of what we might enjoy. The new towns experience is a cheap instruction, if we care to use it, at many points. The failures as well as successes, the earthy problems of water supply and sewage disposal as well as those of finance, industrial location, relation to existing cities or to natural resources, distribution of population by age or income, of "home rule" vs. central or regional powers, as a part of that experience, are here to instruct us and suggest clues and hints to put alongside our own native brands. I am grateful therefore that Mr. Rodwin has made this book, both for its substance and for the way in which he has gone about it. He has worked patiently, modestly, and hard to record a ten-year experience when it was happening. He has kept both sympathy and skepticism in balance. And the essence of his study is of universal importance: how can we all live more safely, less wastefully, more richly, in our urban and rural landscapes?

JOHN M. GAUS
Professor of Government
Harvard University

CONTENTS

CONTENTS

CONTENTS

NEW TOWNS: PROMISE AND REALITY

PART | **I**

"What would you ask of Philosophy? To feed you on sweets and lull you in your errors in the hope that death may overtake you before you understood anything . . . Did you think because I would not spare you that I never felt the cold steel? Has not my own heart been pierced? Shed your tears, my son, shed your tears. The young man who has not wept is a savage, and the old man who will not laugh is a fool." (G. Santayana, **Dialogues in Limbo**)

CHAPTER 1

The British New Towns Policy

New towns have been built and old ones renewed since the earliest times. But a national policy of building within a few years complete communities to serve new needs and to help recast our urban environment is something unique in urban history. Only in 1946 in Britain did this first become official government policy.

Fifteen towns are now underway. More and more persons are curious about the evolution and adequacy of the ideas, the workings of the administrative mechanism, the problems encountered, the prospects for adaptation to different needs. Many countries are beginning to explore similar policies. Whether justified or not, the belief is spreading that guided urban growth and decentralization with government assistance can transform the quality, the efficiency, and even the possibilities for defense of our physical environment. Some of these prospects have caught the attention and even influenced the policies of leading planners in Sweden, Greece, India, Ceylon, Canada, Columbia, the United States, and many other countries.

This interest is not surprising. There are times when certain ideas can be more easily grasped, when their application is especially feasible, when the world is peculiarly susceptible to their influence and appeal. That is the present significance of building new towns. The world is ripe for the dissemination of these ideas. In Asia, Africa, the Middle East, South America, and still other developing areas of the globe, technological and economic development spells urbanization on a gigantic scale. In Western countries, too, new cities will be built because of changing utilization of resources, new industries, and technological innovations.

3

There is widespread discontent with slums and congestion, ugliness and squalor, waste and inefficiency. Population growth, economic progress, and the rise of real income are creating the conditions and the incentives for urban reconstruction. These trends are being reinforced by the increasing scope of government action, the growing importance attached to housing and environment in the politics of welfare, and the support of decentralization in some quarters as one of the means for reducing urban vulnerability if war should occur.

But building new towns is no easy task. Fascinating, frustrating, inadequately explored, the problems range from the mechanics of administration, financing, and development to intriguing normative issues. Should such towns be built? How? What kind of organization can best guide their development? What should be their role and scope? Who should make the decisions? How are policy conflicts to be resolved? What range of experiment should be permitted? How will the costs be borne? What kinds of cities are desirable? What makes a town attractive? How practical or feasible is this goal of comprehensive planning of functions and purposes, growth and renewal, efficiency and design? These and still other knotty questions face those who are bold or presumptuous enough to proclaim these objectives.

This book examines the British experience with new towns. It is not a comprehensive history of new towns, nor is it a definitive description of their operating characteristics. Instead it might be described as a case study of an important planning experiment. It is a retrospective evaluation of the problems of British new towns, problems associated with the ideas as originally formulated, problems encountered in their operating experience, problems which seem destined to emerge in their future development. This emphasis on the problems was deliberate. The basic question motivating this study is whether new towns make sense, taking into account the severest criticisms that can be leveled against the policy.

The analysis is divided into four parts. Following this section (Part I), the original garden city ideas are examined including the subsequent experiments with Letchworth and Welwyn, and the extraordinary convergence of forces that thrust these ideas into the arena of national policy. Then in Part III the present new towns policy is considered, i.e., the principal provisions of the legislation, the present position and characteristics of the program, and the reasons for the shift of emphasis that occurred with the subsequent town development legislation.

In each part of the study there is also a critical scrutiny of the ideas and policies under consideration. For example, following the historical analysis of the development and current status of the garden city ideas, the original hypothesis is re-examined taking into account empirical inadequacies, dubious assumptions, and fuzzy ideas. Similarly, an evaluation is made of the major problems of the new towns and town expansion policies. The analysis ranges from questions of organization of national planning and resource allocation to regional and local operating problems of timing, costs, rents, social organization, design, and the like. Case studies are also added to show how the individual experiences of the new towns reflected weaknesses dealt with earlier in more abstract terms. Some of the limitations of the planners themselves and of planning education are considered in the Appendix.

Only in Part IV is an estimate ventured of the positive accomplishments and ultimate significance of the new towns. These contributions are substantial. Offsetting the errors and discouraging limitations are the imponderable potentials of the policy: its spur to effort, its fruitfulness as a hypothesis with lessons for the future, its pioneering of the entrepreneurial phase of town planning, its importance as a technical tool for enriching the variety of our present urban environment, its possible use for channeling growth in underdeveloped areas and for reducing the vulnerability of our large cities, its significance as an idea in the history of planning.

Possibly a "systematic error" or bias may follow from the method of analysis and point of view. If so, perhaps it may help to counter the conclusions in favor of new towns. Despite blunders, disheartening setbacks, and some undeniable failures, the new towns policy looms as one of the most imaginative, fascinating, and even promising of the planning experiments in contemporary Britain. Some of the experiences to date are, alas, melancholy to contemplate. But the fault was not entirely the planners': certainly Britain's postwar economic crisis must share the responsibility. Nonetheless, the building of new towns has disclosed more frustrating limitations and problems than were anticipated by the planners and has required far more flexible tools, subtle understanding, and calculated foresight than were brought to the task. The weaknesses are evidenced by the assumptions, the experiences, and some of the changes in direction and emphasis. To the extent that these weaknesses persist, the program may fail to achieve its ultimate promise.

But the promise is rich indeed; and some rewards in technical experience and specific accomplishments have already been harvested. No final judgment is yet possible; but perhaps a confession and word of warning are in order. Like others this writer has been bewitched by his subject;

5

yet it is easy to see that the absurd, fumbling idealism often evident in the story may too easily confirm prejudices and dampen enthusiasm. Those apt to deride the idea should perhaps be reminded that there is at its core a luminous sanity which can teach us much and may some day mock the thoughtless detractors. The basis for this view is set forth largely in the last chapter; and no one has gauged the real worth of the policy who has failed to ponder deeply these considerations.

THE GARDEN CITY IDEA: A HISTORICAL APPRAISAL

PART | II

CHAPTER 2

Ebenezer Howard and the Campaign of History

The notion of recasting our urban environment in the form of garden cities owes its contemporary formulation to Ebenezer Howard. It was conceived in Britain in an age of repentant industrialism. But almost fifty years of further urban growth occurred, climaxed by a grave reconstruction crisis, before this idea received recognition as a desirable national policy. Perhaps another half-century or more may elapse before any significant transformation of the urban environment is visible. Whatever the future prospects may be, few ideas have ever presented such a forthright challenge to our thinking about a more sensible and coherent arrangement of the existing metropolis.

Ebenezer Howard and the Garden City Idea

Ebenezer Howard not only devised the idea of garden cities: he also founded the Garden Cities Association and journal; prompted the building of the two experimental garden cities, Letchworth and Welwyn; and indirectly was responsible for the adoption of the new towns policy. Howard's book, *Tomorrow: A Peaceful Path to Real Reform,*[1] outlining his proposals for a new form of urban growth and organization, is a planning classic. Still influential, it has been read by many planners throughout the world and has exerted a strong hold on many minds. Numbered among Howard's many distinguished supporters are George Bernard Shaw, Sir Raymond Unwin, Lewis Mumford, and Clarence Stein. In recognition of his contributions, this modest court stenographer was knighted and elected president of the International Housing and Town Planning Federation. These are no mean accomplishments: indeed they

9

are a remarkable commentary on the contagious quality and historical force of his ideas, and they make one wonder how this came to be.

Howard, according to one of his chief lieutenants and disciples, "was not of a masterful type, not brilliant or rich in conversation or intriguingly obscure, not learned, nor obviously clever." [2] In fact, almost nothing in Howard's nondescript background would tempt one to predict his future role.[3] His parents were thrifty, moderately prosperous shopkeepers, of earnest and somewhat conflicting religious views. They lived in the City of London, ran two shops, and managed to keep the family life happy despite the differences in their churches. Their tranquil life was not marred by the distracting controversies of the period: the ferment of reform bills; Chartist, Corn Law, and socialist movements; and the revolutionary ideas and outbreaks on the continent.[4] Howard, the second child of a family of nine, was born in 1850. A large part of his early education was received in small charming communities like Sudbury, Cheshunt, and Ipswich. Failing to achieve a distinguished record at school, he quit his studies at the age of fifteen. During the next six years he drifted through a series of odd jobs, developed his knack for invention, taught himself the Pitman shorthand system, and served for a short period as secretary to a noted evangelist, Dr. Joseph Parker. Concern about his lungs and his future prompted him together with two friends to migrate to the United States and take advantage of the homestead legislation. The three youths staked out adjoining sections of one hundred and sixty acres of virgin Nebraska farm land, "cooperatively built a one room shanty to sleep in and started farming." [5] The experiment for Howard and for one of his friends was a failure. They sold out and moved to Chicago, then rapidly recovering from its disastrous fire of 1871. Howard quickly secured employment as a shorthand writer, and his work "in Chicago and later in London took him into law courts, arbitration hearings, parliamentary debates, commissions and committees and introduced him into the worlds of business, administration and law." [6]

The period abroad decisively shaped his thinking. After experiencing the bleakness and frustration of farm life on Nebraska's prairies, he had sought better opportunities in a hectic, booming Chicago. New, grandiose schemes for development were being actively discussed. One of these, interestingly enough, was the idea of extending the existing belt of parks around the city, a feature which had already earned Chicago the title "The Garden City." [7] Apparently because of homesickness, Howard returned to London in 1876. He continued his work at shorthand, started and then dropped a connection as a partner of a shorthand firm, married in 1878, and had a happy family life while he continued to expend much time on his inventions, particularly a device for variable spacing of type-writers. Except for the adventure abroad, there is nothing in Howard's career up to this point that was particularly noteworthy or unconventional.

It was near the end of the century that Howard began to think of an ideal and practicable living pattern easily within grasp. What turned Howard's mind in this direction? Certainly not books. He was not a scholar. True, Edward Bellamy's concept of utopia, *Looking Backward*, a book which was sent to him by a friend, left a profound impression. But he was generally *au courant* of the ideas of others from the controversies of the time: the debates about the living conditions of the poor, the drift from the farms, cooperative ownership, socialism, anarchism, land taxation and nationalization, the conflict between religion and science, and the like. In this way Howard became familiar with E. G. Wakefield's and A. Marshall's proposals for colonization; with the views of T. Spence, H. Spencer, J. S. Mill, and Henry George on land tenure; with J. S. Buckingham's model city. But F. J. Osborn reiterates:

> That the idea of these writers entered into his thought is no doubt true; but they did so indirectly, . . . through the discussion of the period in societies and newspapers. It is a misconception to think of Howard poring patiently over the literature of the land question, colonization, and utopian projects, and working out where they are wrong and where they were right. No man ever had a less organized knowledge of the background of the subject to which he was to make a distinguished contribution.[8]

The gist of Howard's views was aptly summed up in his metaphor of the three magnets representing the town, the country, and the most felicitous combination of town and country. The country magnet had little power to attract: the beauties of nature and the advantages of sunshine, fresh air, and low rents were largely offset by long hours, low wages, crowded dwellings, deserted villages, and lack of society and amusements. The town's attractions were deceptive. There were alluring jobs and wages, palatial edifices and places of amusement; but there were also the isolation of crowds, distance from work, high rents and prices, costly drainage, foul air, slums, and gin palaces. "Combining the advantages of both and the disadvantages of neither"[9] was the third magnet, Howard's garden city. Like the holy synthesis of Hegelian dialectic, garden city offered both the beauty of nature and social opportunity; low taxes, prices, and rents; pure air and water and good drainage; easy access to fields and parks; no smoke, no slums; brighter homes and gardens, enterprise and high wages, freedom and cooperation.

More specifically, Howard proposed to build healthy communities of modest size, each owning its own land and surrounded by greenbelts beyond which a group of satellite communities might be formed. Metropolitan areas like London were to be emptied of their *excess* inhabitants. A balance was to be struck between home and industry and between town and country. Residents were to enjoy the advantages of access to the country and closeness to work, while additional markets would be made available to farmers. The plan was to be carried into effect at first by starting one or two demonstration projects to prove that it was feasible, and to show by example what needed to be learned and to be done. Once this was accomplished, public and government support was expected to follow readily enough.

The main objectives, W. A. Eden points out, accorded well "with the ordinary aspirations of the class to which Howard belonged, the somewhat earnest, chapel going or chapel emancipated lower middle class which had lately acquired political power and was destined to inaugurate a revolution by returning the Liberal Party with its high majority at the General Election of 1906." [10] It is scarcely necessary to remark how much these proposals reflect Howard's personal experiences in Britain and the United States; how much they also embody the British love of the countryside and loathing of the nineteenth-century factory and slum; and how much sympathy they exude for the attempts of eminent leaders like Lord Rosebery to stem the drift to the "Great Wen," to the "elephantiasis sucking into its gorged system half the life and the blood and the bone of the rural districts." [11] The proposals also afford, particularly to the proponents, another illustration of the British propensity and ingenuity at compromise, in short, "the English mind at its best: always in touch with the practicable, always in sight of the ideal." [12] Of all Howard's inventions, this one proved to be the most successful. How great an impact these ideas had on the thinking of some persons is brought out forcibly by Lewis Mumford's observation: "At the beginning of the twentieth century two great new inventions took form before our eyes: the airplane and the Garden City, both harbingers of a new age: the first gave man wings and the second promised him a better dwelling place when he came down to earth." [13]

The Garden Cities: Letchworth and Welwyn

Upon the publication of his book Howard received favorable reviews, attracted considerable public attention, and acquired some influential supporters. He lectured throughout the country, formed a Garden City Association, interviewed a number of prominent persons, and persuaded some of them to try out his ideas. In 1903 a company was formed to build Letchworth, the first garden city, to demonstrate its feasibility. It had an authorized capital of £300,000, and share dividends were limited to 5 per cent. However, only £100,000 of shares were subscribed at the end of the first year beyond the £40,000 pledged by the directors. The cost for the initial site alone was £150,000. The rest of the funds were secured from mortgages, entailing heavy interest charges in addition to administrative expenses before any revenues were earned.[14]

Development proceeded slowly. The management was not too vigorous, the organization weak, and there was some internal dissension between the business and ideological leaders.[15] The site too was badly located. It had few attractive natural features, was on a branch line of a railway, and at that time was quite distant from London. There were also financial difficulties, partly a consequence of the shortage of capital which harried the enterprise. In the method of keeping accounts, heavy interest payments and other capital expenditures were charged as operating costs before the project produced income. This led to disheartening balances. These difficulties were not offset by any signal accomplishments easily understood by the public; and soon interest in Letchworth, never too great, dwindled to a point where its objectives and possibilities were ignored, misunderstood, or associated with more traditional suburban developments. Twenty years were to elapse before the shareholders were to receive "their modest 5% per annum." [16] Though the waiting period was far too long for ordinary investors, the small band continued their efforts. At the end of forty-three years all of the accumulated dividends were repaid. It was this indefatigable faith which made Letchworth survive, despite all the difficulties, neglect, and derision.

When the government showed no interest in backing the policy following World War I, Howard, always skeptical of securing government assistance, cavalierly took an option in 1920 on some attractive land which had suddenly come up for sale. He decided to embark on a second demonstration project, this without enough funds, without any assurance of securing some additional adjoining land indispensable for any such scheme, and of course without consulting his supporters. However dismayed Howard's friends were by the thought of embarking on another slow, risky enterprise, which incidentally lessened the pressure on the government to back the garden city policy, they were obliged to follow his lead. Thus Welwyn Garden City, only twenty miles northwest of London and on the same main highway and railway system as Letchworth, came into being.[17]

Difficulties were encountered almost from the start.[18] Understandably enough, the Letchworth directors feared the competitive effects of Welwyn's development. This was one reason why there was little cooperation between the two enterprises. Far more serious were the problems of raising capital. The company dividends were limited to 7 per cent. This return, though cumulative, was inadequate since 10 per cent and more were being received elsewhere. These difficulties were compounded by the postwar depression and by the failure to raise more than £99,000 during the first year, whereas the site alone cost £106,000, not to mention approximately £16,000 incurred as expenses. The company would have foundered if the directors had not personally subscribed for an additional £100,000. Though another £22,000 were raised in the next two years from the sale of shares to the public, the company was forced to borrow additional funds. Another £150,000 was sought by issuing debentures bearing interest at 6 to 7 per cent per annum. The interest charges were paid, although they were treated as capital costs. As a result, "it was not possible in the early stages to show a revenue position that made the security sufficiently attractive to the investor who had no particular interest in Garden Cities." [19]

For these reasons, government funds were sought. They were eventually obtained from the Public Works Loan Commissioners, by taking advantage of a clause written into the Housing Act of 1921 which provided for loans to garden cities. Less money was made available than was expected; and the loans were made grudgingly, erratically, and always subject to approval from the Treasury. The assistance also entailed unwelcome obligations and supervision. Differences of opinion developed over the management of the enterprise and complicated the affairs of the company. The slow development, policy conflicts among the board of directors, and the failure to earn profits resulted in administrative changes, financial crises, and heavy losses. A major reorganization occurred in 1931, when a large proportion of the debentures (approximately £400,000) were converted from securities bearing fixed interest to income stock entitling their holders to returns only out of the surplus revenues. A year later, selling the sewage works, the main sewers, and the water undertaking to the local authority and raising some additional private funds enabled the directors to free themselves from government control by repaying the public loan. But this did not suffice, and in 1934 there was a further reorganization. About £420,000 of the company's share capital was written off. Restrictions on dividends were also removed, thus dropping Howard's principle of giving the residents an equity in the development. In addition the authority of the local urban district council to appoint three directors, a special arrangement voluntarily introduced in Welwyn's original charter of organization, was abrogated. From then on the company earned small profits, until the transformation of the enterprise into a public development corporation under the new towns program.

Unawareness of many of the pitfalls, coupled with the extraordinary loyalty to the idea of garden cities, ranks high among the factors which account for the survival of the two towns. Whatever judgment one may form of the experiment, the fact is that the leaders succeeded in their initial objective.[20] Despite all the mistakes and obstacles, the towns were built; and because they were built, they have provided an enduring three-dimensional expression of the general ideas for all the world to see. In the process of development, the towns also pioneered some significant planning innovations, including use and density zoning, a form of ward or neighborhood planning, employment of an agricultural greenbelt to control urban size, and unified urban land ownership for the purpose of capturing rising land values for the benefit of the residents. A body of experience was also accumulated which gave some inkling of the difficulties ahead and some of the necessary conditions for execution of any larger program.

Emergence of the New Towns Policy

Upon Howard's death in 1928, the responsibility for promoting his ideas fell upon his little group of devoted associates, including C. B. Purdom, who has provided the most authoritative record of the experience of development of the garden cities,[21] and F. J. Osborn, Howard's chief lieutenant, now editor of *Town and Country Planning*,[22] whose forsenic and literary talents have made him the irrepressible pamphleteer and gadfly extraordinary of the Town and Country Planning Association. The campaign was slow and tortuous, and the failure to influence government policy on the general pattern of development was often dispiriting. But the two demonstration projects continued to arouse discussion, to attract some supporters, and to spread the idea to curious visitors. Meanwhile dissatisfaction with existing urban trends of development was mounting, and other events were occurring which were soon to provide the occasion for a wholesale revaluation of existing policies.

The housing shortage following World War I led the central government to adopt a policy of subsidies encouraging housing production by private builders and local authorities. This subsidy policy continued during the thirties, with emphasis on slum clearance and elimination of over-crowding. Though the policy was more or less effective in blunting the edge of the shortage and improving housing conditions, it also created miles of dreary housing which often bore no sensible relation to employ-ment and recreation areas, to schools, shops, or other facilities.[23]

In another branch of government, a separate set of policies was de-vised in the mid-thirties to deal with the then declining economic regions of Wales, Scotland, Cumberland, Lancashire, and northeast England. Activities in these areas, especially collieries, shipbuilding, and cotton mills, proved particularly vulnerable to depression. Younger men and women left the areas in droves. But most of the workers and their fam-ilies remained, and government leaders were apprehensive because of the mounting and persistent unemployment. There was considerable de-bate whether the workers should be encouraged to leave for the metro-politan areas in the South which offered greater economic opportunity. Retraining and other assistance programs were advocated and estab-lished. But there was also pressure to salvage the wasting resources of labor and social capital which remained in the depressed areas.[24] The government experimented with schemes for bringing employment to the workers. A Commissioner for Special Areas was appointed. Planned sites, industrial facilities, and assistance in various guises were provided. Plants were built, favorable credits extended, housing provided for key workers, and special subsidies made available for improving services and ameni-ties, including water and gas supplies, power, transport, the clearing of derelict land and its conversion to industrial and recreational land uses.

Meanwhile London and the surrounding counties continued to grow. After Howard first developed his ideas, the automobile was invented and has helped to spread suburbs even further in the distance. New roads, utilities, houses, and other facilities were built to accommodate the steady increase of population and economic activities. The journey to work grew longer and more costly. Development burgeoned along the major transportation routes, arousing angry but ineffectual protests. Agri-cultural interests fought the indiscriminate loss of good farm land; lovers of the countryside railed against the rape of natural areas of great beauty; recreational interests deplored the lack of parks and playing fields; trans-portation experts fumed at the congestion, accidents, and general reduc-tion of traffic efficiency occasioned by "ribbon development." [25]

In dealing with these problems, whether of housing, industrial es-tates, ribbon development, or preserving the countryside, the approach was piecemeal. Emphasis was always on remedying a particular evil.

16

There was scarcely any recognition of or interest in the possibilities of a comprehensive solution. Town planners, one of the groups most likely to adopt a broader approach, were an unimportant minority, frustrated by lack of money, power, and effective jurisdiction. Under the basic planning legislation, the Town and Country Planning Act of 1932, only a demoralizing amount of local action was possible. Adoption of plans was time consuming and difficult; modification was equally cumbersome. Power existed to prevent something from being done, but not to ensure desirable development along lines and in places deemed desirable. Refusal to allow private development carried the risk of charges for compensation. Planning powers were fragmented, being wielded by 1441 councils of counties, county boroughs, and local authorities in rural areas, with scarcely any coordination. As a result "only 5% of England and 1% of Wales were actually subject to operative schemes, and there were important towns and cities, and large county districts for which not even the preliminary steps had been taken." [26]

In response to these dilemmas, the garden city advocates had a plausible, even persuasive solution. Why build isolated housing schemes or trading estates, they argued, or incur heavy expenses for repeatedly expanding roads, water supply, sewage, and other municipal facilities? Why not limit the size of cities? Why not plan houses, industries, commercial activities, recreational and municipal services in some sensible coordinated pattern? Why pile further developments on a London already monstrous in size? Why not build in some other location where land is cheaper, where development is easier and more desirable, where people can be closer to the ground and to the countryside? By the end of the thirties the prospects of war and aerial attack excited fears concerning the size of London and its concentration of population and resources, lending even greater force to these arguments.

The matter finally came to a head in 1937 with the appointment by Neville Chamberlain, then Prime Minister, of a Royal Commission on the Distribution of the Industrial Population. Chaired by Sir Montagu Barlow, its assignment was

> to inquire into the causes which have influenced the present geographical distribution of the industrial population of Great Britain and the probable direction of any change in that direction in the future; to consider what social, economic or strategical disadvantages arise from the concentration of industries of the industrial population in large towns or in particular areas of the country; and to report what remedial measures, if any, should be taken in the national interest. [27]

17

The Barlow Commission, as it was popularly known, held lengthy hearings and deliberations. Accompanying its report published in 1940 were twenty-six volumes of testimony. The commission concluded that rapid urbanization had led to "a disastrous harvest of slums, sickness, stunted population and human misery";[28] plus higher costs because of higher site values, congestion, reduction of efficiency due to fatigue and long journeys to work; and military liabilities because of the density of population and economic activities. Chief among the policy recommendations was a proposal for a new agency, independent of any existing government department, a central authority with powers of fact gathering, research, publicity, and the like. The functions of this agency were to facilitate redevelopment of congested urban areas, to decentralize or disperse both industries and industrial population from such areas, and to encourage a reasonable balance and diversification of industrial development throughout the various regions of Great Britain. Among the methods advocated in pursuing these objectives were garden cities or garden suburbs, satellite towns, trading estates, and further development of existing small towns or regional centers. A warning was issued that if such developments were to be successful, unnecessary competition must be avoided and adequate account taken of the requirements of industry, the social and amenity needs of communities, and strategical considerations. Without excluding action by private enterprise or quasi-public limited dividend companies, it was recommended that municipalities should be encouraged to undertake such development, where necessary, on a regional basis with the cooperation and approval of the central authority. Though the commission was unanimous about the objectives, there were strong differences of opinion among the members concerning the power and organization of the proposed central authority: whether it should exercise negative or positive controls of the location of industry, whether regional organization of the authority was desirable, and whether any of these powers should be applied to other parts of the country than London.

The Barlow Report and its aftermath became the cornerstone of the postwar town-planning policy for a variety of reasons. Problems resulting from the dispersal proposal led to a major inquiry in 1941 by the Committee on Land Utilization in Rural Areas (the so-called Scott Committee) to explore the impact of such development, particularly industrial location, on agricultural land use.[29] The Barlow findings also instigated another committee, equally famous, the Expert Committee on Compensation and Betterment. Headed by Justice Uthwatt, the committee was instructed to find a solution for the heretofore baffling problems of compensation, which had handicapped any firm regulation of land use or any positive guidance of development.[30] Both the Scott and Uthwatt committees endorsed the Barlow Commission's proposal to establish a central authority. They also added a spate of specific recommendations on agricultural land use, industrial location, compensation policy, and town planning. If past experience was any guide, one might have expected these reports and their dramatic conclusions to be consigned for a long time to the limbo of good intentions: witness the fate of previous recommendations, such as those of the Unhealthy Areas Committee (1920) headed by Neville Chamberlain, and the Marley Committee Report (1934).[31] These committees had also commented favorably, but ineffectively, on garden city development and the barring of new factories in London. However, the war, the bombings, the need for reconstruction, and the prevalent desire to provide some tangible recompense for the sufferings and sacrifice of the period created a mood of expectancy; and as a consequence the Barlow, Scott, and Uthwatt proposals acquired an exceptional timeliness and relevance. The Greater London Plan also exercised a powerful catalytic effect, rising as it did like a phoenix out of the ashes of London, with proposals for reconstruction and for the accommodation of more than one million of the population in new towns and expanded small towns.[32]

Throughout the war years there was a vigorous discussion of these issues. To give some effect to the recommendation for a central authority, the Town and Country Planning Ministry was established by the coalition government in 1943. The new ministry fell heir to the planning functions of the Ministry of Works and Planning and the Ministry of Health. Additional specific functions were acquired later, enlarging the ministry's over-all responsibility to ensure "consistency and continuity in the framing and execution of a national policy with respect to the use and development of land throughout England and Wales." [33] Some interim planning measures were also passed to control development pending the preparation of planning schemes (the Town and Country Planning Act of 1943) and to acquire easily land necessary for redeveloping war-damaged or obsolescent areas at 1939 prices (the Town and Country Planning Act of 1944). A few policy pronouncements were also issued in the form of white papers. Otherwise no decisive action occurred before the end of the conflict.

One reason was that the coalition government had been loath to spark any controversies during the war on these issues. When the coalition dissolved, the succeeding Conservative government hesitated or appeared to hesitate in taking bold, drastic measures to control the location of industry, to tackle the problem of compensation, and to press for a policy of dispersal, though there was general acceptance of these principles as a basis for future policy. What action ultimately might have been taken in any of these directions had Winston Churchill's government not been abruptly overturned is hard to say. That there was doubt and uncertainty about the intentions and prospects is undeniable. This uncertainty vanished when the Labour Party came to power. The change of government wrought a radical transformation of the possibilities.

In the first flush of enthusiasm following their overwhelming victory, the new government possessed a contagious dynamism. It was eager to act promptly and was friendly to the town planners' objectives, consistent as they were with the Socialist government's credo that the state must increasingly take the initiative in production and development. There was another specially favorable circumstance. The new government still wielded many of the war powers, including control of building licenses and materials priorities; and so aside from the numerous prewar precedents for government controls and for government participation in development, particularly in housing and trading estates, controls never appeared more feasible, if not less irksome. There was also at hand an efficient civil service, ready to shoulder ambitious responsibilities and to a considerable extent sympathetic with the aims and objectives of the new ministers.

The mood and the circumstances made almost all goals appear within reach. Everything seemed to favor quick and bold innovations: the war and the reconstruction crisis; the overwhelming public recognition of, in fact insistence on, the need for action; the presence of an energetic group of political leaders ready to put into effect any policy apparently suited to the requirements of the situation and not inconsistent with the broadly defined objectives of the group in power. With an enthusiasm reminiscent of the early days of the New Deal, the Labour Party pressed for and succeeded in enacting a vast amount of legislation. The bulk of the measures dealt with the nationalization of the Bank of England, of coal, gas, electricity, airlines, railways, and medical services; but there was also much that was done about land use planning. The more important of these acts provided new procedures to facilitate prompt land acquisition by local authorities for housing and planning; more generous housing subsidies coupled with still higher housing standards; additional powers over industrial location to offset the costs of moving firms and their workers to development areas; and authorization to

establish national parks and encourage local nature reserves. Possibly
most important of all was the decision to create a new framework for
planning, the Town and Country Planning Act of 1947.[34] In broad outline
the new code contained the following provisions: (1) it consolidated
basic planning powers in the hands of the councils of 145 counties and
county boroughs, with provisions for delegation of these powers to
smaller authorities and for joint action where necessary to deal with still
larger areas; (2) it called for the preparation of comprehensive development plans by 1951, with provision for at least quinquennial revision
thereafter; (3) it required for all new industrial building of 5000 square
feet or over, industrial development certificates from the Board of Trade
indicating that the proposed developments were consistent with industrial location policy; (4) it dealt with the compensation problem by
transferring all development rights to the community and by making all
development subject to permission of the local planning authority or of
the central government; (5) it established a fund of £300,000,000 for
owners who incurred hardships under this legislation. (The last two provisions were repealed in 1953 by the Conservative government.)[35]

Despite this hectic and momentous legislative program the policy of
building new towns received astonishingly prompt attention. The Labour
Party took office in July 1945. By October 19, Lewis Silkin, the new
Labour Minister of Town and Country Planning, appointed a New
Towns Committee:

> To consider the general questions of the establishment, development, or-
> ganization and administration that will arise in the promotion of New
> Towns in furtherance of a policy of planned decentralization from con-
> gested urban areas; and in accordance therewith to suggest guiding prin-
> ciples on which towns should be established and developed as self con-
> tained and balanced communities for work and living.[36]

The new towns policy, it was felt, could attack in one stroke a whole
group of problems, including reconstruction, housing, and dispersal. London's growth and congestion would be halted; housing, a major postwar
need, would be rapidly provided in new balanced communities; population and economic activity would be redistributed for the benefit of other
areas. For a while many planners were emboldened to believe that national planning in Britain might well be coupled with the three-dimensional vision of a New Jerusalem which inspired some of the members of
the new government.

Led by the highly respected Lord Reith, former Minister of Works
and Planning,[37] and aided by the memoranda of a previous technical

committee of the Civil Service, the New Towns Committee submitted three reports in rapid succession, replete with recommendations of principle and detail. The committee knew the die was cast and acted swiftly. But it also took its responsibilities seriously. It was not enough, it asserted, "to avoid the mistakes and omissions of the past. Our responsibility . . . is rather to conduct an essay in civilization, by seizing an opportunity to design, solve and carry into execution for the benefit of coming generations the means for a happy and gracious way of life." [38] By the first of August 1946, the New Towns Act was passed: the building of new towns had become the official policy of the new government.

Summary Observations

New towns owe their existence to a man, a movement, and a unique set of historical conditions. Ebenezer Howard had witnessed the sprawling urban growth of the nineteenth century, had struggled to eke a living out of virgin soil, had personally experienced the attractions of the cities and the drift from the farm; and he was in a general way aware of the varied proposals for land reform, model cities, and cooperative enterprise which had been bruited about by the age. His distinctive personal contributions were (1) "a unique combination of proposals" [39] geared to substitute for the existing metropolis a cluster of small garden cities varied in activities and population, with each city administratively independent, owning its own land, limited in size, and surrounded by an agricultural greenbelt; (2) a mesmeric quality capable of infusing his book and his personal appeals with that indefinable contagious vitality which excites men's imagination and attracts their allegiance; (3) an empirical bent of mind which prompted him to develop Letchworth and Welwyn garden cities as specific examples of the ideas he espoused for all the world to see.

But Justice Holmes once observed, "A great man is a strategic point in the campaign of history, and part of his greatness consists in being there." [40] As decisive as Howard's unpredictable, creative personal response were the circumstances which gave Howard's ideas a heightened appeal and which provided the occasion for the transformation of his ideas into a national policy. It is unlikely that new towns would have been built in Britain were it not for the war, the bombings, and perhaps even the Labour Party's postwar victory. Indeed, adoption of the policy marked the culmination of many trends: the perennial dissatisfaction with the disorder, congestion, dirt, slums, and dangers of the overcrowded metropolis; the urge to guide urban growth and to replace a negative drift with a daring constructive policy; the concern over the loss of fertile agricultural soil to housing, commercial, and industrial development; the discontent with the monotonous housing built before the war, housing unrelated to employment centers or community facilities; and the impatience with the single-minded trading estates policy that encouraged industries in depressed economic areas but slighted housing and community facilities and also industrial development in other areas. The Barlow, Scott, and Uthwatt reports focused attention on these issues and some of the policy proposals. Wartime destruction and suffering aroused popular interest. The London plans fired the debates and gave rise to high expectations; they also sparked the legislation by calling for seven to ten new towns in the London region. Later housing and reconstruction crises helped to overwhelm the prestige of Churchill's wartime leadership; and thus new towns, an idea sponsored by the dissident housers and planners of the country, provided a novel attractive policy for the Labour Party suddenly catapulted into control of government.

CHAPTER **3**

Newtopia versus Megalopolis

Clarence Stein has warned us that "one can never accept a planning or architectural solution as final. . . When an idea becomes conventional it is time to think it through again. Never ending exploration
and the charting of new ways is the life force of the architect and the
New Town planner whose shield of battle should bear the simple device
— a question mark." [1] This is wise advice, which might be applied to some
aspects of the garden city thesis.

To begin with, one wonders how much of the persuasiveness of
Howard's ideas lies in the reminiscence of a golden past, in sheer nos-
talgia for small communities in a rural setting, for simple joys and virtues
missed in a metropolitan milieu. And how much of the attractiveness
comes from the foreshadowing of a modern utopia, from the apparent
reconciliation of technology and nature, town and country, place of residence and workplace, workers and employers, the needs of children and
the imperatives of the balance sheet? The aura of these romantic qualities tends to affect our critical sense. One almost hesitates to mention or
stress the flaws. Yet there are many and they are serious.

Thus the garden city proposals clearly stem from the problems of existing cities yet in some ways tend to slight them. Similarly, the means
suggested to secure the goals may contribute to failure to achieve them.
And though the object was to enlarge men's choices and opportunities,
the prospect appears disturbingly Procrustean. Possibly these limitations
may be better understood if we examine Howard's approach to existing
cities and a few of his more important assumptions.

24

Garden Cities and the Metropolis

Fundamentally Howard wanted to build new cities. Existing wealth is fugitive, he argued. Old physical patterns need not prevent the building of new modern towns. According to his views,

> These crowded cities have done their work; they were the best which a society largely based on selfishness and rapacity could construct, but they are in the nature of things entirely unadapted for a society in which the social side of our nature is demanding a larger share of recognition. . . Each generation should build to suit its own needs; and it is no more in the nature of things that men should continue to live in old areas because their ancestors lived in them, than it is that they should cherish the old beliefs which a wider faith and a more enlarged understanding have outgrown. The reader is, therefore, earnestly asked not to take it for granted that the large cities in which he may perhaps take a pardonable pride are necessarily in their present form, any more permanent than the stagecoach system which was the subject of so much admiration just at the very moment when it was about to be supplanted by the railways. *The simple issue to be faced, and faced resolutely, is: can better results be obtained by starting on a bold plan on comparatively virgin soil than by attempting to adapt our old cities to our newer and higher needs?* [sic] Thus fairly faced, the question can only be answered in one way; and when that simple fact is well grasped, the social revolution will speedily commence.[2]

The last chapter of *Garden Cities of Tomorrow* dealt with London as an example of how all the large and unwieldy cities might be treated. To add realism to his argument Howard asked his readers to assume that many new garden cities were springing up all over the country. Then he outlined his view of how the change might occur. Families would be attracted to the new towns from London and other large cities. The initial migration would be followed by even greater migration since the tax burden could be expected to increase for the population that remained. Faced with disaster, many landlords would bow to the inevitable. Rents would fall. The countryside would invade London. Its population would drop to one-fifth of what it was in 1900 — to less than one-fifteenth of what it is today.

But Howard believed that reconstructing London and similar cities would be a gigantic task, much harder in fact than creating new cities. Building on virgin soil, moreover, would avoid the problem of compensation and allow greater freedom in reconstruction. This tactic would also split the "selfish vested interests." Many landlords and capitalists would be willing to stake their fortunes on the new communities. Still others

25

would bow to the inexorable march of progress. These defections, plus the strength of the workers and farmers united in favor of the program, would presumably render opposition ineffectual. So he proposed building first a model garden city, then a group of "social" cities growing out of the parent city. He expected the reconstruction of London and other cities ultimately to follow. The principal emphasis was on building the garden cities; and the beneficial effects were presumably to filter down to existing cities. "Inevitably," said Howard.[3]

Actually about thirty to fifty years have been spent in getting the first two cities started. Letchworth was begun in 1903; Welwyn in 1920. Both experimental garden cities were in the London region. During this period London and the home counties increased by more than 5,000,000 persons. Letchworth and Welwyn together achieved barely three-fourths of one per cent of this increase: their total population in 1950 was 38,000, with 20,000 for Letchworth and 18,000 for Welwyn.[4]

Howard and his followers misjudged the time and resources required and also the growth and development which would occur outside of such cities. This could be illustrated in a simple way. Suppose, for example, twenty-five years was allowed as a reasonably generous period for building new towns after World War II. Assume also government help and encouragement. That would mean a generation had passed; and the next generation, as Howard suggested, might want to build differently.[5] Meanwhile, what would have been the prospect of realizing Howard's goal? How many towns would be built? At present there are only fifteen. Even if the number of new towns planned in Great Britain were more than doubled it seems doubtful whether Howard's program could have been realized; and whether large cities would not continue to grow. Between 3,000,000 and 4,000,000 homes were needed in England for the ten-year period following the war. Assume twenty new towns were built, each with a population of approximately 50,000. If there were three persons per family, 333,000 houses would be required. Any higher average number of persons per family, say four persons per family (which is the present new towns estimate), would lower still more the number of houses for new towns. Indeed, if forty to fifty towns including about 750,000 houses were built, it would still follow that most of the new construction would probably occur in existing urban areas and their extensions. Forty to fifty towns would be added to the 874 cities of approximately 75,000 or less in England and Wales, without significantly reducing the ninety-one larger cities or the fourteen cities of 250,000 or more.[6]

26

In these statistics no account has been taken of the probable short-ages of capital, technical talent and knowledge, the necessary rationing of resources, the desirability of building fewer towns more rapidly, and the well-nigh fatal political obstacles and counterpressures, especially if population and economic activity failed to increase significantly or if location trends moved in other directions. These observations do not prove that the new towns are undesirable, or that the influence of such a program may not be enormously constructive. They do suggest that we should not delude ourselves about what could probably be accomplished.

Municipal Government and Administration

Howard's mistaken emphasis on the new towns is well illustrated by his plan of government.[7] Each community was supposed to have an independent administration run somewhat along the lines of the commission plan, which was just becoming popular then. The passage of time has brought to light many defects of government by multiple executives, including poor coordination, lack of centralized control, and the understandable inability of the public to inform itself about efficient expert administrators. However, the most serious defect in Howard's proposal was not the commission plan but the stress on separate, self-contained towns. For the major problem was and still is [8] to transform the limited corporate jurisdictions of cities like London, Liverpool, Manchester, and Birmingham into more efficiently organized metropolitan regions. Even in Howard's plan for groups of garden cities, such an integrated political framework would have been indispensable for coordination between the various satellites and the original parent community.

Apparently Howard did not quite grasp the significance of adequately distributed political power and jurisdiction for independent communities. In commenting on the creation of these communities he indicated that "for administrative purposes there would be two cities" though "the people of the two towns would in reality represent one community." [9] It is precisely the failure of corporate boundaries to cover the requirements of what is essentially a single community that accounts for many critical problems of local government. Howard probably failed to emphasize these relationships because the new cities were thought of as outgrowths of the original garden city built on a virgin site. The parent city was more or less "perfect." The new garden city was only a replica, the latest model forced by growth. But the new community would presuppose different relationships if one of its principal functions were to facilitate the redevelopment and redistribution of the population of the

27

existing metropolitan community. Important differences would result in the timing and financing of development, the administrative controls, the services provided, the sharing of costs, the adequacy of the revenue base, etc. By stressing the independence of the garden city and the need for a decisive break with the existing community, the ties have been neglected and their importance underrated. There has been some recognition of this faulty perspective by the editor of the garden city journal, *Town and Country Planning*. "I am afraid," he observed, "that the Garden City Movement has itself been partly responsible for the neglect of the periphery of London. We have perhaps stressed too much the full blooded conception of the detached, isolated Garden City and we have not urged sufficiently the need for control of suburban development on Garden City lines." [10]

Population Trends

As population trends changed in Britain, many of Howard's ideas also acquired a different meaning. The chaotic era of city building had reached its climax long ago. With the rate of growth tending to level off, creation of new cities has assumed less importance. Of course, some new cities will develop because of interregional migration of industry and population, resource development programs and new inventions, processes and products. For better or worse, however, the major job of the foreseeable future will be to improve existing cities and hence to deal with existing social, economic, and political facts.

The consequences of these changes were reflected in two unanticipated developments. First, the plan proposed by Howard as a technique of building new small cities has become one of the approved methods of existing metropolitan growth. The principle of encouraging new communities surrounding the parent city has been accepted. But, as in the case of the Greater London Plan, the "Great Wen" is serving as a substitute for the parent garden city. [11] True, Howard contemplated siphoning out the population of London; but his plan of development, originally and fundamentally intended for garden city growth, has become one of the methods for guiding the growth of London, now more than twice as large as the metropolis he deemed too big.

The possibility of declining economic regions is the other unexpected circumstance. In the past, while London grew other areas were growing as well; but now with differential growth patterns — coupled with sharpened competition in international trade, the decline of the extraction industries, the emergence of new industries geared to a large home market, and possibly the migration of many Britons to Canada and Australia — "depressed areas" have developed instead. During the past twenty years, there has been much concern about the concentration of population in a few areas like London and the home counties; and there have been many efforts to puncture that concentration for the benefit of existing towns in other regions. When Sir P. Malcolm Stewart, first Commissioner for the Special Areas in England, argued in favor of discouraging further industrial development around London, it was not just to make London more livable and manageable but also to preserve and build up other parts of the country.[12] Similarly, studies by Political and Economic Planning (PEP) and other groups have objected to the spawning of new communities while there was a geographical shortage of economic opportunities within the existing economy. PEP contended that because "there are not enough mobile industries to go round, it will be impossible to satisfy the employment needs of existing individual communities, but . . . it may be possible to provide a better balance if several communities are considered together." [13]

Industrial Location

Reading Howard's plans for establishing new communities, one might suppose that garden cities could be located anywhere. There were few reasons for thinking otherwise if the workers walked to work and if the new town were basically self-contained. Indeed F. J. Osborn, one of Howard's chief lieutenants, has implied that the site of Letchworth was chosen almost deliberately without a search for any special advantages, in order to test the theory.[14] Though this may be true, to the outside observer it appears more likely that the site was not consciously selected to test the theory but was chosen because the theory ignored the importance of location.

Since industries tended to move away from areas of high rents and taxation, Howard assumed that they would be able to establish themselves wherever cheap land and "rates" were obtainable. Actually these factors alone are relatively unimportant for most industries. Many economic activities, including public utilities, central retail establishments, financial centers, amusement, cultural and government activities, and certain types of wholesaling and light industries have strong ties to central areas. Moreover, the bulk of the shifts which occur, even if outside the corporate limits, are usually not far from the city. Maximum distances from the center vary for different industries and with the development of transportation and improved technology. Probably far more intelligent

29

location and steering of industries is possible and even desirable. But there are some significant advantages in the present locations, and there appear to be certain limits beyond which most economic activities will not go. On the basis of fairly general location trends, distinctions have been drawn between movement to the periphery as opposed to diffusion within the surrounding counties and dispersal into other regions.[15] Noting these locational impulsions is important, since they suggest some of the reasons for urban concentration and they caution us against extravagant illusions on the subject of dispersal and location of cities.

Quite some time elapsed before the implications of the locational relationships were recognized by the leadership of the garden city movement. Some curious inconsistencies can be cited illustrative of this lag. Perhaps the most striking was an advertisement in *Town and Country Planning*, the official periodical of the garden city movement. It was an appeal to entrepreneurs, the aim being to attract industries to Letchworth by stressing the enormous advantages of the London market.[16] What a curious anomaly! Here were the evils of the "Great Wen" being used as a necessary and permanent bait to build the garden city of the future.

In his testimony before the Barlow Commission, which was investigating the distribution of the industrial population, Sir Edgar Bonham Carter, chairman of the first garden city, Letchworth, pointed out that Letchworth was approximately thirty-five miles from London, whereas most firms usually settled within a fifteen-mile radius. Many of Letchworth's development difficulties were attributed by Carter to this fact. Replying to a direct question, Sir Edgar agreed "that if Letchworth were to be planned again, it should be nearer London." [17] Similarly Theodore Chambers, chairman of Welwyn Garden City Company, emphasized with regard to Welwyn, the second garden city promoted at Howard's instigation, that "there is little doubt that proximity to London has been an important influence in promoting its growth." [18]

Journey to Work

Howard hardly bothered to argue the merits of the journey to work, so convinced was he of its utter lack of justification.[19] Increasingly wearisome travel was quite naturally linked with the evils of the hasty and amorphous expansion of enormous urban centers like London. The permanent necessity of riding to work was considered by Howard and others as one of the more important factors responsible for the deterioration of living conditions.

Since Howard's time, the invention of the automobile has added a new dimension to the problem. However bad it must have seemed then, the situation has apparently worsened, judged on the basis of congestion and the loss of time, energy, and money by the commuter. It is equally "costly" to the community, which has to provide expensive transportation facilities and services of all kinds to mushrooming peripheral areas. Howard's reaction in favor of communities that would abolish congestion and keep the worker's home within reasonable walking distance of employment was therefore quite understandable. Probably this is another reason why he neglected the relationships between the garden city and the existing metropolitan community.

Nonetheless, there are advantages in travel and commuting possibilities which merit more thorough exploration and reappraisal.[20] Part of the responsibility for burdensome and unnecessary trips lies in failure to control development at the outskirts of a city, poor location of factory and residential sites, unsatisfactory transportation facilities, and other results of poor or no planning. To some extent, the difficulties can be reduced by palliatives like staggered working hours and better train schedules. More long-range improvements can also be effected by foresighted guidance of urban growth and systems of land use.

Granting that necessary travel could be cut to an efficient minimum through such efforts, the daily journey would still appear to be indispensable for the functioning of the economy. For employers it means a welcome mobility of labor as well as a flexible labor market. Expansion of industries for the war effort would have been literally crippled by shortages in housing accommodations and labor unless industries had been able to rely heavily on a wider labor and housing market; and this would have been clearly impossible without resort to the journey to work.

Comparable elasticity is possible during peacetime when industries find it necessary to expand or contract, as, for example, in seasonal operations. Howard's program, to the extent that it presupposed keeping the size of cities modest, if not small, tacitly assumed a relatively small and stabilized labor force. But these limitations are often incompatible with the present needs of many economic activities. Larger cities are necessary for industries requiring a large, skilled labor force, ancillary activities, huge markets, highly specialized facilities, and the like. The size of future cities should depend far more on the functions performed and on the relative efficiency of scale, about which we know much too little, than on any a priori predilections.

For workers, the journey to work opens the prospect of varied, more, and better jobs. It likewise facilitates adjustment to changing circumstances such as factory relocation, residential shifts to preferred neighborhoods, flexibility for home ownership, and necessary opportunities for secondary wage earners. Until our economic system or social institutions reduce these uncertainties or requirements, the effects have to be reflected in one's planning.

PEP's report on the location of industry, which was largely concerned with general employment problems, has claimed that "it is even in theory impossible to reconcile the need for a maximum variety of industry and occupation with the need for a minimum journey to work." [21] Only groups of communities can furnish the flexibility required to maximize employment and stabilize the economic base of the region, or segments thereof. Within this "employment orbit" a satisfactory variety of industries and opportunities might be achieved. Kate Liepman, in her authoritative study, *The Journey to Work*,[22] approaches the problem from the point of view of the individual. She suggests that the journey must ultimately be accepted as the necessary price paid for greater industrial stability, superior employment possibilities, and a higher standard of living.

The Cost of Garden Cities

Howard and his followers conveniently assumed that garden cities could be justified on the grounds of cheaper costs. Since the evidence available is still skimpy and inconclusive, the issue will probably continue to be resolved by affirmation or by citing congenial facts.

There are several ways to analyze the problem. One might ask whether investments in garden cities would give higher returns, however that might be defined, than investments in education, health facilities, new industrial plants, roads, research, projects like the TVA, or perhaps general urban redevelopment. At least two types of measurements are possible. The comparative impact on productivity or output might be one guide. Relative consumer preferences could be another. To date, few adequate measures or data have been developed to assess the comparative effect on productivity of these or other alternatives. Evidence now available suggests that in the short run the returns are meager; over the long pull the benefits may be far more significant, but we really don't know.[23] Nor are we able to say whether any of these possibilities will contribute more to welfare as expressed in consumer preferences, except by crude and dubious measures such as questionnaires or votes; and even these rough indices have not been adequately explored.

Another approach might be to treat garden cities simply as one of several technical solutions for additional housing developments or for replacements which are necessary or unavoidable. The question then is whether garden cities are less expensive than other physical patterns which would be developed anyhow. To this question too a firm answer is not possible. Comparison is hazardous since other types of development vary considerably. There are many other possibilities besides the alternative of high-rise buildings in central areas, which is usually considered. There may be several ranges of intensity of development of the large city from the core to the periphery. There can also be linear alignments of residential, industrial, and service areas; the concentration of residential centers in the core and employment areas in the suburbs; the creation of clusters of industrial and shopping areas in the periphery, surrounded by residential areas; and still other unexplored possibilities.

Difficulties of comparison abound, even when similar standards are assumed. Account must be taken of capital and operating costs, private and public costs, overhead and "waiting" costs, short- and long-run costs, hidden costs of wasted facilities, and the like. These costs are not easy to establish: the data are generally inadequate; they also may change markedly with variations in the scale and speed of development, the relative efficiency of the building industry in handling different types of construction, the existence of surplus capacity in the existing municipal plant and services, and the relative costs of adding to plant and services. Moreover, the burden of these costs varies with the accounting unit used for their allocation and with the pattern of subsidies for building different types of housing or for purchasing and eliminating existing land uses in the metropolis.

Some persons think that garden cities are cheaper because lower land costs, plus profits from rising rents and land values of municipally owned land, would redound to the benefit of the public. Others emphasize the advantages of having more persons grow their own food, the savings from low density and planned development, or the closely aligned employment, residential, shopping, and country areas all within walking or short commuting distance. But even if correct, few of these claims are decisive.[24] Cities like Liverpool and Stockholm, which own much of their surrounding open land, reap similar benefits without necessarily building along garden city lines. On the other hand, a capital value tax system, like that of the United States, is in a sense a form of municipal land ownership, with increasing revenues for the community resulting from a formula geared to rising assessed values and tax rates. Labor spent in gardening is a cost, especially for those who prefer to occupy their time otherwise. It may often be less expensive (although not necessarily

33

more desirable) to get food commercially.[25] Presumed savings from low density, lower land costs, or planning may occur in many types of suburban development; and some of these savings may be offset by higher costs for roads and higher transportation costs for private and public services. Also, closeness to one's place of employment and to residential and rural districts may not necessarily involve lower costs, if closeness is defined not as a relationship between the principal wage earner and his present job but as the accessibility of many or of all wage earners to maximum opportunities for employment, shopping, and cultural activities.[26]

The most frequent argument of all is that as the scale of the city increases, costs rise. Doubtless efficiency decreases as a city grows beyond a certain size, just as it is equally true that costs increase if cities do not grow beyond a certain size. But it is not at all certain when these points have been reached; nor how they vary for different types of cities, regions, economic systems, technology, and the like. The claims are shrill, the answers not at all certain, and the difficulties surrounding analysis explain why no authoritative data are yet available to end the controversy. True, quite a varied assortment of criteria and data have been developing on aspects of how much different-sized cities cost.[27] But the variability in services has vitiated most of the comparisons. Suitable measurements of the quality, scope, efficiency, and need for public and private facilities are either unavailable or discouragingly inadequate. Conclusions from the surveys that have been made are generally partial, indeterminate, inconsistent, or dubious because of the limitations of the assumptions, methods, or data.

Certainly if the foregoing observations correctly represent our knowledge at this time, few persons who have strong opinions in this field are under any particular obligation to change them. At best they need only to mind the tenacity with which their views are espoused. Just as an example, when it can simultaneously be argued that transportation systems increase living costs but multiply employment opportunities, extend the area and costs of government services but widen the tax base, help to solve the problem of transportation but add to the possibilities of congestion, place further drain on our energy and health but enhance the possibilities for better services and a richer social life, it should be clear that prejudices are being confirmed while analysis is being shirked.

About the only sure item of agreement is the inability of private investors to finance garden cities without the privation and dangers of undercapitalization. The operation is too huge and takes too long. Possible advantages of long-run economies are counterbalanced by the initial capital outlays for plant and other facilities which are not self-liquidating, at least during the long development period. Hence there is a readiness to assume that the program will benefit the large neighboring city or the country generally, though on this score too the data are of course inadequate. But it is ironical that on the issue of financing, even the most ardent proponents will not insist that the garden cities should be independent or self-contained.

Procrustean Characteristics

There is a persistent tendency of the human mind to universalize personal solutions or ideals. In some ways Ebenezer Howard's proposals reflect this frailty; and in this sense his solution is on a par with Wright's "Broadacre City," Borsodi's "Sevenacres," Le Corbusier's "Ville Radieuse." All of these "solutions" are alike in their presumption and their Procrustean implications.

When one contemplates the variety of cities that may be desirable, the differences that may be involved in functions, preferences, technology, economic systems, cultures, time scale, and the diversity of tools that ought to be available for urban growth and redevelopment, the possible narrowness of Howard's simple recipe may give one qualms. Why impose an urban straitjacket? Why not have big, medium, and small cities; dormitories and self-contained cities; unitary, satellite, linear, star, finger, and ring shaped cities? Why not new towns of low and medium density, and high-density redevelopment schemes such as Lansbury?[28] Why may not all of these and still other possibilities prove adequate in varying circumstances and lend a welcome variety of physical environment for different needs and temperaments?

One is reminded of Sherwood Anderson's parable, "The Book of the Grotesque." The theme, it will be recalled, was

> that in the beginning when the world was young there were a great many thoughts but no such thing as a truth. Man made the truths himself and each truth was a composite of a great many vague thoughts. All about in the world were the truths and they were all beautiful. . .
>
> There was the truth of virginity and the truth of passion, the truth of wealth and of poverty; of thrift and of profligacy, of carelessness and abandon. Hundreds and hundreds were the truths and they were all beautiful.
>
> And then the people came along. Each as he appeared snatched up one of the truths and some who were quite strong snatched up a dozen of them.

35

It was the truths that made the people grotesques. The old man had quite an elaborate theory concerning the matter. It was his notion that the moment one of the people took one of the truths to himself, called it his truth, and tried to live his life by it, he became a grotesque and the truth he embraced became a falsehood.[29]

Garden cities embraced too fervently could also become grotesque.

Summary Observations

Some of Howard's proposals, penned even before the automobile appeared on the scene, are still highly suggestive and provocative. Examples are the notion of urban size limited by an agricultural greenbelt; the insistence on a plan of use and growth, not aimless settlement and sprawl; the emphasis on unified, balanced development of a whole community, not solely on residential, industrial, or commercial expansion.

But these more fruitful views might easily be discredited if they were not separated from those containing serious inadequacies. Howard misjudged the advantages, strength, and momentum of existing cities, trends in population growth, the strategy of urban location, the positive benefits of the journey to work, the problems of financing and of metropolitan organization. And like too many reformers, his solution gave short shrift to other alternatives.

These failings are understandable. There are always horizons to human vision. The wonder is that Howard formulated an ideal so persuasive even though partial. Possibly the explanation is that "the city has become indispensable to civilized existence, but at the same time subjects man to so many frustrations of his deepest longings [that] the notion of an ideal mode of life lying somewhere between the two extremes has been a force ever since cities have been in existence." [30]

But different tools and difficulties confront those who must work within an already established structure. Urban patterns will be as much a product of the past as of the future. Thinking, however imaginative, must reflect continuities as well as mutations, if it is to find practicable expression. He who would help build the city of tomorrow must reckon with the lives and living habits of human beings: with jobs and security, homes and population trends, esthetics and economics, politics and social drift. Prophets are sometimes exceptions: inspiration has its own intrinsic virtues and justification. But prophets should never be taken too literally, especially by subsequent generations.

NEW TOWNS AND TOWN DEVELOPMENT:

PROBLEMS OF EXECUTION

PART | III

The New Towns Act and the New Towns

With the passage of the New Towns Act, the building of cities for the first time in contemporary Western history became a concern of long-term *national* policy. The form, the growth, the character of the city as a whole had for a long time escaped national attention. Not that there weren't numerous building, planning, and other local regulations; but in the past, despite these regulations, the key characteristics of the city emerged from decisions of the private developers, the policies and practices of private landlords, of private builders, industrialists, traders, and property owners guided largely by markets, prices, and profits.

The new legislation relied on a different set of premises. Local and national policy was to decide the essential character of the community in advance. Private decisions were to be made within the framework of an over-all plan which embodied these social goals. The position, in short, was to be reversed. The city was no longer to be an incidental by-product of countless individual decisions made in the market with other ends in view. Instead it was to be the framework, presumably a more economical framework, within which other decisions were to be made.

There was some experience to aid the new policy: the earlier nineteenth-century community experiments with Saltaire, Port Sunlight, Bourneville; the more recent pioneering of the garden cities; the various activities and policies in housing, trading estates, and planning. But it was another matter to engineer a suitable administrative mechanism. To build new towns, machinery had to be created for organizing, planning, and decision making, for financing, site acquisition, building, and managing. This instrument had to be responsive to policies of the central gov-

3 9

ernment, yet able to serve local and regional needs and at the same time cope with all the traditional entrepreneurial problems on a vaster scale. It was a long-term job; and there were of course many possible ways of doing it. These included the use of one or more development agencies for all of the new towns, the choice of private or public corporations or local authorities, and a varied range of powers, financing devices, and design approaches. The task required an exacting combination of daring and restraint. Ideally what was needed was the efficiency and flexibility of the private corporation, the tough-minded financial calculus of the entrepreneur, the social and administrative accountability of the public authorities, and all the foresight and imagination with which the planner at his best should be endowed. In the light of these prerequisites, what in fact was actually done?

The Procedure for Building New Towns

Public corporations became "the chosen instrument" of the program. The New Towns Act authorized the creation of development corporations to plan, build, and for a certain period of time to manage each of the new towns whenever such action appeared to be "expedient in the national interest." [1] The decision whether such corporations were needed was to be made by the Minister of Housing and Local Government and by the Secretary of State for Scotland.[2] No limit was set on the number of new towns to be built, but not more than fifty million pounds could be encumbered in the first five years. Though the local authorities concerned had to be consulted, the use of local authorities and "authorized associations" for this purpose, which the Reith Committee had recommended, failed to receive the government's support.[3]

Initiative for the formation of these towns has come from the local or the central authorities. In the future, however, since "the county councils have become firmly established as the local planning authorities for their areas and are carrying out the surveys prescribed by the 1947 Act, it is expected that the first proposals for sites will come from them, either on their own initiative or in conjunction with their urban neighbours." [4] Before a town can be established, the minister has to prepare and publish a draft order and provide for hearings allowing an opportunity for objections to be heard. The hearings are not formal ratifications of previous decisions. They set the stage for vigorous discussion and controversy. On occasion they have retarded or modified the initial plans: the minister's designation orders were challenged by the residents of Stevenage, Hemel Hempstead, and Crawley and led to court battles; and the sites of Harlow, Crawley, Bracknell, Corby, and Hemel Hempstead were reduced because of forceful objections.

Site selection was made the responsibility of the ministry, though the development corporations exercise the compulsory purchase powers. Since the act requires the site to be designated before the development corporation is appointed, the ministry usually makes a rough sketch of the possible layout for guidance in land acquisition. The Reith Committee, assuming a range of population of 20,000 to 60,000 persons, suggested that the sites should usually vary between 5,500 and 11,000 acres. It felt that the site should include the entire built-up area and also a peripheral belt three-quarters of a mile across. Actually, the ministry has tried to keep the sites as small as possible because of the discouraging effects which the designation usually has on activities in the area, on farming especially. It also is confident that any undesirable development outside the area can be prevented by using the new planning powers.[5]

Acquiring suitable sites has proved to be one of the most vexatious tasks. It has not been easy to find several thousand acres of level land not valuable for agriculture, not subject to subsidence, reasonably serviced by roads and railways, relatively economical to supply with water, drainage, and sewerage, attractive to industry, and relatively accessible to congested areas — to mention some of the many factors that guide this choice. Many sites have been rejected because of their value for agriculture; and in other cases, to minimize the taking of fertile land or the sterilization of valuable mineral resources, the sites selected have been drastically cut in size to the detriment of subsequent planning.[6]

Final plans are made by the staff of the corporation, often after the initial plan has been prepared by outside consultants. The plans consist principally of the master plan, which indicates the comprehensive layout of land uses and transportation, the stages of development, and the necessary supporting data; and maps on topography, geological features, basic services, traffic, etc. In addition, specific development plans are also submitted to the minister. Preparation of these plans requires close consultation with the existing local officials and with many other groups affected by the program. When the comprehensive plan is completed, hearings are generally held to gauge public support and to discover any possible objections overlooked by the planners.

The minister must consult the local authorities before giving his approval of the plans. To avoid a second review, the new town corporations have been freed of the obligation to secure the approval of the local planning authorities as well. Since the corporation has a dominant interest in the area of the new towns, the minister generally requests the local planning authority to consult with the corporation on any formal requests it may receive for developing or changing the land use in the area. If there is any disagreement on the handling of the request, the issue must be referred to the ministry. These can be somewhat touchy matters because the powers of the local planning authority are being superseded by the development corporation. Fortunately experience thus far has been quite favorable.

To build the town, the act gives the corporation the "power to acquire, hold, manage and dispose of land and other property, to carry out building and other operations, to provide water, electricity, gas, sewerage and other services, to carry out any business or undertaking in or for the purposes of the new town, and generally to do anything necessary or expedient for the purposes of the new town or for purposes incidental thereto." [7] However, these powers are actually more circumscribed than the language seems to imply. The corporations are strictly confined by a provision obligating them "to conform to the general law." [8] They can plan and build houses, factories, and shops; and it "is relatively easy for them, where necessary, to obtain sewerage and water supply powers normally vested in local authorities or water companies, but beyond this, in general development corporations cannot exercise the functions which elsewhere would be undertaken by local authorities." [9] Construction is usually handled by outside contractors.[10] As the program has matured, a huge labor force has been built up. Some of the London new towns have had as many as 1,500–2,500 persons employed on their sites.

The act allows the corporation, with the minister's approval, to make financial contributions to offset costs incurred for services rendered by local authorities or statutory undertakers.* In cases where these authorities are unable or unwilling to provide the services, the development corporation may accept the responsibility, with the expectation of receiving some financial payments from the authority responsible for the service. The basis for such payments has never been spelled out. Since there is considerable interdependence in the timing of the provision of the water supply, sewerage, roads, schools, and other services, serious delays may be the consequence when disagreement develops over the sharing of costs.

Financing is entirely the responsibility of the central government. The corporations cannot borrow money independently. This has been a

* Statutory undertakers are concerns authorized by law to carry on transport undertakings and supply electricity, gas, and water services. They receive special privileges from Parliament in recognition of their public obligations.

mixed blessing since the terms are inflexible.[11] Neither the minister nor the Treasury can approve the advance of funds for any specific development proposal unless it is likely to secure "a return which is reasonable having regard to all the circumstances." [12] Financial control is exercised through the ministry by detailed examination of the justification for any major proposal and by supervision of the budgets submitted by the corporations. These budgets include proposed expenditures and receipts, anticipated costs of each project, and future expenditures estimated to be necessary.

The loans have to be repaid "over such periods and on such terms as may be approved by the Treasury." [13] At present the corporations secure sixty-year loans at Public Works Loan Board rates. Interest rates, formerly 3 per cent, have risen beyond 4 per cent. The corporation would prefer the shorter-term loans and lower interest rates enjoyed by the local authorities.[14] The minister has also permitted deferment of the payment of capital, but not interest, for a maximum period of five years. All of the corporations have naturally taken advantage of this arrangement.

In addition to the repayable advances, grants too are provided by the minister. These grants, which meet 50 per cent of the deficits incurred in the first year of operation and 25 per cent in the following year, are intended to cover part of the initial organizing expenses. The remaining deficits are carried on the capital accounts and thus charged to the cost of the town. The corporation also receives the customary central government subsidies for housing, and the ministry has arranged to give to the corporation the share of the housing subsidies normally paid by local authorities. In 1953, the ministry also made it possible for congested local authorities to pay the usual local housing subsidies for approximately ten years; and in return these authorities received the right to nominate tenants for housing in the new town. (The reason for this later arrangement and its significance are discussed in more detail in Chapter 9.) Save for these grants, the investment is expected to be self-liquidating.[15] After ten or fifteen years, when the town is expected to be completed, the corporation will be dissolved and the assets handed over to the appropriate local authority. No one quite knows whether controls can or will be imposed to see that the new towns do not thereafter veer away from their established objectives.

To do its job, the development corporations have an administrative staff ranging in size from about sixty to seventy-five for towns like Corby and Aycliffe to approximately three hundred for the larger towns like Hemel Hempstead, Harlow, and Crawley. Usually the key administrative officials are the general manager, who is the chief executive officer responsible directly to the chairman of the development corporation, plus the chief architect, the engineer, the estates officer, and the legal officer. This staff serves the corporation members who are responsible for the basic policy decisions. There can be not more than seven members in addition to the chairman and vice-chairman. At least one of them must live in or have special knowledge of the area; the others are presumably men of wide experience representing many points of view. Men of distinction and ability have already served or are serving part time on the corporations, including Lord Beveridge, Lord Reith, Sir Ernest Gowers, Sir Thomas Bennett, Sir Lancelot Keay, Mr. Henry W. Wells, Mr. Richard R. Costain, and many others.

The ministry to which the corporations are responsible was created in 1943. Established as the Ministry of Town and Country Planning, it later was assigned responsibility for housing and local government and became the Ministry of Housing and Local Government. The ministry is the over-all organization coordinating the National Parks Commission, the Central Land Board, and the new town development corporations. Interdepartmental and regional committees are used to integrate policies of the several ministries concerned with transportation, industrial location, agricultural land use, and public works — functions that lie outside the jurisdiction of the junior ministry. Of the total staff of approximately 1200 persons employed, almost one third are professional or specialized personnel.[16] There is also a small research section in the ministry, staffed by persons trained primarily in geography, geology, and town planning. Almost all of the research, however, consists of surveys and fact gathering for decisions on administrative policy.

This, in brief, is the machinery devised to build new towns. Development has frequently faltered during the first five years, but the "creeping stage" is now over. Whatever limitations may affect its operation it is at least functioning as a going concern.

The Present Position

Of the new towns under construction, ten are intended to relieve congestion in metropolitan areas. (See Map 1: New Town Sites in Great Britain.) There are eight in the London region: Harlow in West Essex; Basildon in South Essex; Stevenage, Hatfield, and Welwyn Garden City, north of London in Hertfordshire; Hemel Hempstead, northwest of London; Bracknell in Berkshire; and Crawley in Sussex, south of London. (See Map 2: London New Towns.) In addition, there are five "independ-

44

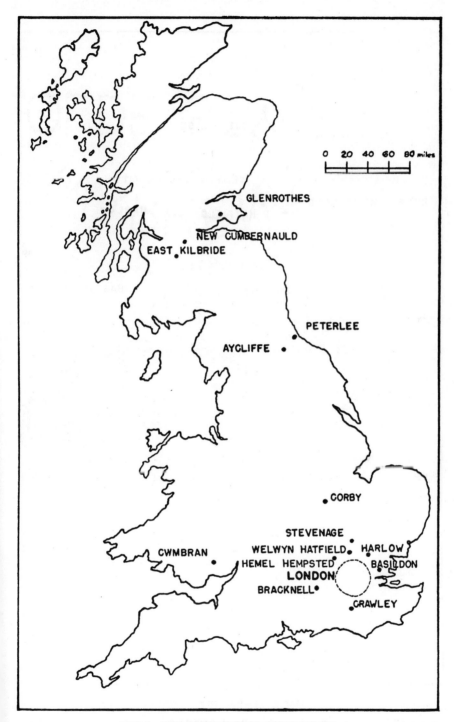

MAP 1. NEW TOWN SITES IN GREAT BRITAIN

Source: Ministry of Local Government and Planning, Town and Country Planning, 1943–1951, Cmd. 8204 (London: HMSO, 1951), p. 138; L. E. White, New Towns: Their Challenge and Opportunity (London: The National Council of Special Service, 1951), facing p. 17.

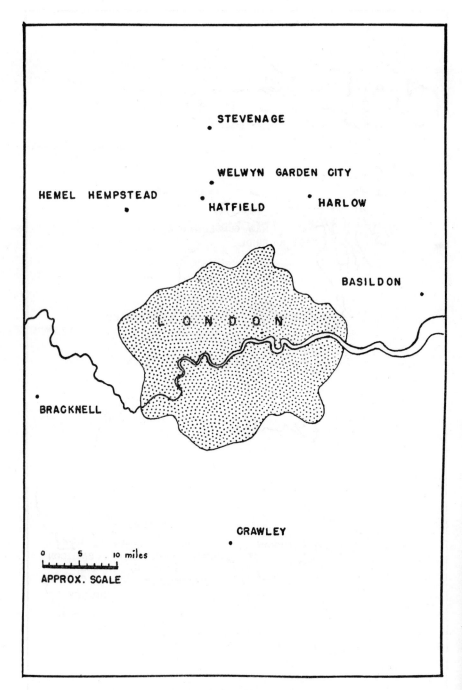

MAP 2. LONDON NEW TOWNS

Source: Ministry of Local Government and Planning (1951).

ent towns": Corby in Northamptonshire; Cwmbran in South Wales; New-ton Aycliffe and Peterlee, both in County Durham. There are also three new towns in Scotland: Glenrothes in Fifeshire; East Kilbride, six miles southeast of Glasgow; and New Cumbernauld, the most recent new town, designated in the summer of 1955, twelve miles east of Glasgow.

For the present, few, if any, additional new towns are contemplated. Since the Committee of Public Accounts has complained of the extraordinary ministerial discretion contained in the New Towns Act, Mr. Macmillan, the former Conservative Minister of Housing and Local Government, promised that in the future no new towns would be started in England and Wales without prior Parliamentary approval.[17]

During the first three or four years, the rate of building was depressingly slow. The corporations were principally preoccupied with their organizations, the making of plans, the building up of a labor force, and the solution of some of the ticklish problems of securing water, sewerage, electricity, roads, and the like. When the program had been under way little more than a year, the economic crisis occurred. The impact on the program was almost fatal. Losses of foreign markets, shipping, and investments during World War II, coupled with steadily shrinking gold reserves and the specter of insolvency, made rapid increases of exports and immediate gains in productivity overriding necessities. They offered the only way to secure the necessary imports, including half the nation's food. Investment was concentrated on dollar-earning projects. All other activities were sharply curtailed, including work on new towns not serving "immediate industrial needs." [18] The policy affected mainly the four London new towns: Stevenage, Crawley, Harlow, and Hemel Hempstead. The labor force was cut. Only a minimum amount of site preparation was permitted. Since Peterlee was held up for other reasons, and the other new towns had not yet come into being, Newton Aycliffe (the smallest of the new towns) and East Kilbride near Glasgow were the only ones able to push ahead.

As economic conditions improved, the reins were gradually relaxed and by 1950 were almost fully removed. At the present time, most of the towns have entered the phase of large-scale construction, attraction of industry, and securing adequate schools, community centers, pubs, recreation areas, and other facilities for their expanding population. Problems of management are also coming to the fore, and some towns have established or are anticipating the establishment of a local urban authority for their population.[19] A few statistics may help to point up these trends. (See Tables I–III.) From December 1947, when the first new

47

I PROGRESS OF NEW TOWNS TO DECEMBER 1954[1]

Name	Corporation Appointed	Designated Area (acres)[1]	Population			Shops		Schools (In brackets: number of school places)			Estimated Capital Expenditure[2] by Development Corporation	
			Original	Proposed	At 31 Dec. 1954	No. of original traders (approx.)	New Shops completed 31 Dec. 1954 (In brackets: sq.ft of floor area)	No. before designation	New Schools completed 31 Dec. 1954	Under construction 31 Dec. 1954	Housing since designation to 31 Dec. 1954 £	Total (inc. housing) to 31 Dec. 1954 £
LONDON RING												
Basildon	Feb. 1949	7,834	25,000	80,000	31,000	294	29 (23,660)	6 (not available)	2 (1,120)	2 (1,160)	4,343,000	7,936,000
Bracknell	Oct. 1949	1,860	5,142	25,000	8,403	85	10 (7,050)	4 (1,260)	1 (560)	2 (1,160)	1,949,000	3,196,000
Crawley	Feb. 1947	6,000	10,000	59,000	23,500	177	77 (59,930)	11 (1,480)	8 (2,870)	6 (3,092)	10,000,000	15,000,000
Harlow	May 1947	6,320	4,500	80,000	22,500	90	59 (50,600)	5 (815)	5 (3,120)	3 (2,080)	9,950,000	18,140,000
Hatfield	June 1948	2,340	8,500	25,000	12,500	104	none	4 (1,500)	4 (2,050)	1 (340)	2,050,000	2,770,000
Hemel Hempstead	Mar. 1947	5,910	21,200	60,000	35,900	368	82 (60,960)	11 (3,520)	7 (2,330)	7 (2,540)	9,000,000	14,600,000
Stevenage	Dec. 1946	6,100	7,000	60,000	17,000	140	12 (13,500)[3]	3 (730)	5 (1,960)[4]	6 (2,080)	6,425,000	13,225,000
Welwyn	June 1948	4,231	18,500	50,000	23,000	51	18 (25,100)	5 (2,040)	5 (2,160)	1 (600)	2,920,000	7,000,000
OTHERS												
Corby	May 1950	2,677	15,700	40,000	21,000	107	63 (66,146)	7 (2,940)	3 (900)	4 (1,550)	1,760,000	2,464,000
Cwmbran	Nov. 1949	3,160	12,000	35,000	16,000	155	14 (8,666)	6 (2,269)	1 (600)	4 (1,290)	2,539,025	4,169,287
East Kilbride	Aug. 1947	10,250[5]	2,300	45,000	11,000	40	19 (11,900)	1 (400)	2 (1,300)	3 (2,410)	5,900,000	7,500,000
Glenrothes	Oct. 1948	5,730	1,150	32,000[6]	5,850	3	19 (14,624)	1 (200)[7]	2 (945)	1 (1,000)	1,942,000	2,661,000
Newton Aycliffe	July 1947	887	60	10,000	6,061	none	18 (15,257)	none	2 (840)	1 (450)	3,231,400	4,337,500
Peterlee	Mar. 1948	2,560	200	30,000	5,500	1	17 (9,710)	none	2 (560)	2 (740)	2,721,000	3,974,000
Total			131,252	622,000	239,214	1,615	437 (367,103)	64 (17,154+)	49 (21,305)	43 (20,492)	64,721,425	106,972,787

[1] In some cases the area includes part of a green belt, not to be built on.
[2] Expenditure by local authorities and private persons on housing is not included. Nor is county council expenditure on schools etc. or expenditure by private enterprise on factories, etc.
[3] Not including 6 temporary shops or additional premises in Old Stevenage.
[4] Plus one temporary school.
[5] Area to be built up is 2,500 acres.
[6] Target population of present stage is 18,000.

ILLUSTRATIONS OF MASTER PLANS,

NEIGHBORHOODS, AND TOWN CENTERS

IN THE NEW TOWNS

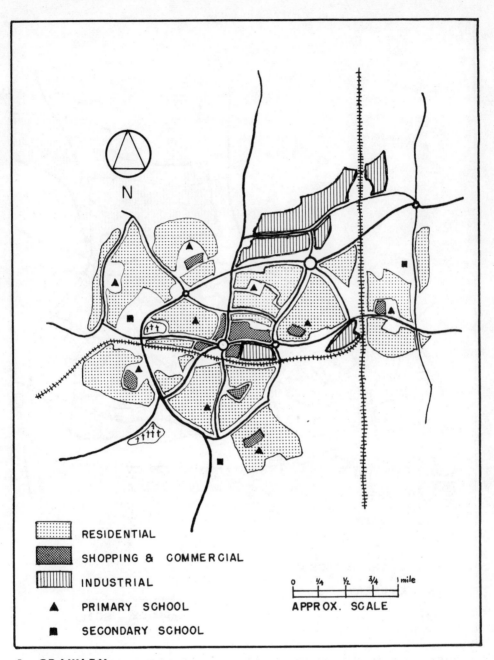

N

RESIDENTIAL

SHOPPING & COMMERCIAL

INDUSTRIAL

▲ PRIMARY SCHOOL

■ SECONDARY SCHOOL

0   ¼   ½   ¾   1 mile

APPROX. SCALE

1. CRAWLEY

Source: Crawley Development Corporation, *The Changing Face of Crawley* (pamphlet; Crawley: Courier Printing and Publishing Co., Limited, 1953).

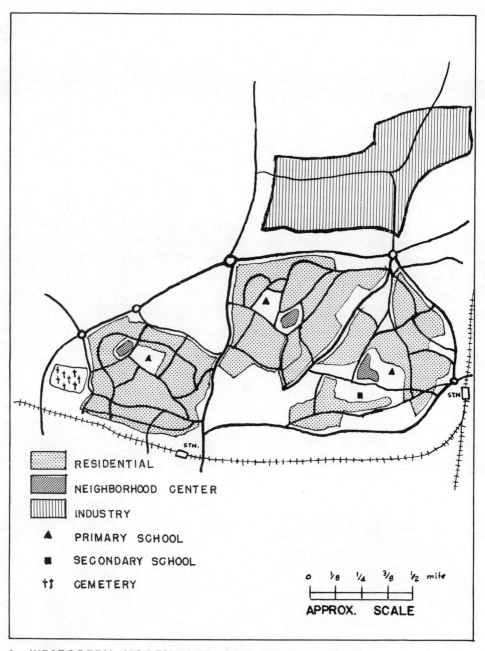

RESIDENTIAL

NEIGHBORHOOD CENTER

INDUSTRY

▲ PRIMARY SCHOOL

■ SECONDARY SCHOOL

†† CEMETERY

0   ⅛   ¼   ⅜   ½ mile

APPROX.   SCALE

2. WESTGREEN, NORTHGATE, AND THREE BRIDGES NEIGHBORHOODS IN CRAWLEY

Source: *RDC* (March 31, 1951), facing p. 148.

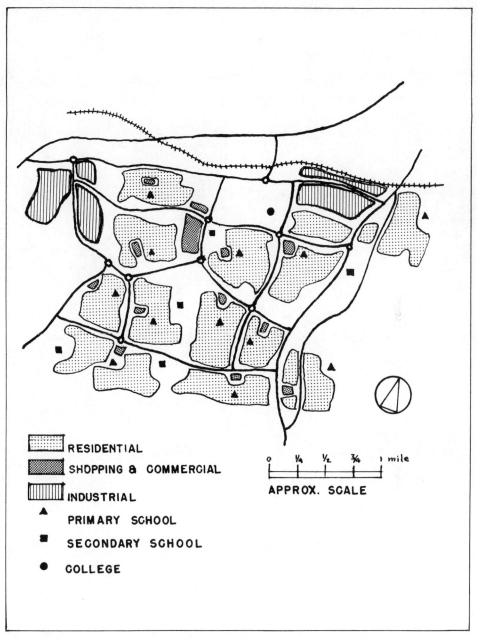

RESIDENTIAL

SHOPPING & COMMERCIAL

INDUSTRIAL

▲ PRIMARY SCHOOL

■ SECONDARY SCHOOL

● COLLEGE

0   ¼   ½   ¾   1 mile

APPROX. SCALE

3. HARLOW

Source: Harlow Development Corporation, *Harlow New Town* (pamphlet; reprint from *Architectural Times*, date and volume not indicated).

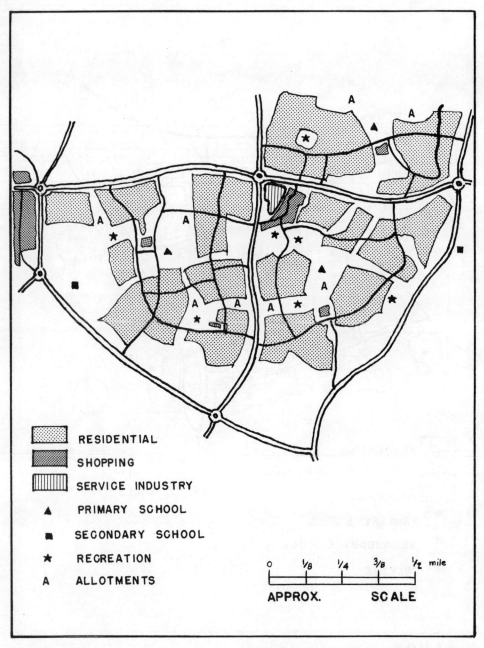

RESIDENTIAL

SHOPPING

SERVICE INDUSTRY

▲ PRIMARY SCHOOL

■ SECONDARY SCHOOL

★ RECREATION

A ALLOTMENTS

0   1/8   1/4   3/8   1/2 mile

APPROX.   SCALE

4. MARK HALL AND NETTSWELL NEIGHBORHOODS IN HARLOW

Source: Harlow Development Corporation, *Harlow New Town* (pamphlet; reprint from *Architectural Times*).

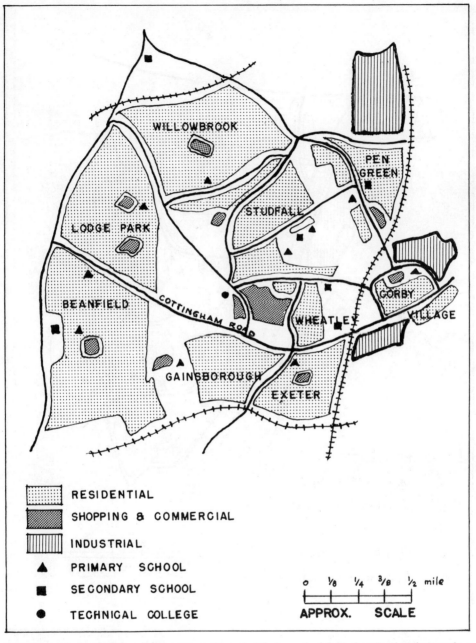

RESIDENTIAL

SHOPPING & COMMERCIAL

INDUSTRIAL

▲ PRIMARY SCHOOL

■ SECONDARY SCHOOL

● TECHNICAL COLLEGE

0   1/8   1/4   3/8   1/2   mile

APPROX.   SCALE

"Neighborhoods do not exist as distinct entities in the part of Corby north of Cottingham Road, and play only a limited part in the proposals of the Corporation... The Wheatley, Exeter, and Gainsborough subdivisions together form the South-East Neighborhood."

5. CORBY SUBDIVISIONS

Source: W. Holford and H. Myles Wright, Corby New Town: A Report to Accompany the Master Plan of the Corby Development Corporation (December 1952), p. iv.

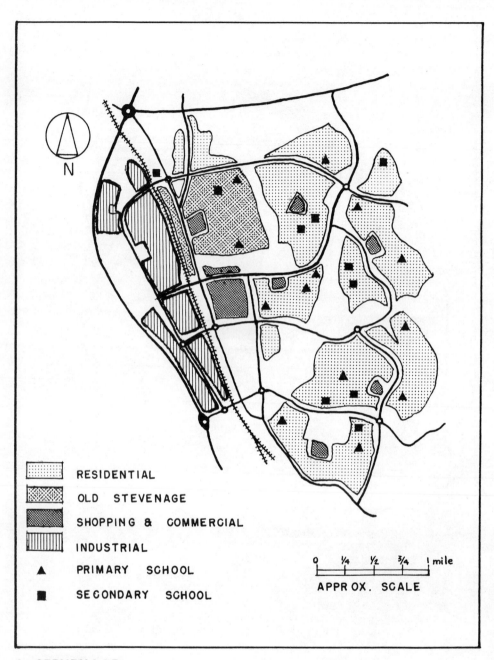

RESIDENTIAL

OLD STEVENAGE

SHOPPING & COMMERCIAL

INDUSTRIAL

▲ PRIMARY SCHOOL

■ SECONDARY SCHOOL

0   ¼   ½   ¾   1 mile

APPROX. SCALE

6. STEVENAGE

Source: *RDC* (March 31, 1954), p. 392.

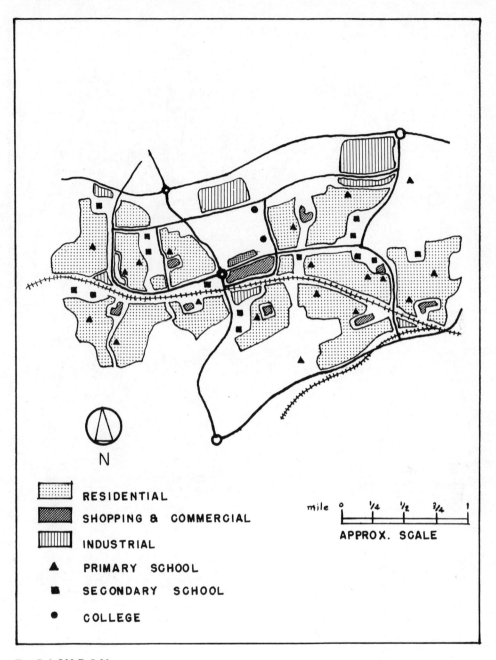

RESIDENTIAL

SHOPPING & COMMERCIAL

INDUSTRIAL

▲ PRIMARY SCHOOL

■ SECONDARY SCHOOL

● COLLEGE

mile 0 ¼ ½ ¾ 1

APPROX. SCALE

7. BASILDON

Source: *RDC* (March 31, 1951), p. 48.

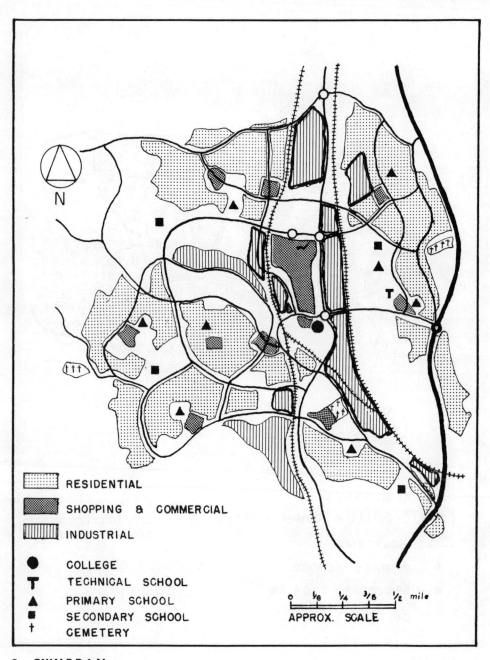

LEGEND

RESIDENTIAL

SHOPPING & COMMERCIAL

INDUSTRIAL

● COLLEGE

T TECHNICAL SCHOOL

▲ PRIMARY SCHOOL

■ SECONDARY SCHOOL

† CEMETERY

N

0   ⅛   ¼   ⅜   ½ mile

APPROX. SCALE

8. CWMBRAN

Source: *RDC* (March 31, 1951), p. 168.

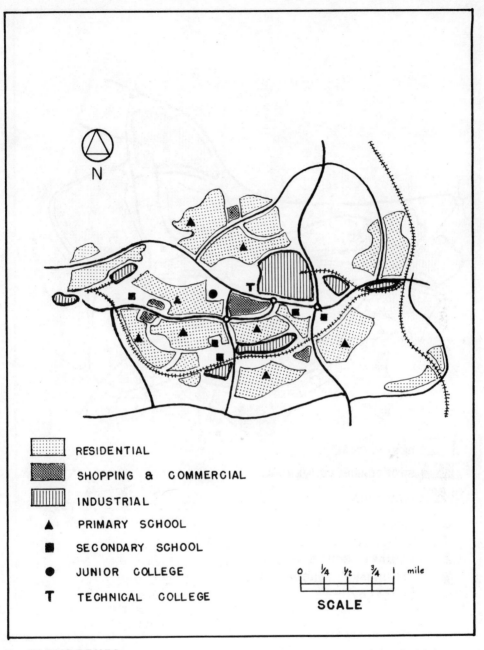

N

RESIDENTIAL

SHOPPING & COMMERCIAL

INDUSTRIAL

▲ PRIMARY SCHOOL

■ SECONDARY SCHOOL

● JUNIOR COLLEGE

T TECHNICAL COLLEGE

0 ¼ ½ ¾ 1 mile

SCALE

9. GLENROTHES
Source: *RDC Scotland* (March 31, 1954), p. 44.

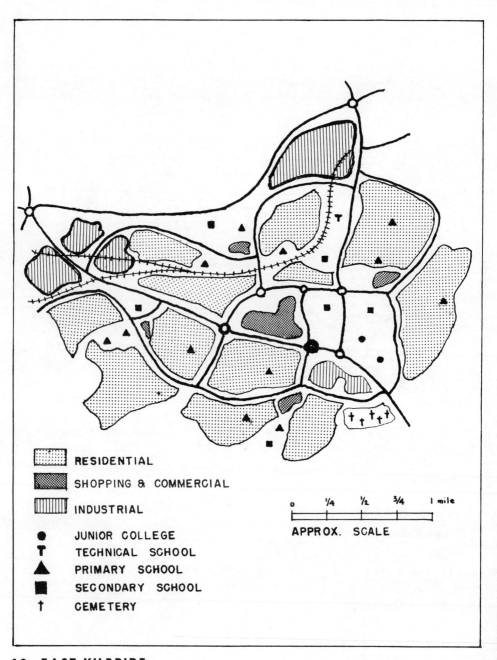

RESIDENTIAL

SHOPPING & COMMERCIAL

INDUSTRIAL

● JUNIOR COLLEGE
T TECHNICAL SCHOOL
▲ PRIMARY SCHOOL
■ SECONDARY SCHOOL
† CEMETERY

0 ¼ ½ ¾ I mile

APPROX. SCALE

10. EAST KILBRIDE

Source: East Kilbride Development Corporation, *Industrial Facilities* (East Kilbride, 1949, no page numbers).

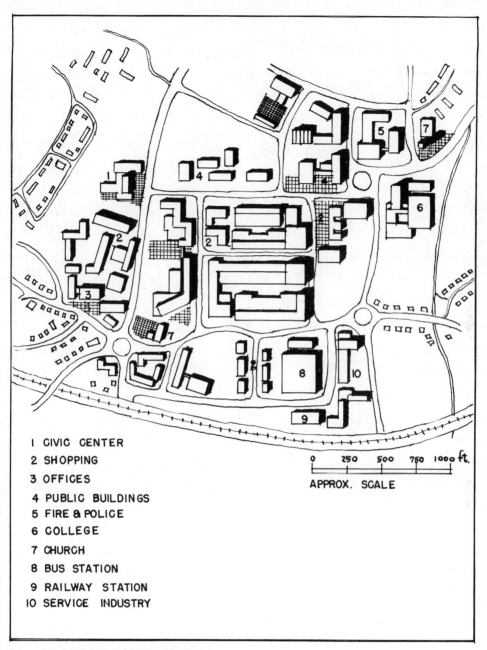

1 CIVIC CENTER
2 SHOPPING
3 OFFICES
4 PUBLIC BUILDINGS
5 FIRE & POLICE
6 COLLEGE
7 CHURCH
8 BUS STATION
9 RAILWAY STATION
10 SERVICE INDUSTRY

0   250   500   750   1000 ft.

APPROX. SCALE

11. CRAWLEY TOWN CENTER
Source: *RDC* (March 31, 1952), facing p. 182.

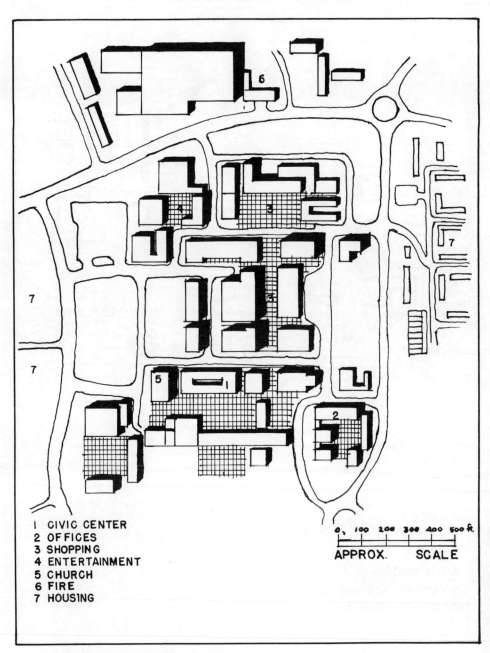

1 CIVIC CENTER
2 OFFICES
3 SHOPPING
4 ENTERTAINMENT
5 CHURCH
6 FIRE
7 HOUSING

APPROX.   SCALE
0   100   200   300   400   500 ft.

12. HARLOW TOWN CENTER
Source: *RDC* (March 31, 1952), facing p. 264.

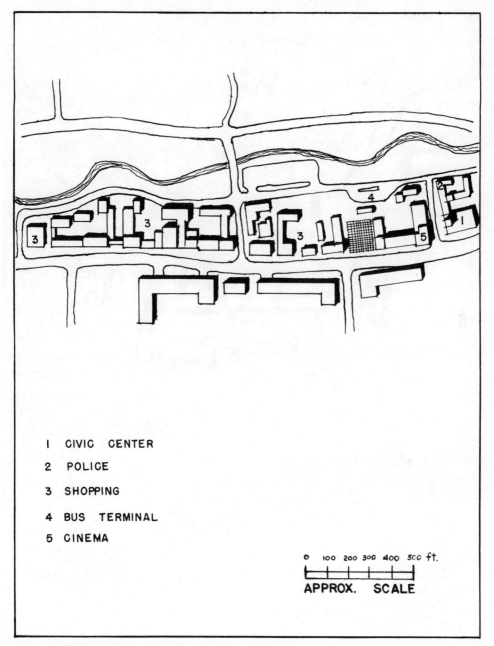

1 CIVIC CENTER

2 POLICE

3 SHOPPING

4 BUS TERMINAL

5 CINEMA

0 100 200 300 400 500 ft.

APPROX. SCALE

13. HEMEL HEMPSTEAD TOWN CENTER

Source: Hemel Hempstead Development Corporation, *Getting to Know Hemel Hempstead* (Hemel Hempstead: Benham and Co., Limited, no date), pp. 28–29.

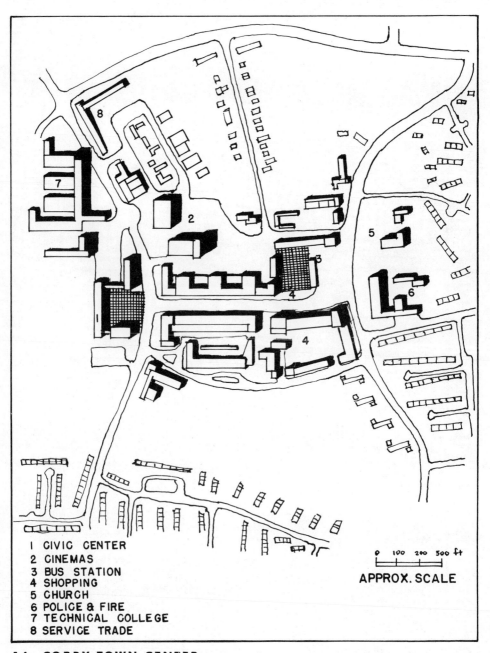

1 CIVIC CENTER
2 CINEMAS
3 BUS STATION
4 SHOPPING
5 CHURCH
6 POLICE & FIRE
7 TECHNICAL COLLEGE
8 SERVICE TRADE

APPROX. SCALE

0   100   200   300 ft

14. CORBY TOWN CENTER

Source: W. Holford and H. Myles Wright, *Corby New Town: A Report to Accompany the Master Plan of the Corby Development Corporation* (December 1952), p. iv.

II HOUSING IN THE NEW TOWNS TO DECEMBER 1954

	Completed at 31 December 1953 (from date of designation)			Completed during 1954 (est.)			Total completed at 31 December 1954 (est.)			Under construction 31 December 1954 (est.)			To be completed 1955 (est.)		
	Dev. Corp.	L.A.	Others	Dev. Corp.	L.A.	Others	Dev. Corp.	L.A.	Others	Dev. Corp.	L.A.	Others	Dev. Corp.	L.A.	Others
LONDON RING															
Basildon	1,106	504	89	700	170	29	1,806	674	118	960	196	25	1,400	220	25
Bracknell	372	94	49[1]	560	none	13[1]	932	94	62[1]	820	none	13[1]	600	none	15[1]
Crawley	2,525	440	28	1,775	48	141	4,300	488	169	1,500	90	70	1,500	90	110
Harlow	3,373	235	7	1,967	165	3	5,340	400	10	1,700	112	none	2,150	112	3
Hatfield	676	397	15	414	101	3	1,090	498	18	117	157	5	488	163	5
Hemel Hempstead	3,036	531	74	994	236	38	4,030	767	112	1,250	82	29	1,450	108	50
Stevenage	1,842	320	11	1,150	40	6	2,992	360	17	2,200	60	1	1,600	60	not known
Welwyn	866	455	96	687	243	17	1,553	698	113	745	none	13	949	50	13
OTHERS															
Corby	464	1,358	20	396	281	5	860	1,639	25	400	98	4	500	120	4
Cwmbran	460	498	23	625	122	18	1,085	620	41	742	48	10	725	171	40
East Kilbride	1,505	none	none	1,100	none	none	2,605	none	none	1,400	none	1	1,000	none	1
Glenrothes	655	306	none	345	none	2	1,000	306	2	660	none	none	409	none	1
Newton Aycliffe	1,318	none	1	547	none	none	1,865	none	1	450	none	1[2]	450	none	6[3]
Peterlee	1,239	none	none	379	none	none	1,618	none	none	426	none	none	500	none	none
Total	19,437	5,138	413	11,639	1,406	275	31,076	6,544	688	13,370	843	172	13,721	1,094	273

[1] Including Air Ministry married quarters.
[2] One vicarage.
[3] Four police houses, vicarage, and manse.
Source: *Town and Country Planning*, vol. XXIII, no. 129 (January 1955), p. 31.

III MANUFACTURING INDUSTRY IN NEW TOWNS TO DECEMBER 1954

	Before Designation			New Factories Completed by 31 December 1954			Under Construction 31 December 1954	
	No. of occupiers	No. of employees	Size (sq. ft)	No. of occupiers	No. of employees	Size (sq. ft)	No. of units	Size (sq. ft)
LONDON RING								
Basildon	20	not known	not known	16	2,600	498,900	7	373,000
Bracknell	11	not known	not known	8	1,005	286,639	7	64,023
Crawley	17	1,300	159,000	31	3,999	898,900	15+3 extns	745,600
Harlow	6	333	not known	4[2]	3,496	708,825	17	566,529
Hatfield	8[1]	1,500	100,000	1	49	10,000	9	58,240
Hemel Hempstead	36	6,200	not known	19	3,650[2]	736,150	6	111,400
Stevenage	4	not known	350,000	11[3]	1,468	375,200	5	285,550
Welwyn	69	8,000	1,994,594	2	1,000	189,091	5	235,248
OTHERS								
Corby	none[4]	none	none	4	300	21,310	3	67,280
Cwmbran	30	17,000	not known	2 (extns)	195	81,000	2	44,425
East Kilbride	3	380	155,000	5[3]	3,610	804,000	1	210,000
Glenrothes	4	1,650	750,000	none	none	none	none	none
Newton Aycliffe	none[5]	none	none	none	none	none	none	none
Peterlee	none	none	none	1	335	70,000	1	50,000
	208	36,363+	3,508,000+	140	21,617	4,680,015	78	2,811,295

[1] This does not include the de Havilland Aircraft and other factories outside the designated area.
[2] Actual present employment. Potential employment 4,550.
[3] These figures include the non-manufacturing DSIR establishments — Stevenage, 49,700 sq. ft., 100 employees; East Kilbride, 77,000 sq. ft., 360 employees.
[4] Stewarts and Lloyds' steel works which employ 8,700 persons adjoin the designated area.
[5] The Newton Aycliffe industrial estate adjoins the designated area.
Source: Town and Country Planning, vol. XXIII, no. 129 (January 1955), p. 34.

town (Stevenage) was designated, to December 1951, 2,385 houses were
built in all the new towns. By September 30, 1952, the number had risen
to 7,888.[20] At the beginning of 1955, if private houses and those built by
the local councils are included, the total completed had passed the 38,000
mark and the population served was almost 240,000. During 1955, a
building rate of more than 12,000 houses a year is expected for England
and Wales and perhaps another 1,400 or more for Scotland. This rate is
close to the peak performance expected for the corporations.

In addition, at the beginning of 1955, 140 factories had been built,
providing 4,680,015 square feet of factory space. Approximately 3,000,000
square feet was to be provided by the seventy-eight factories then under
construction. Almost 22,000 persons were employed in the new factories
already in operation. Add to this the provision during the same period
of 437 shops, forty-nine schools, plus roads and other necessary services.
These included a few churches and social centers, though the number
was almost negligible because of the restrictions imposed by the crisis.

The New Towns

Although many changes will occur over the next few years, enough
of the plans have been formulated and enough development has occurred
for the key features of the towns to come into focus. (See Appendix C:
The Look of New Towns, and the plans at the end of this chapter.) Perhaps the first characteristic which should be noted is the disparity between
the towns reflecting differences in purpose, location, and direction. The
most obvious dissimilarities are between the London towns and those in
the provinces. Thus Peterlee and Glenrothes are attempts to substitute
urban communities for straggling mining villages; Newton Aycliffe serves
as a residential addition to a trading estate; Corby is trying to channel a
flood of development resulting from the expansion of a steel works;
Cwmbran is an effort to tidy up industrial development by providing
housing and community facilities for many industries which located in
the area before and during World War II; and East Kilbride and New
Cumbernauld presumably represent outlets for Glasgow's decentralization.

The London new towns also differ from each other, though their
common purpose is to relieve the congestion of the metropolis. To illustrate their variety, compare Hemel Hempstead, an ancient town of 20,000
which is being expanded, with Basildon, an effort to transform a loose,
shoddy, residential binge into a community; and with Welwyn, the second garden city sired by Ebenezer Howard, now fostered by a development corporation for the express purpose of hastening its growth. Though

51

THE BRITISH NEW TOWNS POLICY

the other towns are somewhat more comparable, many differences are
still evident: in their varying sizes, their approach to neighborhood
modules, their choice of building types, their emphasis on contemporary
design and sculpture, and the like.

Despite these differences, the towns have enough in common to
justify their characterization in a broad way. Thus most of the towns
are relatively small, with target populations of 35,000 to 60,000 representing the modal size. Almost all have what Professor Lynch has called a
"coarse grain," [21] i.e., the major functions — housing, industry, shopping
centers, recreational areas — are laid out on a broad scale. The residential
areas are generally divided into several neighborhoods, each containing
one or more primary schools, shopping areas, and different kinds of playfields, and all grouped around the principal town center. Secondary
schools are usually between neighborhoods, close to the main circulation
system. The industrial areas, served by rail and road connections, are
close to routes which pass near the town center. Requirements for waste
disposal, easy building on flat land, and possible expansion also influence
their general location. Ring roads circle the town, with secondary roads
connecting the principal neighborhoods and districts. Smaller and often
curved streets knit together the neighborhoods. As a rule, the emphasis is
more on pedestrian and public service routes than on convenience to the
private car.

The shape is irregular, and generally not easily distinguished except
from the air or by reference to maps. Open space abounds. Densities are
relatively low. In nine of the towns they range from twelve to fourteen
houses a net residential acre; in the remaining towns they vary from
sixteen to eighteen and one-half houses an acre.[22] There are many children's and young people's play areas, larger playing fields for cricket,
football, and tennis, and usually agricultural greenbelts surrounding the
town. Because of criticism, high costs, and the desire to achieve a more
urban setting, the densities are being increased; and emphasis is being
placed on compact town centers to heighten the sense of urbanity.

Though in some ways there is considerable variety of design, possibilities are generally channeled and curbed by limited income, family
needs, public taste, and other factors. About 50 to 70 per cent of the
dwellings in towns are usually three-bedroom, one- or two-story terrace
(row) houses of about 800–950 square feet. Another 15 to 40 per cent
have two bedrooms, and most of the remainder contain one bedroom.
There are also some three-story houses, but taller buildings have been decisively rejected by the residents, and earlier forays in this direction have

been reined.[23] Almost all houses have fenced gardens used for sitting out and for planting flowers and vegetables, and some are even large enough for exercise and recreation.

The rents for the standard three-bedroom house in new towns range from 30s. to 42s. a week, including rates (taxes for local government). These rents may be a reasonable, and indeed economical, reflection of the costs of building houses of such quality in Britain today. Nevertheless they are quite high in relation to prevailing rents. According to a survey by the Oxford Institute of Statistics, an average rent of 15s. a week, including rates, is paid by families in Great Britain who live in unfurnished houses and flats.[24] On the average such low rents are paid even by higher income groups. Thus manual workers in the highest income category, who are earning £1000–£1999, pay rents, including rates, which average 17s. a week. Families in the salaried and self-employed categories pay 21s.; and for tenants in council houses the average is 18s. Rent control is responsible for these low rents; but even the rents of newly built council housing, for reasons discussed later, are significantly lower as a rule than rents in the new towns.

Most of the houses cost less than £2000. Only about 15 to 20 per cent of the houses cost between £2000 and £3000. A very few larger houses of about 2000 square feet are being provided for top executives on larger, more attractive sites, with garages; these generally cost between £3000 and £4000.[25] In some cases sites are also made available on long leases and even freehold for "custom" housing. The better houses are built in separate groups or in areas set off from the more modest dwellings. A few corporations have already asserted that "in practice cheek by jowl development of houses for the lower and middle income groups is not always welcome by either group and in present and future schemes particular care is being taken to ensure that the siting of the various types of housing will meet the tenants' wishes." [26]

The corporations tended to stress the early development of their industrial areas. This was partly because they wished to avoid "bedroom developments" and partly because it takes more time to organize an industrial area than to build a neighborhood. The residential districts are generally insulated from the industrial areas. Even when the factories are not objectionable on the grounds of noise, smoke, or appearance, residential and industrial uses are not being mixed because of traffic and other considerations.

Generally the corporations prefer to offer sites on ninety-nine year leases for firms wishing to do their own building; but they have built

53

many standard factories for small and medium-sized firms preferring to rent. Such facilities, of course, are quite attractive to organizations with limited capital that must be ploughed back into their enterprises. But well-planned industrial areas with utilities, housing, and modern community facilities, plus good communications and easy access to a large market, have appealed to many other firms and particularly to those huddled into cramped quarters during the postwar years. The experience of firms which have moved has been quite favorable to date. More than half the employees have tended to move with their establishment. Prosperity is general and the establishments are expanding. If this prosperity continues, the development corporations hope to reap handsome returns from their industrial estates. Indeed, this phase of the program has fared so well that some persons have wondered whether the new towns shouldn't also accommodate some of the less stable, less efficient, or less prepossessing establishments.[27]

The town center with the shops, offices, and transportation foci is expected to be the most profitable area of each new town. Rents are generally set by competitive bids. Though the towns are only partially developed, the returns are already satisfying. For similar reasons the transfer of the pubs from state to private control delighted the corporations. State control would have meant loss of the profits. Indeed, the corporations are still vexed because the general policy of the government makes it possible for other government departments to acquire valuable land in the new towns at existing use value.[28]

In addition to the shops, the offices, and the pubs, the town center will eventually have civic buildings, a community hall, one or more churches, and perhaps a health center providing medical and dental services and clinic accommodations for maternity and child welfare. Most of the new towns, and especially their architects, are eager to complete their centers. It is undoubtedly one of the high points of the community's development. One corporation report has declared that it is

> perhaps the most important and also the most difficult individual piece of planning in the building of the Town. In the past there has been little attempt to plan Town Centres — they have grown haphazardly into prominence and importance. Many have charm and most have faults. In a New Town in present times of shortage of materials and economic difficulties, to emulate the former quality and eradicate the latter is both a challenge and a problem.[29]

As the towns have grown, the meager provision for automobile traffic and garages has become embarrassingly evident. Also, the shortage of social facilities has become more and more troublesome. Without sewers, water, roads, and factories, there can be no towns; but without the necessary schools, churches, community buildings, and recreational facilities, the towns could hardly fulfill their promise. Till recently the new towns have been shorn of these social facilities because of the postwar economic crisis. The policy was to add only a bare minimum of the community buildings and recreational facilities until the bulk of the population arrived. This was partly because the ministry in its interpretation of the New Towns Act only approved outlays on which a reasonable return could be anticipated.[30] Fortunately this policy is in process of being reversed. Grants for playing fields and community centers have been resumed and it is expected that the development corporations will act vigorously to correct these shortcomings.[31]

Summary Observations

The New Towns Act set new goals for British town planning. It fashioned a novel instrument for town building. It sanctioned a new class of towns, easily identifiable in physical and social characteristics.

The new goals, broadly speaking, were the exercise of development powers to control the form and character of the city. More specifically, London was to be decongested. Balanced new towns were to aid the process by ringing London's periphery. And still other new towns were to be built to correct specific urban disorders.

The new instrument was the public development corporation. Presumably engaged in a self-liquidating operation, it could plan, build, acquire, manage, and dispose of property; it had access to long-term, low-interest government funds; it was the recipient of the customary local and central government housing subsidies. Its functions were entrepreneurial, its powers public; its term of life limited; its immediate aims: efficient and socially approved methods of town development.

The new class of towns was the "balanced" small city or metropolitan satellite. Features the towns shared in common were moderate size; relatively low density; gross unmixed land uses; unified public land ownership; fairly rapid comprehensive development; and an emphasis on more open space: private and public open spaces, playgrounds, playfields, gardens, parks, and countryside.

Measured on the basis of things done and planned, of services provided, houses and factories built, expanding population and the like, the program is showing prodigious vitality: this despite the most lamentable handicaps and adversity during the early years. There is every likelihood that the towns will be completed. Also, the houses, the space standards, the schools, and other facilities are of relatively high quality: indeed the towns are being planned by some of Britain's most competent professional talent. This is a great achievement, if as yet a limited one. It is evidence that public development is feasible. They may serve as one of several tools for town building or for remedying desperate urban problems. But the ultimate worth of the enterprise is still a matter of controversy. To understand why, it will be necessary to examine the difficulties encountered and to review the more recent legislation and the changing perspectives on urban growth and renewal.

CHAPTER **5**

New Towns: National Policy Issues

$\mathbf{O}$n the whole, the New Towns Act of 1946 represents Howard's ideas translated into a national policy. In the process there were changes of emphasis, of course. One example was the acceptance of London's vast metropolitan status; another was the role of new towns as satellites of London; a third was the eventual adaptation of new towns for other purposes than channeling growth or redistributing population of the giant cities. Still other differences lay in the scale of the program and many of the unexplored details of execution. Nonetheless, Howard's ideas on the object, the size, and the essential characteristics of new towns are everywhere in evidence. This is all the more striking, considering that the legislation was a response to a complex array of forces and that the act owed much of its legislative expression to contemporary political leaders, civil servants, professional planners, and miscellaneous experts.

But before long the new towns were engulfed in difficulties which nearly wrecked the program. Though rapid expansion is now occurring, it is in fact still uncertain whether the initial hopes will be fulfilled. Many, perhaps most, of these difficulties could not be blamed on Howard. They were often the result of pioneering errors, postwar dislocation, and administrative inadequacies. Still the burdens were not lightened by the emphasis on independent new towns, by the crude assumptions and expectations, financial and otherwise, and by the oversimplification of the tasks and strategy for urban reconstruction. It is fascinating to examine some of these problems. It is also quite instructive, since they provide many insights for interpreting and guiding future planning policy and action.

Organization for National Planning

Jobs, houses, services, and utilities are necessary ingredients for a new town, that is a new town which is not primarily a dormitory, a workshop, or a recreational or other specialized area. Development corporations cannot build such "complete" towns by themselves: they lack the staff, the organization, the experience, and the financial resources or subsidies. To a much larger extent than is often realized, their task is to enlist the help of other organizations, private or public, that can provide these types of assistance. They must also have the cooperation of other agencies of government to bring jobs, families, and necessary services to the sites of the new towns.

It is clear that development corporations ought to be closely associated with the strategic ministries and other government agencies whose decisions directly and vitally affect physical development. They include among others, the Board of Trade, the Ministry of Transport, the Ministry of Agriculture, the Ministry of Labour, the Ministry of Works, and the Ministry of Housing and Local Government. There is at present no central planning agency with power to require the various national agencies to adapt their policies and programs to a national planning and development policy. Such coordination as is achieved comes through informal Cabinet decisions and policies adopted by interdepartmental committees.

There would have been some advantages in making the development corporations responsible to the Board of Trade rather than to the Ministry of Housing and Local Government. The Board of Trade is a senior ministry. It administers, among other responsibilities, the government's industrial location policy. It has substantial industrial location powers,[1] especially for encouraging industrial development in declining areas. It also exercised substantial influence on the issuance of building licenses by the Ministry of Works, a form of control abandoned November 11, 1955. Nonetheless there are some strong reasons in favor of the present administrative location of the corporations. Housing constitutes most of the physical built-up area of a town. Housing costs and problems in new towns are serious and will receive sympathetic consideration from the Minister of Housing and Local Government. So, too, will questions involving local government and boundaries. But the present organization creates certain difficulties for the corporations. One or two examples will illustrate some of the handicaps under which they operate. Final decisions on location of sites for new towns are made by the Ministry of Housing and Local Government. Such decisions should be based on economic as well as other factors, but there are scarcely any trained economists in the ministry. At least *pro forma* the Board of Trade and the Treasury are closely associated with the program and committed to its implementation. In fact, neither the board nor the Treasury have had the staff or the time to do more than casual research or analysis to check decisions on site location.

L. E. White and other new town proponents have charged that the policy of the Board of Trade has not been helpful to the new towns or conducive to the policy of dispersal.[2] This accusation may be true, but it is less a reflection of hostile attitudes than of inconsistent policy commitments. Postwar economic difficulties, depleted resources, the "dollar gap," shortages of labor and materials, and the general policy of austerity slowed the tempo of development and led to restrictions. The board used its power over steel and plant construction and its special development powers to encourage exports, to expedite defense construction, and to strengthen the development and unemployment areas.[3] (See Map 3: Development Areas of Great Britain.) New towns were at the end of the queue.

Equally difficult is the creation of a diversified economic base for new towns. The task is all the more exasperating without the full assistance of the Board of Trade. At present, town planners can do scarcely more than hope that varied economic activities will be lured to their town and that they will prove adept in overcoming the obstacles placed in their path.

A special organizational problem was created by the restriction on capital investment. A ceiling was set on the amount of resources which could be employed for various types of activity. These were grouped "under familiar headings, such as housing, factory building, public utility services, school building and so forth."[4] Since new towns were just additional claimants on these resources, they had enormous difficulties in securing at least balanced, if not sympathetic, attention. Mr. Hart has explained that

> national policies, controlling these resources and designed, naturally enough, to deal with the normal areas have been applied by the appropriate Departments to the abnormal areas of new towns. This process has been seen over and over again: housing, classified roads, industrial development, factory building and school building are illustrations. And it is not until some administrative arrangement is made, under which the total resources available for new towns are segregated and their detailed allocation made subject to the practical direction of the Deparment re-

59

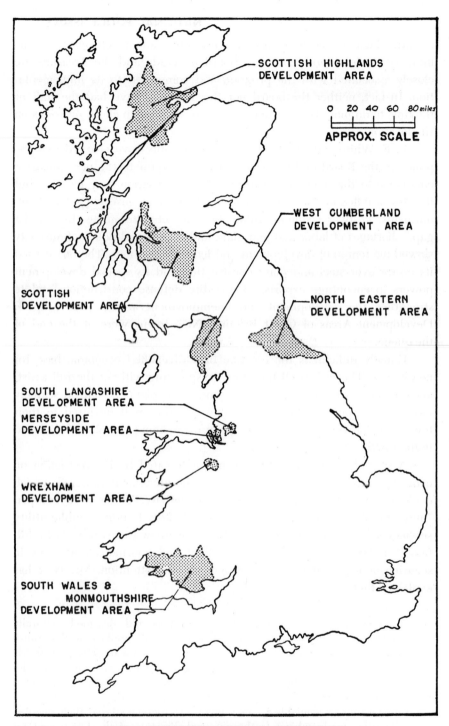

SCOTTISH HIGHLANDS
DEVELOPMENT AREA

0   20 40 60 80 miles
APPROX. SCALE

WEST CUMBERLAND
DEVELOPMENT AREA

SCOTTISH
DEVELOPMENT AREA

NORTH EASTERN
DEVELOPMENT AREA

SOUTH LANCASHIRE
DEVELOPMENT AREA

MERSEYSIDE
DEVELOPMENT AREA

WREXHAM
DEVELOPMENT AREA

SOUTH WALES &
MONMOUTHSHIRE
DEVELOPMENT AREA

MAP. 3. DEVELOPMENT AREAS OF GREAT BRITAIN

Source: Location Planning Room, Board of Trade (January 1950).

sponsible for New Towns, that there can be a reasonable hope of a balanced and programmed development of the new towns taking place.[5]

Resource Allocation

Once a policy of building new towns was adopted, some basic questions had to be faced if the ministry's decisions were not to appear embarrassingly haphazard. One of the most important was the proportion of the nation's resources to be devoted to new towns. Although the minister had carte blanche to create an indefinite number of new towns, financial support had to be secured from Parliament, and sooner or later the scale of the program was bound to become a matter of controversy. The onset of Britain's grim postwar economic crisis only underscored the urgency of this issue and heavily weighted the short-term considerations. Every proposal for capital investment had to be judged by its contribution to "dollar earning and dollar-saving projects." [6] The stark question was whether the payback from new towns then and in the next few years compared favorably with other possibilities, such as retooling, industrial expansion, new industries, shipbuilding, research, allocation of more land for agriculture, and the like. This hard, inescapable choice was disheartening for the new towns advocates, but there were few protests. The gravity of the situation was understood; and however sound the development of new towns may have been considered in the long run, no one doubted that many years had to elapse before the program could pay dividends.

As economic conditions improved, the reins were gradually relaxed, and were largely removed in 1950.[7] However, there was still some skepticism whether new towns were the best financial investments even in these relatively more normal circumstances. It was not easy to still such misgivings, partly because of the absence of any persuasive financial analysis. Undertaking such a chore did not seem rewarding for many reasons, including its inherent complexity, the uncertainties of future outlays and prices, and the assumptions that ultimately the undertaking would be self-liquidating and that comparable developments would be necessary in any case.

In addition, the soaring estimates of the expenditures required for new towns did not help to allay the doubts. About £15,000,000 was the first rough guess of the necessary Treasury outlays for the average new town (excluding investments by private and local authorities). After being subjected to scrutiny by the Committee of Public Accounts, the figure was later hoisted to £20,000,000–£25,000,000. More recently, taking

61

into account rising price levels, it is expected to approximate almost £40,000,000, or a total of more than £500,000,000 for the fifteen new towns undertaken to date.[8] However, G. D. M. Block, the author of a Conservative Party pamphlet on new towns, observes:

> The investment involved is big. But the investment need not necessarily be ill spent. . . . If the development were not undertaken in New Towns the whole or part of it would have to be undertaken elsewhere. There are therefore cases where it can be claimed that the New Town method of providing what is needed will be the cheapest in the long run.[9]

This Conservative view is nothing more than a lucid restatement of the position developed by the Reith Committee and later by the accounting officers of the ministry in their reports before the Committee on Public Accounts;[10] and it is correct as far as it goes. But strictly speaking the arguments are not decisive; and this should be recognized even if understandable limitations of time and data precluded any better justification. Investments in activities are not warranted simply because they are self-liquidating, or profitable, or even because similar developments would have to be undertaken in any case. For the government may have to choose among many activities which satisfy these criteria. It also has to decide upon the scale of the investment and determine whether the objectives achieved with a given scale of investment compare favorably with the benefits realizable from other alternatives. Unless special considerations dictate otherwise, investments ideally should be directed toward activities which yield the highest rate of return, measured on the basis of either profits, alternative costs, or social gains.

To develop such a technique of analysis is an extremely difficult task, and one which is still not common practice even for well-managed companies geared primarily to maximizing profits. The results of a survey by one keen student of this subject indicate that the executives of many efficient firms still show a "lack of defensible objective standards of an acceptable investment [and] . . . are still forced to play by ear to a distressing extent."[11] It is not surprising therefore that the government and the ministry, even in a program dedicated to planning, still betray a scant appreciation of this point of view and of the need to forge better tools for the future.

Regional Development

Tied to the appropriate resource allowance for new towns were several other closely related issues. Take, for example, the number of new towns to be built. Should there be one or two, with emphasis on speedy development and the lessons derived from this experience? Or ten, twenty, thirty, or forty? Also, how much development should be in the form of new towns and how much in the expansion of existing towns? And what were the best locations for the new towns, considering such factors as their functions, the need for speedy development, the facilities and services available to support their expansion, the various regional requirements and priorities? Were the new towns only to decentralize London? What about the other giant cities and the other uses of new towns? And if several regions were to be served, how many new towns were needed for the Midlands, for the North, for Scotland, and for Wales?

Most of these questions fell within the jurisdiction of the ministry. But they do not seem to have been adequately resolved. The original objective of the New Towns Act was to help decentralize London. Other new towns were authorized later in response to special problems and pressures. And so the list of designated towns steadily increased. Unfortunately there were no comprehensive long-term *national* physical development plans. Nor were any undertaken. Neither was there any long-term capital expenditure plan geared to national and regional physical development policies. As a result one wonders how much chance and pressures influenced the allocations that were made; whether policies and programs might have been undertaken that were incompatible with other commitments; indeed, whether the wrong number of new towns may have been started in the wrong places at the wrong time.[12] There is evidence, as we shall see, to show that some of these speculations are justified. Yet what is the object of planning if not to minimize such waste?

To say that the central government must decide many of these issues does not imply either dictation by the central government or the absence of local initiative. The central government would have had this obligation even if it did not act until the local authority requested assistance or until conflicting claims emerged. The question is not whether the central government should make such decisions. Rather it is the basis on which the claims are to be decided or the assistance given, if orderly regional and national development is to be encouraged.

Under the Town and Country Planning Act of 1947, the counties and county boroughs are preparing development plans for the next twenty years. The Ministry of Housing and Local Government must review these plans, analyze their regional and national implications, and check them for consistency. But actually major economic analyses are outside the purview of the ministry. The Board of Trade deals with economic activities generally, with industrial location, with permits for new plant construction and location, and with trading estates and development areas. At present it would be the most logical central agency to evaluate the economic structure and potentials of each region and the relevant aspects of the development plan, but it lacks the authority to do so, and many of its personnel are skeptical about their capacity to handle this assignment — aside from any lingering ideological distaste for planning. On the other hand, the Ministry of Housing and Local Government is not in a good position to conduct this review because a coherent national development policy has not been formulated and because the data are skimpy, the techniques of analysis primitive, and the ministry's technical staff largely unprepared for such responsibilities. The ministry to date seems to be relying on a planners' version of "the unseen hand." In its review, *Town and Country Planning 1943–1951*, it asks:

> Will plans of this kind dovetail into a sensible pattern of land use for the whole of England and Wales? . . .
>
> What has been done to ensure that the development plans of 62 counties and 83 county boroughs make up a pattern rather than a patchwork quilt and that the joins are not too obvious?
>
> The regional projects of Government departments, nationalised industries and public authorities . . . are being notified to planning authorities as they prepare their plans. But the greater part of the work of dovetailing and reconciling plans must be left to the local planning Authorities themselves, either through the formal machinery of joint advisory committees or by other means, and with such help as the Ministry can give them through its Regional Controllers. The work involves a great deal of consultation with neighbouring authorities, with statutory undertakers, with representatives of industry and with all kinds of bodies having regional as well as local interests. It is hoped that, by the time plans are submitted for the Minister's approval, the national and regional aspects will have received their due attention and that the adjoining plans will agree.[13]

Perversely enough, there is disturbing evidence that the regional considerations are being ignored. Robert B. Black, after reviewing the problems and experience of the northeast region, concluded that "at present there is no Regional machinery whatever, and little Regional Planning."[14] The London Planning Administration Committee declared unanimously that "if the overall Plan is to be carried through, some kind of [local] regional authority must be set up."[15] And R. Vance Presthus, in "A Note on British Town Planning Coordination," observed that

> the two principal [regional] co-ordinating committees [of the central government] . . . are not very effective . . . and such co-ordination as

occurs is the result of *ad hoc* consultation between senior civil servants and the more powerful local planning authorities. In the latter case, however, the conflict of interest between great cities, such as Manchester and Liverpool, and their respective county planning authority throws the burden of co-ordination in many cases on the central government. . .

In sum, despite the great strides which have obviously been taken, it seems fair to conclude that effective town planning will await an extensive overhaul of the national and regional machinery which presently seeks to co-ordinate Whitehall and the local planner.[16]

Planned Decentralization

It was assumed that the decongestion of London would occur with the building of new towns. Also, better balanced community developments were expected to replace the suburban dormitories of the past. However, the means devised leave much to be desired. Difficulties already in evidence in the initial stages of the growth of new towns bid fair to become even more serious if the program is carried forward.

Development corporations started from "scratch." They were new, independent agencies. They had to develop their plans, their building organization, their labor force. No effective building record could have been anticipated during the first two or three years. In the meantime, existing local authorities, possessing experience, organization, and political prestige and harried by housing shortages, proceeded to build typical housing estates and to build them very quickly. As a result, a large portion of the new housing has been and is still being built outside of new towns.

Similar attitudes were soon characteristic of the development corporations. The effort to attract industries, the need to house construction workers and key employees of migrating industries, and the desire to secure a variety of skills and income groups in new towns have tended to make housing available for many families without high housing priorities. True, an ingenious selection scheme was devised to maximize recruiting of workers, whenever possible, from families on the housing lists of local authorities. But the pressing immediate problems often spurred the development corporations to get on with the job of building their towns and to be concerned more with successful building performance than with the collateral benefits the new towns might confer on existing metropolitan communities.

Since these prospects were fairly obvious, it is surprising that the minister ignored the wise recommendations of the Reith Committee and of the Barlow Commission to permit local authorities as well as develop-

65

ment corporations to build new towns. Only a few larger local authorities would have been interested and would have possessed the necessary resources, leadership, and initiative to lend aid.[17] Of course opposition was expected from neighboring authorities determined to resist the expansion of Liverpool, Glasgow, Manchester, the London County Council, and other capital cities of a metropolitan region. But it was an open question whether incursions by the development corporations would receive much friendlier receptions. A high official has already characterized new town corporations as "cuckoos" in the nests of local authorities. Considering the price that had to be paid if local authorities were denied such development powers, the legislation might at least have been flexible enough to allow participation where feasible.

Suppose, however, that these difficulties were overcome and these and still other new towns were built. It seems likely that the country would continue to be faced with the ancient problem of many small jurisdictions within a single metropolitan region. One of the important tasks today, particularly in the London region, is the development of a suitable organization to handle regional problems.[18] The London Planning Administration Committee appointed by the Ministry of Town and Country Planning was unanimous on this score. The purpose is not to absorb local governments but to set up some workable arrangement for the handling of regional problems and services. The present program moves in the opposite direction. It will create new independent communities. For when the corporations, in the judgment of the minister, have largely completed the task of development, the new towns will be turned over to the local authorities of the areas in which they are located.[19]

The financial problems likely to arise also underscore the importance of participation by local authorities. Many authorities are reluctant to export any important source of potential income. They have rising financial commitments and they try to avoid the loss of any possible revenues. If the new towns were not entirely outside the corporate jurisdiction of the local authorities, the redistribution of economic activities might have been more easily encouraged.[20] Some financial dilemmas of new towns would also have been avoided if they had the status and resources of local authorities: utilities could have been more easily financed, rent restrictions avoided, and the forbidding costs of new construction could have been cut by a more flexible use of local rates and existing housing subsidies.[21]

What is perhaps most frustrating is the failure of new towns to promote effective decentralization. Success appears dubious even if the program is tremendously expanded. Such expansion appears unlikely: at present, no more new towns are planned and not more than a handful are contemplated, even by their proponents. Moreover, no one in a responsible position seems to take seriously the policy of accelerated decentralization for defense. In the first six years of the program, the pace of construction for *all* the new towns was only a small fraction of the building in the "Great Wen's" suburbs.[22] Even by 1955, when building in the new towns reached its stride, the total houses produced approximated the capacity of the London County Council's housing program. Under the circumstances, it would be Pollyannish to think that the character of London will be significantly altered or improved by the present new towns. Actually most of the development has occurred or is occurring largely in other ways. Indeed, when relocation does take place, existing houses and plants are infrequently demolished. In a period of shortage or prosperity, empty housing and sorely needed plant facilities easily attract newcomers; and the prohibitive acquisition costs impel local authorities, reluctantly perhaps, to acquiesce. New families and expanding economic activities have therefore replaced those departed. With such a big and obvious loophole, the total population of the region is expected to increase. At present the top officials confess sadly that they are helpless and simply have little power to cope with this dilemma.[23] The reason is that the hidden cost of purchasing and eliminating these facilities has never been reckoned as part of the price of new towns.

As for the other metropolitan areas, the new towns policy has been surprisingly indecisive or indifferent. Until 1955, only one town served Glasgow; and a cynical official observed that it could have been built anywhere since it is scarcely serving Glasgow's needs, in the decentralization of either industry or population. No new towns have been authorized for Manchester, Birmingham, Liverpool, and other large cities, though some have been proposed. Although more than 340,000 houses were built in 1954, mainly in the large cities, only about 13,000, or about 4 per cent, were in the new towns.

Considering this record, the conclusions of the original Advisory Committee for London Regional Planning in its *Report to the Minister of Town and Country Planning* seem remarkably prescient. The committee said:

> In the process of investigating the various centres of population in the Greater London Area, it was brought home to us that, in a large number of existing towns, redistributed population could be received to a greater extent than proposed in the Plan and yet the larger additions could still be integrated with the existing centers so as to form reasonably balanced

67

communities. This still appears to be the view generally shared by the Constituent Authorities. Furthermore, as a result of our investigations we have reached the conclusion that New Towns cannot be justified solely as being necessary to accommodate redistributed populations, because the whole of the redistribution could, if necessary, be effected in the existing communities within 50 miles of London. We agree, however, that a certain amount of redistribution should be dealt with by the development of New Towns, as these will have intrinsic planning advantages and will form valuable examples for guidance in planning extensions of existing towns.[24]

This view was rejected by Lord Silkin, the former minister. He insisted that "the provision of New Towns [was] an essential part of the regrouping of the population and not merely . . . a valuable example in planning." [25] But actually, as the committee proposed, only a limited amount of redistribution has occurred in new towns. And meanwhile the emphasis on the role of existing towns has increasingly commanded attention. Indeed, the Town Development Act of 1952, whose purpose is to facilitate such expansion, was a tardy and limited step in this direction.[26]

Research

When a long-term investment involving several million pounds is to be made, it would seem penny-wise and pound-foolish to scrimp on a research program costing a few thousand pounds that might ensure more economical and wiser decisions. Most efficient large-scale business organizations make a practice of setting aside a sum of money for research on improving their products. When the government engages in activity as a public entrepreneur, it might do well to emulate this common-sense business policy.

The Ministry of Housing and Local Government did make a brief stab at socio-economic research in 1948 in a program that dealt with the size and growth of towns; population, households, and dwellings; employment and industrial structure; and the neighborhood pattern. Coordination with the new towns was handled by a monthly conference of social development officers. Apparently the results were not impressive, at least to the principal officials. Inadequate data, lack of previous research, and the uncertainties of policies relating to new towns and their rates of development handicapped the research. Scarcity of qualified personnel, personality difficulties, and the time-consuming character of such inquiries may also have contributed to the failure. Whatever the reasons may have been, the program was discontinued.

The present research staff is largely assigned to day-to-day fact gathering. A few social studies have been sponsored: an investigation by the Social Survey on the people who would go to new towns;[27] an inquiry on the use of the shopping facilities in Bourneville by the Village Trust; a study of the output and value of garden produce and their variation with density and other variables. Some work has also been done on special overlay maps with socio-economic data; air photographs; and the like. There has also been considerable exploration of planning standards and of the geology of new towns areas, but even these efforts have been somewhat curtailed. The ministry contends that research contributing to thought and to knowledge about town planning

> is primarily the responsibility of universities and nongovernmental bodies, although the planning authorities must be concerned with the collection and analysis of information, and also with the observation of current practice and experience. For the Ministry and for local planning authorities, concerned as they must be to keep their staff demands to a minimum, the question must always be whether any particular study makes a direct and demonstrably useful contribution to their planning administration. Judged from this point of view, the true "research" in which either party should engage must be small, though accurate knowledge of the physical conditions of areas to be planned is always necessary.[28]

Unfortunately there is little basic research in town planning now under way at the universities or in nongovernmental bodies.[29] Since the ministry is aware of this situation, and since it is not pressing or stimulating the universities to do research, it is distressingly obvious that a dangerous gap exists.

Almost every aspect of the new towns program could profit from research. Criteria governing the scale and priorities of new town development require review. Policymakers are not at all sure what an optimum-size city is or whether there are several optimum sizes for cities. Many persons are also beginning to ponder the limitations of the neighborhood concept and the extent to which planners should take into account arguments and evidence of dissenting students on this subject. Techniques of improving building efficiency on the site could likewise benefit from exploration.[30] Statistics, too, need to be improved. Present data are crude and unreliable.

Obviously the list of necessary research can be extended in many directions. There are other technical, social, and economic questions, some perhaps even more pressing than those that have been mentioned. What is almost beyond dispute, however, is that the new towns program is embarking on an extremely novel and ambitious operation involving great risks and great possibilities of achievement. Only the crudest outlines of the goal are known. Planners face to face with these responsibilities would be presumptuous to rely on pat solutions or on the existing fragmentary rules of thumb.

The experience on which to base analysis does not exist for many points, but that is not an argument against a research program. An experimental approach to town building can nonetheless be maintained. On occasion, alternative solutions can be deliberately developed for test purposes. As Professor R. K. Merton has pointed out,

> In the world laboratory of the sociologist, as in the more secluded laboratories of the physicist and chemist, it is the successful experiment which is decisive and not the thousand-and-one failures which preceded it. More is learned from the single success than from the multiple failures. A single success proves it can be done. Thereafter, it is necessary only to learn what made it work.[31]

Too often new experimental achievements do not become part of our heritage because the nature of the success has gone unrecorded.

Summary Observations

The idea of building new towns is deceptively simple. It has the allurements of the virgin site, of new administrative machinery, and of public power and financing. But one must also reckon with existing agencies and policies, and with existing cities, attitudes, and trends.

Experience so far has turned up some difficulties that are sobering. The most obvious are the limited powers of the development corporations and of the Ministry of Housing and Local Government. To establish a relatively "balanced" community presupposes power over many forces, including industrial location and general economic development. Both are outside the purview of the ministry and the development corporations. Other national objectives, such as the promotion of development areas, the encouragement of export trade, or even the expansion of agriculture, have features that are inconsistent with the policy of establishing new towns; and the existing machinery is not geared to anticipate or resolve such conflicts.

In addition, problems of resource and regional allocation require more attention. New towns are being built without any long-range analysis of how many should be built, of where they should be built, and of what priorities should govern the growth of different regions.

Links with existing cities are also inadequate. The new towns were primarily intended to serve the existing cities; but the administrative organization, the emphasis on new towns, the need to build quickly, the failure to permit local authorities to participate in the process of building, and the absence of control over the replacement of population and economic activities siphoned from the central areas make the attainment of this objective improbable.

And the neglect of any significant research program, other than surveys and fact gathering for immediate administrative purposes, suggests that there is not sufficient awareness of the gaps in understanding and of the costly and avoidable blunders that may be made.

One of Ebenezer Howard's ideals, which has proved appealing to a whole generation of planners, is the "balanced" city. It is one of those notions, like virtue, which all embrace though few fully comprehend. Still it has been a suggestive concept and has prompted fruitful questions. Indeed it leads one to wonder whether Howard's views and the contemporary new towns policy did not possibly suffer from "imbalance." The approach does not seem to be sufficiently comprehensive. The interest has been largely in the new community. The balance sought has been largely between place of work and residence, between town and country. Not enough emphasis has been placed on the varying functions and sizes of cities; on the interrelationships of existing and new cities; and on an evaluation of development prospects and requirements from a regional and national point of view. Howard himself once remarked near the end of his career that when he conceived the idea of garden cities, practically no one had any "conception whatever of regional planning. A colossal mistake might be made if in starting New Towns the importance of their interrelationships has not been sufficiently recognized." [32] Exploring this wider, more "balanced" view would appear to be one of the major tasks of the present generation of planners.

CHAPTER 6

Problems of New Town Development

To many persons in the early postwar period, the new towns program stood for the boldest vision of contemporary British town planning. Then within a few years it had become a wavering policy in the hands of skeptical administrators. Still later, as Britain emerged from its dangerous economic crises and as the problems of development were solved, attitudes became more buoyant again. New town reports began to exude confidence, even enthusiasm. Building grew in volume. Many of the corporations even expected to complete the towns within the ten- to fifteen-year period originally envisioned. Some of the bitter obstacles and failures encountered during the initial development period were responsible for the doubts and forebodings which assailed the responsible officials. These problems, which threatened demoralization, warrant careful scrutiny. Some of them still handicap the program today.

Administrative Relationships

New towns are being built by a relatively new type of entrepreneur, the public corporation. The aim in establishing the corporations was to create a more efficient and flexible instrument for the tasks ahead. Many of the existing local authorities would not have been willing or able to handle the novel and more exacting responsibilities of the program. But sound as the corporate device may be, it has evidently not avoided certain administrative snags, and it has even raised others, judging from official reports and the comments of key administrators.

Thus, ministry officials are often incensed that the members of the development corporations, appointed by a minister of the Crown to spend millions of pounds on a new town, could be completely blocked by an aggrieved local town clerk or by other local officials or groups. Activity in Stevenage, as is well known, was held up for years because of stolid local resistance. Opposition by a strong and ancient local authority in Hemel Hempstead has resulted in sniping and bitterness and a dangerous gulf in local authority and corporation relations. Welwyn, the second garden city, is still bitter about the ministry's decision to supplant the original limited-dividend corporation. Crawley, Corby, Aycliffe, East Kilbride — indeed almost all of the corporations — have been hampered in varying degrees by such friction.[1]

However exasperating and time consuming the administrative entanglements may be, they generally cannot be avoided. Development corporations have limited powers. They must consult with and secure approvals from local district councils on building bylaws, on plans for sewerage, open space, and sometimes water. They must engage in similar negotiations with the county council for roads, surface water drainage, education and health services; with statutory undertakers for special services such as gas and electricity; with the Ministry of Health on water and sewage disposal; with the Board of Trade on industrial developments; with the ministries of Labor and Works on labor and materials; with the Agricultural Land Commissioner and the County Agricultural Executive Committees, and so on. Moreover, since sites for the new towns were chosen presumably for technical and socio-economic reasons, the boundaries of local authorities were often slighted, if considered at all; and as a result some of the above complications were multiplied because of overlapping boundaries and multiple jurisdictions.[2]

Satellite towns have still other administrative chores. Liaison must be established with officials of the neighboring cities to facilitate their "exporting" programs. Proper timing of the physical and financial arrangements is necessary. And in towns like Basildon and Hemel Hempstead, where existing built-up areas are part of the new towns, a tremendous number of *ad hoc* decisions must be made by the local authority exercising the 1947 planning powers. All of these decisions require close consultation with the new town corporation. To this list must be added the countless meetings and conferences with private groups and organizations affected by the program.

It is not surprising that the 1950 Crawley Report pointed out "with restraint" that all these activities "consume a great deal of time and effort." Appendix E of the 1949 Report of the Crawley Corporation attracted some attention.[3] It set forth the following list of public consultations and approvals:

Appendix E

a) CONSULTATIONS AND APPROVALS REQUIRED FOR THE EXECUTION OF PLANS.

County Council

Town Planning approval
Approval to roads standards
Approval to road surface water drainage
Approval to school proposals
Approval to health center and maternity and child welfare proposals
Approval to community buildings

Parish Councils

Street lighting

Ministry of Health (HQ)

Approval of houses for subsidy
Approval of sewerage proposals
Approval of water supply proposals

Ministry of Transport

Approval of classified roads
Approval of junctions of estate roads with classified roads
Approval of street lighting for classified roads

Ministry of Labor

Approval for labor and materials

Rural District Councils

Building by-laws and new street by-law approvals
Town Planning approval (as agents for the County Council)
Approval to sewers
Approval to open spaces

Ministry of Health (Regional Office)

Approval of house plans
Approval of housing site development works
Permission to go to tender
Approval of tender

Ministry of Town and Country Planning

Acquisition of land (Section 5)
Proposal for development (Section 3 (1))
Financial approval (Section 12 (7))
Starting dates
Licences for scarce materials

Board of Trade

Distribution of Industry Certificate

Ministry of Works

b) AUTHORITIES WHOSE PLANS AND PROJECTS HAVE TO BE COORDINATED WITH THOSE OF THE CORPORATION.

County Councils

Schools, health centres, clinics, police buildings and housing, fire hydrants and fire stations, classified roads and bridges (with the Ministry of Transport).

Ministry of Works

Buildings for Government Departments

Rural District Councils

Public conveniences, bus stations, car parks, playing fields

Parish Councils

Street lighting

Ministry of Fuel and Power and Gas Companies

Gas mains and supplies

South-Eastern Electricity Board

Electricity mains, sub-stations and supplies

British Railways

Goods and passenger facilities

Four Water Authorities

Water mains and interim supplies

South-West Metropolitan Regional Hospital Board

General Hospital

Transport Commission

Road passenger service, bus stations, bus lay-bys

Thames Conservancy Board

Works to rivers and streams

The following year Sir Ernest Gowers, Chairman of the Harlow Corporation, sharply complained that these consultations and approvals

> create machinery which is in some respects cumbrous almost past belief and which produces in profusion officials doing one after another work that one official could well have been trusted to do by himself. Development Corporations have too many masters.[4]

Ministry officials were also excoriated. Although Sir Ernest acknowledged that controls are necessary, he still felt obliged to declare that the corporation's progress

> has been unnecessarily delayed and its expenses unnecessarily swollen by prolonged scrutiny on the part of Ministry officials of matters of detail

7 5

which might reasonably have been left to the Corporation's discretion. As has been recorded in this report, the Corporation's proposals for the development of part of the Mark Hall Neighborhood were with the Ministry for nearly five months before being approved and the Corporation has only just received approval (9th May, 1950) of a plan for the development of the East Industrial Estate submitted to the Ministry on the 1st December 1949. Delays like these can cost money in two ways. So far as they may be caused by examination of detail of no great importance, they mean that the time of Departmental office staff is being wasted, and so far as they impose an unnecessarily long gap between the completion of a plan and starting to carry it out, they mean that staff which is ready to get on with the job cannot do so except by anticipating approval, and so risking a waste of time and labour if approval should eventually not be given. In the two cases referred to the five months' thought devoted by the officials of the Ministry to each project ended in acceptance of both, subject to slight modifications which effected a reduction of some £3000 in programmes estimated to cost nearly two million pounds.

The Corporation recognizes, of course, that there are two sides to this question. The problem of how much control is proper for a Government Department to exercise over a statutory board is exceedingly difficult, and no generally accepted solution of it has yet been found.

What can hardly be questioned is that the tangled thicket of controls and overlapping duties depicted in the Crawley Corporation's Appendix contains much that serves no useful purpose, and needs to be drastically pruned if Development Corporations are to be given a chance to build New Towns in reasonable time and at reasonable cost.[5]

These lamentations, however, will probably prove futile. Ministers who are politically and financially responsible for a program will insist on adequate supervision and safeguards. Probably a comprehensive review by a royal commission, as Lord Reith suggested to the Committee of Accounts, would be helpful.[6] Certainly ministerial scrutiny could be a little less picayune. But some delay is inevitable. Perhaps this is part of the price to be paid for planned instead of haphazard development, and for democratic procedures rather than dictatorial ones.

Initial Development Costs

Agile handling of initial large-scale development costs has long been recognized as one of the crucial determinants of the success of new towns. One of the decisive reasons for shifting the major development responsibilities to central government corporations was to avoid the frustrations of undercapitalization. But the financial formulas are still inadequate.

Development corporations, it will be recalled, receive loans and grants from the Ministry of Town and Country Planning. These funds are made available by the Exchequer. But the problem does not disappear simply because the corporation has funds at its disposal. The financial burdens imposed on the local authorities and the residents must also be reckoned with. When local authorities must undertake costly expansion of existing plant and facilities to provide the necessary services, they are reluctant to impose such charges on their rate payers. They often refuse to cooperate unless the corporation is willing to pay "a fair share" of the costs. The same reluctance holds true for the services provided by the statutory undertakers.[7] Just what is a fair share is a matter of controversy. Some authorities are content with temporary assistance "with loan charges on large capital works until the growth of the population which will fully justify them." [8] Others, however, are claiming rate stabilization. They want

> reimbursement so far as development is "unprofitable" by producing less rate revenue than their expenditure on the services provided. This may come to be a conflict between the ratepayer as represented by the local authority, and the taxpayer as represented by the development corporation — with all sorts of complicated repercussions — or even as a conflict between the old ratepayer of the area before designation as the site of a new town and the new ratepayer, who may be in danger of paying twice over, once as a ratepayer and again as a tenant, since the rents a development corporation collects must ultimately be the source from which its finances are drawn.[9]

Until these issues are thrashed out, development tends to get stalled. For example, in Aycliffe difficulties were experienced with the parish council on the division of lighting costs and on the provision of necessary sewage facilities. In Crawley the £124,000 river works, needed to prevent the surface water carried from the new towns from causing floods, posed a delicate question about sharing of costs. In Hemel Hempstead prolonged negotiations were conducted for the expansion of the local water undertaking by the town council and for the laying of an enlarged trunk sewer up the Gade Valley by the Colne Valley Sewerage Board — both services required far in advance of need and thrusting heavy capital expenditures on the local authorities. Essex authorities were shocked by the school problems imposed by Basildon and Harlow. And in Stevenage the urban district council would not proceed with the needed sewerage works until adequate guarantees of financial assistance were forthcoming. This is only a small but typical sample. Many other instances could easily be cited.[10]

77

Difficult as these issue are, they are being negotiated and settled by the corporations with the aid of the ministry. What is not yet solved is how to deal with the burden that these capital investments impose on the residents and economic activities of the new town. The services must be built in advance, and usually in scale with the requirements of the future built-up town. Unlike the ordinary speculative development, higher capital costs are inherent in the initial stages of any long-term, efficiently planned development. Until the town has grown sufficiently, an excessive burden may fall on the residents, if the cost is assumed by the corporations. Local authorities and statutory undertakers have no desire to assume any significant portion of these costs. This reluctance is quite understandable. They are corporation problems, and other agencies do not wish to be saddled with them. The alternatives open to the ministry are either an intolerable burden on the rates for the residents and activities of the new towns; or a disproportionate and unlikely assumption of these costs by the local authorities and statutory undertakers; or deferred payments on a long-term loan; or a subsidy.[11]

This difficulty in allocating costs is really the result of a drastic change in the revenue base. In real terms, the costs for these new towns ought not to be much greater, if at all, than for ordinary suburban speculative development. Except for cities with considerable underemployed capacity in utilities or services, the actual costs might be assumed to be approximately the same.[12] When urban expansion occurred in the past, the burden was distributed among the population of the entire urban area. It was not inordinately heavy, unless investments were made prematurely; and then bankruptcy and defaults on municipal bonds resulted. What complicates the new towns' financial problem is their political independence and the installation of services far in advance of actual use. There is no significant supporting economic base. Risks mount if building occurs too slowly or fails to materialize. Heavy "waiting" charges will also be incurred, adding to the expense of new town development, especially if the government does not subsidize these costs.[13] There are fairly good prospects that the outlays will be recovered in the final stages of development; that is often the practice in private real estate operations. But during the early years the local authorities, the Exchequer administrators, and Parliament's Committee of Accounts were understandably restive as the development corporations incurred increasing debts seemingly beyond the income capacity of the towns.[14]

Still another problem of initial development costs has been caused by an awkward accounting formula. Under the present record of accounts, interest is charged on capital invested in sewers, water mains, roads, houses, factories, and other works under construction, before revenue is obtained from the assets. This is the same practice which stumped Letchworth. As a result the accounts of the corporations have shown mounting and forbidding losses during the early development period. For example, Crawley's deficiency on interest for the period ending March 31, 1954 amounted to £40,000; for Hemel Hempstead it approximated £35,000; for East Kilbride during the same period it reached £91,633; and the other corporations were similarly affected. These paper losses mean little. In fact, during 1954 and 1955 these deficits have in some cases begun to decline. The real test will be the earnings of the enterprise in relation to the capital invested, including the interest charges during the early unproductive years. Though the present method of reporting annual accounts does not materially affect the financial position of the corporations, it does exaggerate the deficits and cast unnecessary gloom on the financial prospects. Some of the corporation chairmen have therefore campaigned vigorously to have the interest charges during construction capitalized, i.e., added to the capital costs of the development. It is surprising that this is not done. The present system of reporting gives little advantage from a fiscal standpoint. While it recognizes that money is not a free good, so does capitalization, and the latter does not furnish a misleading estimate of the actual earnings of the enterprise.[15]

Rents

New towns also have a rent problem. This exists despite the corporation's receipt of the customary Exchequer subsidies plus the ministry grants equal to the subsidies provided by the local authorities.[16] Of the 15,000,000 private families in Great Britain, there are 9,000,000 renting unfurnished houses or flats. Nearly 3,000,000 of these families live in council houses or prefabs. Over 6,000,000 live in privately rented dwellings. They paid an average of £39 a year for gross rent.[17] For the standard three-bedroom house in new towns, on the other hand, gross rents range from £81 to £109 a year. The average rent in new towns might be a little lower if smaller as well as larger and better houses were included. In addition, the low average national rent reflects slum rents, houses let at low rents in provincial areas, and the depressing effects of rent controls on older houses. These factors plus price inflation after the war account for most of the difference in the rents of houses in new towns compared with prevailing rents. But this explanation does not eliminate the problem. The fact is that the houses in the new towns are more expensive than new houses built by local authorities. This added straw has aroused some bitterness and calls for an explanation.

Corporation houses, unlike those of the local authorities, were subject to the rent restriction acts. Rents fixed on new houses could not be raised without considerable difficulty. Since higher maintenance costs in the future could have played havoc with low rents, development corporations had to establish rents which also took into account rising price trends. For a long time the government hesitated to tamper with the Pandora's box of rent-control legislation. Rightly or wrongly they feared the aftermath: higher rents, higher wages, higher prices, reduced exports, and, of course, less votes. With revision of the rent-control legislation under the Housing Repairs and Rents Act in 1954, however, this particular handicap has been eliminated.

Development corporations also have no pool of additional council houses or cushion of local rates. Under the Housing Act of 1936, councils with a stock of existing housing can lump together the varying subsidies of all the separate housing acts. They can, therefore, establish more equitable and flexible rent levels for all the available housing. Rents of housing built during a period of high price levels can be reduced; and similarly rents of lower-cost housing can be increased. Development corporations, however, have no alternative but to charge what are comparatively steep rents for their dwellings.

Local authorities, moreover, can avoid charging the tenants the full economic costs for their houses by simply increasing local rates to offset some of the deficits. Presumably the costs are thus distributed more equitably. They can also charge expenses of the architecture department and the costs for roads, parks, and the like to overhead costs for the city. Many years will pass for most new towns before such a reservoir of local rates exists. Besides, for a long time the rates will be heavily burdened because of the initial capital expenditures and the higher overhead costs in the early stages of town growth.

Local authorities are also securing cheaper loans for shorter periods. Development corporations must make sixty-year loans. The corporations are therefore "in a less flexible and less advantageous position as compared with local authorities who are now able to borrow from sources other than the Public Works Loan Board." It has been suggested that the government's advances should be made "for a period of fifteen years or less, i.e., the approximate life of the Corporation at 3¾ per cent (the existing rate for loans repayable to the Public Works Loan Board over such a period); such advances to be repaid at the end of the period out of the proceeds of the disposal of the assets of the Corporation to the authority responsible for taking over on completion of the Corporation development." [18] The savings on interest would reduce rents, and the local authority would not be at a disadvantage in taking over such loans.

Higher labor costs are another reason for the more expensive housing, at least at the outset. Most of the new towns are sited approximately six to thirty miles from the existing cities. To attract the necessary labor to the new towns, extra payments sometimes must be made for travel. There are also additional costs for temporary housing and canteens. Often it has been necessary to reserve permanent housing for part of the construction force to retain key employees. But even if labor were less scarce, some of these additional costs would probably be entailed.

Some development corporations, like Harlow, Crawley, and Newton Aycliffe, have tried to build a few modern flats. They wanted to reach certain densities; to avoid building on good farm land; to provide for childless families and single persons; to achieve a more satisfying architectural variety. But such flats have generally proved expensive; and since they are built on vacant land, they do not qualify for the higher subsidies which the 1946 Housing Act made available for the more expensive high-density flats in central areas. Moreover, most tenants to date seem to prefer houses and will not willingly pay more for flats.[19]

Lord Beveridge, in his 1951 report as Chairman of the Aycliffe Corporation, said that they were previously perturbed by the "steadily rising building costs." He added that

> this disquiet of mind has recently changed to alarm in consequence of the recent rapid rises in material prices and building workers' wages. . . The recent upward surge in building costs fills us with apprehension that resultant rents will prove to be too much for the workers to pay.[20]

He also observed sadly in a lecture at the University of London:

> One after another, ambitious schemes for making the perfect town fell by the way or are delayed. At Newton Aycliffe we hoped to make a smokeless town with district heating, but we found the costs so high that we could not make it a compulsory addition to the rent of every person in town. We wanted to build a good theatre for community drama but the cost was frightening. We thought of a first class hotel, but we find ourselves reduced to a public house with no rooms for anything but drinking.[21]

Perhaps, as Lord Beveridge believes, families should spend more for better housing. Certainly, despite persistent grumbling about the rents, the tenants appear to like their new homes. At present there are no vacancies. Probably as long as a critical housing shortage persists, most of the houses will be occupied. But occupancy rates alone can be misleading. They may still conceal the fact that many potential tenants with high priority will not be able to live in the new towns; that many families in these towns may live in smaller quarters than desirable; [22] that local authorities are charging lower rents for new housing; [23] and that when the pressure abates, the vacancy ratio may increase unless rents are cut.

Balanced Towns

The negative character of British planning prior to World War II was generally considered its greatest failing. But it is far from certain that the "plenary" powers sought and obtained by town planners after World War II will be adequate to achieve one of their more dramatic, positive objectives: internally "balanced" towns, with an ample variety of industries, shops, population, and different kinds of community, recreational, and social facilities. Quite aside from the merits of this ideal, a combination of obstacles exists that may well prevent the testing of this challenging assumption on how to organize a democratic and socially desirable physical environment.[24]

Balanced towns may not grow automatically. To get such balance, ordinary market and social phenomena may have to be tampered with. If the right industries do not come, then they must be induced to come. Too many or too few shops are taboo. And one ought to get the "right" occupational skills, the "right" distribution of income, sex, and age groups. Then, too, the appropriate community and cultural facilities to serve these needs must be secured. The goals are not quite as difficult as they seem because the "tolerances" are often fairly gross. But neither is the task easy, especially in the complicated circumstances confronting the British planners.

Take the key problem: industrial location. Before a factory could come to the new town, it had to get an industrial development certificate from the Board of Trade. But the board, as already noted, had prior and more compelling commitments in favor of strengthening the development areas and promoting export activities. It can and does "offer substantial financial inducements to industries to go to [Development] Areas. No such power exists in relation to New Towns unless they happen to be situated in Development Areas." [25] These "special responsibilities" are not necessarily consistent with the new towns policy; but they are equally, if not more, important, and they certainly are sensitive to political pressure. Some towns, like Crawley, did quite well in securing industrial activities. Others were seriously disturbed. Harlow and Basildon have been impatient about their difficulties in getting the Board of Trade's cooperation.[26] Hemel Hempstead was worried about new industry and the disproportionate number of unskilled, semiskilled, and female workers in the present labor force. Apparently "a judicious amount of pressure" helped to remedy the situation.[27] Stevenage, the first new town, opened its first factory only in January 1953. Neither Peterlee nor Glenrothes has had much success in attracting the industries it sought. These problems complicated the larger general question of securing the most appropriate, stable, and varied activities for these towns.

Though the type of industries will be important in determining the kind of people who come to the new town, so also will the type of housing. If the housing costs are high, and this has been the case, the town can expect few low-income tenants. Letchworth, the first garden city, labored under this difficulty because it did not even have the advantage of housing subsidies; and it is now tagged as a one-class town. G. D. M. Block, author of a Conservative party pamphlet on new towns, has said: "The danger at present is not so much that of unlettable houses as of difficulty in catering for the lowest paid classes. In 1951 Stevenage Urban District Council was having acute difficulties in recruiting dustmen at £6 a week. The town clerk was reported as saying that he could not expect to recruit at £6 a week from among the newcomers to Stevenage as the rents of the New Town made the proposition look silly." [28]

Other aspects of the government's housing policy contribute to this trend toward homogeneity. The aim was and still is to stretch materials and labor as far as possible to produce the maximum number of houses. Expensive homes were reduced to a minimum and in some cases not even provided; and so the wealthy too tend to be excluded from the new town, assuming that any significant number were even willing to come. When they did come, they wanted their own type of houses in their quarter of the city. In Newton Aycliffe, for example, the original intention was to have families of many income ranges living around a village green. But experience indicated that the higher-income groups would not build expensive houses in neighborhoods of poor houses. So a "West End" is being planned. The chairman of the Crawley Development Corporation pointed out that "there was so much semi-developed land in the country available for building that land in the New Towns at £850 for a quarter acre could not compete with it financially." [29] Though most of the corporations are trying to build three or four types of houses roughly corresponding to the needs of the major income groups, the odds would

83

appear to be in favor of a town with moderate income emerging as the probable end product.

This pattern is reinforced in still other ways. First priority now goes to key employees of the plants locating in the town. These employees are usually in the middle-income group. Equally high priority goes to the skilled construction workers to keep a permanently active labor force in the present tight market. Both often preceded, at least at the outset, the claims of high-priority tenants on council lists. Moreover, even the tenants selected from the housing lists generally earn higher income. They tend to be the skilled workers in fields like light engineering, since their services are in demand. The much larger groups on the register, such as the transport workers or unskilled labor, earn less and are less sought as employees in new towns.[30]

Other groups are hard to serve. For example, the needs of the aged may be difficult to satisfy in the first few years. Many of the unmarried single individuals, if they stay, may become restive because of the absence of most attractions of the large city, if the experiences of Letchworth and Welwyn are any guide.[31] And it is not at all clear whether the planners could or should ensure other kinds of variety — say of religious, ethnic, nationality, or regional groups; nor is it clear what the right variety is.

All of these problems were further aggravated in the early development period. The austerity policy, which virtually eliminated the provision of community buildings and facilities, was a severe blow. To make matters worse, most churches faced bleak economic prospects and had very limited funds to build adequate structures to serve their diminishing flocks. Fear was expressed that once the character of the town was established, changing its pattern would require strenuous efforts. Welwyn, the second garden city, was faced with that issue in the "Great Divide" of the railroad tracks. On the east side were the workers' homes; and on the west the homes of the middle classes. The corporation is trying to modify the pattern by building houses for sale and middle-income flats on the workers' side, but not vice versa. Since some private building is underway on the east side, the policy is said to be successful. Perhaps the present deficiencies in the new towns will not prove too serious, if in the future the corporations can be equally effective in obtaining the required housing for families in the lowest and highest income ranges.

In a way the new towns kept careening from distortion to distortion: not enough community centers; or churches; or playing fields; or factories; or shops; or schools. As a commentary on planning, these lapses have their ironical aspects; but it is worth remarking that they were temporary and that efforts were always underway to correct the shortcomings. This is more than one could say for most other types of development.

New Town Design

Building on comparatively virgin soil is generally considered one of the indisputable assets of new town planning. Presumably, in such a setting existing physical development and property interests could scarcely compromise the boldness or the freedom of the design. However true this may be, there are fewer advantages than one would suppose. The new freedom has been qualified by new limitations. Aside from the perennial difficulties of costs and the preferences of the consumer, there are the constraints imposed by the judgments of the development corporations, the ministry, and the various local authorities. There were also the dangers of innovation: the dangers implied in the aphorism that the rules of a sonnet do not hamper a good poet but may aid a poor one.

Surely this explains in part why the new towns' response to the three-dimensional challenge has thus far been interesting yet disappointing. (See Appendix C: The Look of New Towns.) They do offer open space, clean salubrious environments, plenty of fresh air, better housing equipment, well-planned industrial and shopping areas, and simple, competent, often good design. The residential areas are generally organized into neighborhoods of low density with elementary schools, playing fields, and green wedges. There are also some deliberate variations. Newton Aycliffe has experimented with village greens, somewhat along the lines suggested by the Reilly Plan.[32] Corby is de-emphasizing the neighborhood module. And planners at Peterlee, to counterbalance the straggling mining villages and to reduce the amount of coal sterilized in the seams underneath the site, are concentrating all development in one area rather than in several neighborhoods.[33] In almost every way the towns, as one commentator has emphasized, are far superior to the worst excesses of British nineteenth-century cities, the Black Country, for example. But that is not much of a boast. Friend and foe alike are depressed by the dearth of urbane qualities, of significant choice, of really original or distinguished site plans or designs.

The towns lack warmth, sensual delight, surprise, stimulus, drama. The few efforts to achieve these effects, with possible exceptions, such as the piazza in Harlow's shopping center, seem strained and only partly successful. The towns, like a bad painting, are apprehended too quickly. The eye has little to feast upon, nor can it take any interesting journeys.

There are few successful examples of a defined or a "masked" approach to the towns; of varied, interrelated, and delightful enclosures; of movement and concealment of space; of throbbing vitality or exciting perspective, panorama, or skylines. There are no sharp divisions between town and country; few alternations of intensity, rhythm, texture, light, color; no breath-taking setting off of forms, of facades, or central foci. The smells and sounds are monotonous; the shops, the signs, the entertainment, and general intellectual fare, Spartan. The metropolis, Professor Lynch says, "is continually 'talking' to the observer; it is full of written or pictorial symbols, directing, informing, exhorting. The chatter must be controlled so that the voices can be heard." [34] In the new towns, however, the density of ideas is rather low: the towns are boring.

Others whose judgments command respect deplore even more strongly these limitations. Thus Mr. J. M. Richards, one of the editors of the distinguished British journal, *Architectural Review*, passed the following judgment apropos of the new towns:

> the greatest disappointment, when we come to compare expectation with achievement, is on the architectural side. . .
>
> It should hardly be necessary to emphasize that a town is, by definition, a built-up area, whose role is to provide for a particular mode of living. It is a sociable place, for people who want to live close together, and expresses itself as such through the compactness of the layout, through the sense of enclosure experienced within it and through being composed of streets. The New Towns, by and large, have none of these attributes. They consist for the most part of scattered two-story dwellings, separated by great spaces. Their inhabitants, instead of feeling themselves secure within an environment devoted to their convenience and pleasure, find themselves marooned in a desert of grass verges and concrete roadways. . .
>
> They gain something too, of course, from the move: cleaner air, more up-to-date kitchens, space for children to play. But all these could have been provided in towns planned *as* towns. They could have had these and the cheerful life of the streets, the street corner pub, the market place gossip, the public services and entertainments and the easy access to real countryside (denied by the present suburban sprawl) which a proper town provides; and in addition, they could have had what, as time goes by they will miss, more than any of the foregoing: the sense of being in the center of a community, however small, not on the fringe of it.[35]

Mr. Gordon Cullen, the art editor of the *Architectural Review*, is even more caustic in his criticism of this "prairie planning." He complains of the too

> generous a use, or rather unuse of land, . . . the feeling that the little

two-story houses are far too puny and temporary to match up to the monumental, overpowering space, . . . the eternity of wideness punctuated at intervals by seas of concrete . . . the cult of isolationism . . . the theory that everybody stinks and so you must have as much room as possible between.

Translated into town planning jargon, this quality of ebbiness becomes low density housing — the results are deplorable — footsore housewives, cycle weary workers, never ending characterless streets, the depressing feeling of being a provincial or suburbanite in an environment that does not belong to town or country; and the impossibility of ever getting into the real country which this suburban sprawl has banished. End result — travelling shops and higher rates to pay for acres of unnecessary pavements at twenty-five shillings a square yard. To sum up, the New Towns, except for rather better house plans, have advanced but little on the old housing estates. In the sense that they tend to occupy more valuable land they are actually a step back. Regarded as what their name claims for them, New Towns, in spite of all the administrative energy, publicity and cash expended on them, what should have been a great adventure has come to nothing and less than nothing — and so far with hardly a word spoken in protest.[36]

But these expostulations may be a harking back to another golden age, this time of the sophisticated connoisseur, and perhaps only of the Chelsea type. Mr. Richards, beating his chest and crying *mea culpa* in behalf of the architectural profession, is a puzzling figure. He complains that

Good design by individual architects does not alter the fact that their failure as a body to give society a lead and impose on it the ideas their knowledge and technical resources tell them are the best ideas is the failure of modern architecture itself, a failure the more disastrous for having occurred on the occasion when architecture faced the challenge of fulfilling a vital social need.[37]

But in his contemporary classic *The Castles on the Ground*, Mr. Richards warned that

It will do no good to impose an advanced or academic idiom on people who are already evolving at their own slow pace a vernacular style based on very different standards but suited for their own peculiar needs and aspirations. . .

The present day suburb is peopled with amateur gardeners, amateur landscapists and amateur decorators, with contrivers of all sorts of effects, with handymen and with the individualists from whom the suburban jungle draws much of its vitality and for whose creative instincts it caters in a way that nothing else can as the world is made at present.[38]

87

There is also some reason to question whether the blame has been properly fixed. Mr. Lionel Brett, the gifted architect planner of Hatfield, believes that "Red tape, lack of funds, engineering restrictions, consumers' conservatism, inefficient organisation produced" these results.[39] The astonishing thing, he thinks, "is that the New Towns aren't worse." Others, like Mr. Tom Mellor, have raised searching questions about the possible weakness of the case for urbanity on social, if not aesthetic, grounds.[40] Indeed, it may be as wrong today to seek the older, nostalgic town qualities as to emulate the picturesque charm one finds in the crowded medieval town. Perhaps the values sought are incompatible with the automobile, the rising real income, the contemporary hunger for space and gardens and for houses close to the ground. With the mellowing of age and twenty years' nursing of trees and landscape, the towns may also evolve more winsome features. There might be some justice to Mr. Osborn's rejoinder that

> What it comes to is that the new towns do not comply with a pattern of urbanity laid up in the Heaven of the Review's architectural priesthood. This ideal is variously described as making for "enclosure," "civic warmth," "towniness," "cosiness," "intimacy," "floorscape," "immediacy" . . . The notion that the creation of townscape to assuage a scene designing urge was ever any part of the serious purpose of the new towns is nothing less than ridiculous.[41]

And perhaps there is also some point to his caustic asides on the "Fetish of Urbanity":

> A town can be very open with any amount of public space and garden space and still be in the fullest sense a town with any of the typical urban attributes — many trades and professions, large scale industry, diversified culture, and if you like, ample sophistication, ostentation and vice. None of these things, good or bad, imply or necessitate corridor streets or multistory dwellings, or enclosure or cosiness or stuffiness, any more than they necessitate traffic congestion or theatre queues or smoke palls or the smell of drains or motor exhausts.[42]

There is certainly enough truth in these views to make one pause before a final judgment. Yet something is amiss. Even devoted supporters of the new towns program, such as Lionel Brett, Lewis Mumford, and others, seem to be apprehensive. The shopping centers, Mr. Mumford notes,

> usually provide arcaded walks beside the shops, but aside from that even the best seem to have been conceived without reference to the exigencies of the motor age or future traffic. Nowhere is there the separation

of pedestrian precincts from parking lots and motor avenues one would expect in a mid-twentieth century New Town; nowhere is there sufficient use of the super-block or cul-de-sac street to separate foot and wheeled traffic; rarely are there any of the internal parks and internal pedestrian ways that the pioneering Unwin provided in Hempstead Garden Suburb. . .

Something important in the old towns and villages that these New Towns often surround has been lost in the new design — something that needs to be understood and adapted. The fact is that a city is not primarily a way of providing a vegetable garden for every inhabitant; above everything else, it is a means of providing a maximum number of social contacts and satisfactions. When the open spaces gape too widely and dispersal is too constant, the people lack a stage for their activities and the drama of their daily life lacks sharp focus . . . Because the new planners were mainly in revolt against congestion and squalor, rather than in love with urban order and cooperation, the New Towns do not yet adequately reveal what the modern city should be.[43]

The Opposition

Every new town dislocates, threatens, or wipes out some, perhaps many, existing interests. Opposition naturally develops. This opposition can and must be anticipated, placated, outmaneuvered, or overridden; for if allowed to fester or cumulate, it may kill the program.

The nature of the opposition has varied. In almost every town there are officials who will balk at the invasion and its possible challenge to their power or prestige. Local officials in Hemel Hempstead served a town of 20,000 before the new town corporation arrived. They did not like and they still do not like the activities of the intruding corporation, however thoughtful and sensitive the members of the corporation are to the delicate situation. Sharing of authority by appointing local officials to development corporations sometimes helps. That step was belatedly taken in Stevenage. But there are limits to what tact can do to soothe the outraged feelings of an "invaded" and "occupied" area.

Other interests besides those of the local officials are quickly affected. There may be great shock when existing properties are purchased. Stores, for example, are generally acquired promptly. The corporation wants to capture their increased value as population increases. But the owner of a little store may object bitterly even if the store is leased back to him on fair terms and with prospects of increased trade. The property may have been a family heirloom or a form of security. He may not want or be able to handle the increased business. He may simply want to be let alone.

There are many who have other interests of this nature: the person who has bought or built a quiet place in the choice spot to retire; the owner of a farm who knows and loves the land his family has tilled for many years and who has heard the government ask for increased production and sees his efficient farm going to "waste"; the comfortable middle-class merchant or professional who likes the community as is, with all its faults and virtues, and does not want it balanced according to the taste and doctrines of some civil servant in London or on the development corporation; the landed aristocrat who takes a paternal interest in the area and who dreads the change into something alien; the local politicians and job holders who see their prospects clouding with future uncertainties.

There are, of course, also local interests that are favorably affected, like those of the merchants who foresee increased business and the politicians who anticipate growth, increased prestige, or more voters of their political complexion. These interests are sometimes in the majority. Even then there is often a tendency born of suspicion to propose other "more satisfactory" locations.

Eventually, as the town grows, the hostile interests shrink in relative significance. Some of their representatives may even change their views. But in the early period there is often intransigent resistance. Hearings may be demanded to consider whether the right site has been chosen, whether too much land has been included, whether proper attention has been given to the water supply, to the conservation of agricultural land, to the historic character of the community. Legal battles may be precipitated and development brought to a standstill for years. Effective opposition, as in the case of Bracknell and Glenrothes, may cut drastically the size of the proposed site or turn a bold policy into a timid one.

If the town is approved, rear-guard actions may be fought. Cooperation may end or be reduced to a bare minimum. Bylaws and other regulations may be enforced to the letter. Services required by the development corporation may be provided, but very slowly. If the costs are high, adequate reimbursement may be demanded before such a development is undertaken "in all fairness to local rate payers." For a long time administration can be effectively hamstrung by hostile groups skilled in the potential dilatoriness of democratic processes.

Neglected as well as impaired interests can become a powerful source of opposition. The principal metropolitan communities have not been granted any significant role as developers. Yet they are directly concerned as authorities "exporting" population and industry and as agencies with great building potential for good or evil. If London, for example, is not to grow, the London County Council must either cut its building or build elsewhere. With housing still one of the most sensitive variables influencing voters' reactions, it is politically impossible for the council to discontinue building. If the building potential is not harnessed to the new towns, it will find outlets either in suburban areas, in the greenbelt, or in the construction of flats. Faced with these alternatives, the leadership in existing towns has been skeptical about or even hostile to these rootless new towns, which scarcely seem to help and may even hinder their own programs by diverting materials, labor, and technical personnel. These powerful authorities have friendly representatives in Parliament who often reflect their dislike or distrust of the program, and stand ready to challenge it. These Parliamentary representatives must be added to the list of those who are indifferent to the new towns policy or who respond sensitively to the interests that are injured by it.

Finally, there is the opposition within the government itself. Often it is mistakenly assumed that because a government policy is expressed in favorable legislation, the government has a consistent and a homogeneous view. Actually, the policy may represent a compromise or the cautious, perhaps unopposed response to some special pressure. As the policy is developed later, it may suffer from neglect or from internal attacks because of conflicts with other policies and programs. The new towns policy is no exception. Many persons insist that the Board of Trade personnel and the permanent staff are not sympathetic with the planning ideas. Even more important, the board's commitments, as we have noted, are inconsistent with many of the new towns' objectives. From the board's point of view, first things come first; and with the country slowly extricating itself from its precarious economic condition, it would be surprising if many key officials did not feel that export requirements and other basic policies should not be hamstrung by misguided or overambitious welfare legislation. Similarly, the food specialists, worried about the critical exchange problem, high food prices, and the rest, have looked askance at the erosion of the nation's agricultural resources by the absence of any coherent policy. New towns, developed with what appeared to them to be scandalously low densities, were just another example of the loss of precious agricultural resources. The Treasury staff were equally aghast at the mounting costs and at liabilities authorized by the new towns legislation, during a period of inflation when the Treasury was struggling desperately to reduce costs and maintain solvency. Similarly, the Ministry of Labour, the Ministry of Supplies, the Coal Board, and others were worried about the use of scarce resources for "expendable" programs.

Most of these senior ministries are long established and more powerful than the Ministry of Housing and Local Government. In retrospect, the greatest compliment to the new towns policy makers may be that the program survived while many important government officials and their subordinates and many powerful local interests chafed at the apparent frittering away of resources. It is still uncertain whether this opposition from within the government and from disaffected outside interests can be withstood by new towns adherents possessing only moderate political support. Imaginative industrialists, workers, and consumers may be a tremendous latent force, as F. J. Osborn believes, in behalf of new towns. But even Osborn laments the "paucity and thinness" of their influence in the face of "the organized, determined and affluent" forces in favor of the *status quo* or their own immediate objectives. Put more starkly, if any government ever becomes lukewarm or hostile to the new towns policy, what is there to prevent it from being ignored or swept aside? [44]

Summary Observations

The building of new towns has been handicapped by administrative entanglements: disputes with local authorities, conflicting jurisdictions, overweening ministerial supervision of detail. There were also financial dilemmas posed by unsolved long- and short-term cost allocations. Rents too were high, primarily because of inflated costs, a narrow economic base, and inadvertently unfavorable administrative, accounting, and lending arrangements. The ideal of varied and balanced town development has been upset by inconsistent policies, steep costs, and the inherent difficulties of the task. The towns themselves, although they furnish good healthy environments, have not won enough plaudits, just the reverse in some respects from certain sophisticated connoisseurs of contemporary architecture and town planning. The new towns also have inescapably aroused local opposition or have come into conflict with proponents of other seemingly incompatible policies.

Solutions may be tricky and perhaps even improbable; but almost none of these difficulties appear to be irremediable. Corrective measures may include administrative changes, such as freeing the corporations from unnecessary supervision and perhaps permitting local authorities to participate in the building of new towns; policy changes, such as recasting some of the directives governing the Board of Trade, tightening controls on plant extensions in London and elsewhere, and more systematic decentralization of government offices; fiscal changes, such as arranging for advances on more suitable terms, shouldering more of the less remunerative phases of town development, and providing subsidies to purchase vacant premises.[45] But much depends on whether the idea of new towns can generate enough support to make the program more than an absorbing minor episode in contemporary planning history: in short, an indispensable, not an expendable, policy commitment.

CHAPTER 7

New Towns: Personal History

As one might suspect, each new town had its unexpected fiascoes in getting things underway. They were the usual "teething" difficulties with occasional alarming complications. In different measure they betrayed inexperience, conflicts of interest and personality, defects in the planning mechanism. Some day a richer personal history must be provided than the few scraps offered here. For many lessons can be gleaned from the careful dissection of these episodes. T. S. Eliot once remarked that "Dostoyevsky had the gift, a sign of genius in itself, for utilizing his weaknesses." [1] Such a gift is surely needed for turning new town weaknesses into insights that would strengthen the program.

Stevenage

Consider, for example, Stevenage, the first and most notorious of all the new towns.[2] It was to set an example for the other towns. But the good intentions were of no avail. The first few years were marked by stormy conflict, rankling bitterness, endless delays.

The 6000 residents of the old town of Stevenage, located in Hertfordshire about thirty miles from London, were governed by an urban district council, two-thirds of whose members were Independents or Conservatives. Preliminary inquiries and discussions of the prospects for expansion as a new town were initiated during the closing days of the war. They were marked by a cooperative council attitude. In January 1945, the Town Planning and Development Committee of the Council had recommended "that the proposal to site a satellite town at Stevenage be approved in principle subject to reservations with regard to the financial provisions and any necessary boundary revisions." ³ Receptive gestures and discussions followed.

But this cordiality soon changed. The pleasant abstract prospects began to manifest some harsh realities. Fears were first roused by the somewhat inadvertent disclosure that approximately 5500 acres of land would be acquired soon. This acquisition was to include almost all of Stevenage except for the built-up area. The fears gave rise to shock when the residents in the area where the new town was to develop received blunt, formal notices of the government's intention to acquire their properties, by agreement or compulsion.⁴ All at once unforeseen implications of the program were sensed: the danger of being uprooted, the ending of sentimental, local ties, "invasion" by Londoners, possibly higher rates, changes in the character of the town, decisions affecting the community by "distant" government agencies, the restrictions of "planning," the loss of good agricultural land, and the like. However unfortunate these implications, they might conceivably have been accepted with melancholy or otherwise — as part of the price of change and development. For there were also advantages for some of the local residents: more trade for the shops, more and better job prospects, some of the variety and opportunities of an urbanized community, superior physical plans and layout, etc. But administrative bungling spurred collective resentment, entrenched opposition, stung the victims and the disaffected interests into action, and discouraged or rendered negligible such assistance as the supporters of the program might have given.

Almost from the beginning neither the council nor the public were too well informed. When the council objected and asked for more information, the ministry ventured a few details in confidence. But "leaks" brought protests from the ministry, then a period of caution and secrecy. On many points, too, the ministry had simply not developed a clear policy. Fear and suspicion spread. Though there was scarcely any intention of evicting anyone for at least a year or two, few families knew this. Aside from the difficulty of getting other homes, compensation rules were based on 1939 values. Strict adherence to this policy was a real financial threat to many families and sure to exacerbate their problems of securing new homes. These and other grievances were fanned by the Stevenage Residents Protective Association, formed to protect the objectors' interests.

Matters were not improved when the minister arrived personally on the scene to explain, to pacify the residents, and to enlist support for his program. He faced a hostile audience. His speech was interrupted by whistling, catcalls, and bitter questions. The sympathy he expressed for those who would be displaced and his promise to delay evictions as long as possible fell on deaf ears. His declared inability to change the rules of compensation left many persons troubled or enraged.[5] His picture of a better and more attractive town made no impression on those who were satisfied with things as they were. His firm assertion of his right and responsibility to protect the interests of the town's future inhabitants, and of his authority and duty to see that the town got built whether the populace approved or not, left a bitter imprint on most persons' minds. When the minister left the hall, he found that the tires of his car were deflated and that sand had been dropped in the petrol tank.

After the minister returned to London, he refused for a time to meet with council officials. This attitude, plus a disinclination to keep the council informed of plans, led to even more embittered relationships. At the inquiry requested by the council concerning the selection of the site, the ministry presented no testimony but adhered to the decision to develop the new town despite the objections raised by various local groups. The minister also refused to appoint as a member of the Stevenage Development Corporation a hostile candidate strongly recommended by the local council. He paid no attention to the charges of politics or of loading the corporation leadership with Labour personnel. Whatever the pros and cons, the occurrence of these incidents only intensified the intransigent attitudes.

The council decided to fight the minister's decision in the courts. The grounds for the appeal were that the minister had not given proper consideration to the evidence introduced at the hearings, that he was judging his own cause, that the hearings were defective because the case of the ministry and the reasons supporting the decision were not properly presented.

Some inkling of the temper of the residents was furnished one day by the substitution of Silkingrad for the Stevenage sign on the railroad station, an episode which attracted attention even beyond the nation. When the High Court decided in favor of Stevenage, the case was appealed to the House of Lords, where the minister ultimately won after a delay of approximately a year. Considering the initial objectives, it was a Pyrrhic victory. Instead of a model town, the program turned into a frustrating failure, with the Stevenage Corporation in the position of a successful occupying power. Development was practically at a standstill. The lessons were all negative: a record of how things should not have been!

Before new momentum could be acquired, other obstacles cropped up. Shortly after legal clearance had been secured, the national austerity policy intervened to curb further activity. To deal with the economic crisis, capital development was strictly rationed. "Work on the New Towns," Sir Stafford Cripps declared, was "in general to be limited during 1948 to starting the provision of water and sewerage and roads." [6]

Alas, this was not all. For a variety of reasons ranging from resignations to death, there was a succession of chairmen of the Stevenage Development Corporation. It appeared as though there were some evil demon bent on frustrating continuous and clear direction. Fastidiousness within the corporation in developing the program and overzealous regulation by the ministry added to the handicaps. As development proceeded, new baffling problems emerged: high rents, rigid economies limiting experimentation, the dormitory character of the town, the difficulties of securing water and sewage facilities, the insistence of Hertfordshire on adequate remuneration before it would provide services. This combination of obstacles makes it easy to understand why only twenty-eight permanent dwellings were completed by 1950; why the first family only arrived in 1951; and, even more tragic, why the first factory was built only in January 1953.[7] When one considers that a principal reason for placing new town administration in the hands of the central government was to secure speedy, uninterrupted development, it is possible to appreciate the anguish and crises of morale that such delays must have entailed.

Stevenage, in short, was a bad start. But perhaps such a virgin program had to "bleed a little before bearing fruit." [8] The influence of new families will eventually balance and ultimately submerge the views of the original residents. Unfortunately, scars still remain; and many friends of the program, like the distinguished novelist E. M. Forster, have been disturbed because this "meteorite town . . . will obliterate the ancient and delicate scenery," because "something irreplaceable has been lost. . . I wonder what compensation there is in the world of the spirit," Forster asked, "for the destruction of the life here, the life of tradition." [9] Mr. Harold Orlans, whose sensitive painstaking study is the most complete record to date of this experience, remarks in summing up that:

> Ministry and Corporation officials had started work on the New Town with high ideals, great ambition, and no experience. By 1950 they had gained a good deal of frustrating experience which must have served to moderate their ambition and ideals. The New Towns programme was a bold venture for a young Ministry and, if it could not resolve in a score

of years problems created by over a century of urbanization, it could still hope to achieve standards utopian for previous generations. In the move from planning to practice, the planners experienced the recalcitrance of many people to being planned, the compulsion of economic factors, the power of the status quo, the conflict of interests between rival individuals and groups within and without the Government; the importance of "connections" and of personalities; of patience; of power; and of change. In short, they experienced something of the world.[10]

There is heartening evidence, however, that the worst days have passed. Part of the credit for this is owed to Sir Thomas Bennett. Chairman of the Crawley Corporation, he was also appointed Chairman at Stevenage in June 1951 and remained in office until May 1953. Under his leadership there was vigorous promotion of economic development. These efforts were fairly successful and were continued by his successor. At the start of 1955, arrangements were made or pending for the erection of 622,000 square feet of factory space with an estimated employment of 2,700 workers. Another 31,000 square feet of space was to be provided for a water pollution station for the Division of Industrial and Scientific Research, employing approximately 100 scientists and administrative staff.[11] The absence of an economic base has led to the acceptance as tenants of workers recruited from London by firms located in Letchworth and Hitchin. Some employees of firms in old Stevenage have also been given houses. In the future, however, it is far more likely that the employees of these new firms will "occupy all the houses which the Corporation can build." [12]

There are still some exasperating difficulties. Rents are quite high. The corporation is also dissatisfied with the inadequate assistance received from the Ministry of Education and the county council for playing fields and community buildings, and with the lag between population increase, schools, and social and recreational amenities. Traffic problems have also arisen in the shopping center of old Stevenage and in the east-west access route from residential to industrial areas. This is because the Great North Road bypass, which should have been ready in 1947, has not yet been approved. The corporation, too, is skeptical of the extremely expensive sixteen and a half mile sewerage scheme, costing more than £1,500,000, exclusive of the treatment plant. The scheme, however, is necessary to avoid pollution of London's water supply.[13]

Happily, there were other items which the corporation could view with deep satisfaction. Generally, building was moving forward at a rapid pace. About 1600 houses will probably be completed during 1955.

Also, the new towns' boundaries were adjusted finally so that the whole of the designated area fell within the Urban District of Stevenage. Not least, most of the other services necessary for the life of the town have continued parallel with the housing development.[14]

Peterlee

The history of Peterlee, too, was marred by tragic episodes. This is all the more saddening since the demand for the town came originally from the miners' representatives. The miners' jobs were hard, dirty, and in the past poorly paid. They lived in grim, primitively equipped mining and agricultural villages. Many of the houses were overcrowded. They lacked baths, indoor toilets, and even kitchens. Community facilities were negligible or deplorably inadequate. The villages were scattered among the pitheads, close to the sulphurous coke ovens and the collieries' chimneys. In response to opportunities elsewhere, miners were leaving the area in droves. An average of one out of every five households in Easington had an emigrant, and there were few replacements.[15]

With the passage of the new towns legislation, the Easington Rural District Council submitted proposals for a miners' town, a town that would furnish all the needed social facilities which a modern community should have. These proposals were later published as a pamphlet called *Farewell Squalor*. On the suggested site (an area surrounded by mining villages), new houses, schools, shops, and hospital, recreational, and transportation facilities were to be provided. Industries also were to be attracted to furnish employment for the disabled miners, for girls who might leave the mining communities, and for many miners who might lose their jobs because of "rationalization." [16]

The idea of a new town pleased the miners. The ministry too thought it made sense. So a designation order was drafted in late 1947. Hearings were held in 1948. None of the three principal objections raised were considered sufficient grounds for stopping the project.[17] The new town, as envisaged by Mr. Berthold Lubetkin, its first distinguished architect, was to be built at a density of twenty persons per acre. There were some protests that good agricultural land would be taken. But even more might be lost, the minister claimed, if the villages expanded. Still other persons, such as the parish clerks of Horden and Thornley, feared the new town would be built at the expense of their districts: one local official dramatically asked whether the population of his area would be carried in cattle trucks to Peterlee. They recommended that, instead of a new town, strong community ties ought to be encouraged and existing deficiencies of the villages be remedied by providing needed meeting places, houses, playing fields, and some redevelopment. The ministry conceded that these points had merit. But its reply was that the new town would benefit all the villages by providing urban facilities. Finally, the objection that miners would have to travel to work was countered with the fact that about one-fifth of the miners already traveled between villages, and that more intervillage travel was expected. Peterlee, it was hoped, might ultimately reduce travel since it was close to the long-life coastal pits. During the early years, however, considerable difficulties were anticipated.

The corporation was established in 1948, and the new town was christened Peterlee in honor of one of the local mine's leaders.[18] An unusually attractive site had been selected. The plans called for a recreational and shopping center to serve the Easington District; the attraction of industry to provide more diversified economic opportunities; social facilities, including schools, a technical college, a hospital, and better transportation; and the preparation of a site to serve a community of more than thirty thousand persons. Thus the project began with the highest of hopes, the best of motives, and apparently only minor misgivings.[19]

Problems soon cumulated, however. Bitter winds and sea mist posed some climatic limitations that detracted from the advantages of the site. Far more serious, however, was the fact that underneath there was coal; [20] and not only on this site, but on every other available site near the long-life coastal pits. Sterilization of this coal, approximately 30 million tons, meant a huge cost, perhaps even unemployment for the workers. Mining the area, on the other hand, resulted in subsidence, an unstable site, and considerable dangers for the housing erected.

Prior to the establishment of the town, the National Coal Board and the Ministry of Town and Country Planning reached an informal understanding about the pattern of development. No coal was to be mined in a part of the site's northeast corner which was to be the starting point. For this area alone about one and three-quarter million tons of coal were to be sterilized. But in return the ministry promised to erect only detached and semi-detached houses. As for the development of the rest of the town, only a general accord was reached.

The new town's corporation, and particularly its architect, Mr. Lubetkin, insisted that a more satisfactory and comprehensive agreement had to be negotiated, a position which the Coal Board felt was a betrayal of the original agreement. More specifically the corporation advocated extraction of the seam, area by area, and building after the subsidence occurred. According to the corporation's mining expert, Mr. E. L. S. Potts, Mining Reader at King's College, Durham, subsidence was to be expected in two to five years. If rapid extraction occurred in the first few areas and the building program was timed properly, the subsidence danger could then be minimized. But it was recognized that such a program, considering the existing mining of the pits, involved many technical and financial difficulties. So other alternatives were also advocated, including filling in the extracted areas, the sterilization of some areas, and the use of certain unstable areas for low-density residential development.

Mr. Lubetkin ardently desired a compact center with a variety of houses, including flats. Flats for one- or two-bedroom dwellings were cheaper, he insisted; and they could accommodate families in different stages of the family cycle. Sterilize a small part of the area, he urged, and take certain precautionary measures such as putting fill in the mined areas; and then it would be possible to build quickly and efficiently, to reduce the amount of land sterilized, to achieve architectural urbanity, and to provide a social and urban focus for the mining areas.[21]

However, the Coal Board disagreed. They questioned whether expenditures to provide fill were wise or economical. To refute these objections, Mr. Lubetkin imported specialists from abroad who cited the experiences of Holland, Germany, and Poland. Recourse to these foreign experts did not endear him to the board. No development was possible, however, until this issue was resolved. The dispute was therefore referred to a Committee of the Ministry of Works, known as the Webster Committee. Their report, received in January 1949, supported the Coal Board. It recommended that the town should be built while mining continued underground. This report was referred to an interdepartmental working party; and later to a regional working party representing the corporation and the National Coal Board, and chaired by the Regional Controller of the Ministry of Town and Country Planning. Agreement was not secured, despite various modified proposals and counterproposals. So the dispute was referred back again to the interdepartmental committee and then to the Cabinet. In July a ruling was made in favor of sterilization of the land. Quite evidently the Cabinet wanted the miners to get their town and either overlooked or weren't too concerned about the fact that some three hundred acres containing excellent seams of coal were to be lost as a result.

Nobody relished this decision. The source of livelihood of the miners and a valuable resource of the national economy was at stake. Even a small amount of land on the surface meant thousands of tons of coal be-low, employment perhaps for a few hundred miners for many years. Enough opposition developed so that the decision, as expected, was ulti-mately reversed. A smaller amount of land was made available, and the Coal Board was to set the time and pattern for mining the area to make development possible. In effect, Mr. Lubetkin's proposals were jettisoned, and he resigned in despair.[22]

Two years had elapsed. Plans had been made; various surveys under-taken. But no houses were built. Prior to the establishment of the new town corporation, the Easington Rural District Council had an enviable reputation for building houses. But to get the new town it was necessary to limit this program to approximately ninety-six houses a year. Pre-sumably, most new houses for miners were to be concentrated in the new town. The Easington authorities didn't like this decision at all.[23] Housing was a delicate issue in Britain generally. A slowdown in building could have grievous political repercussions. Yet for two years the subsidence controversy raged and no houses rose in the new town. Understandably, some people wondered whether a new town was such a good idea after all, particularly those persons who had originally thought that it would be "their show." It dismayed many of them to find a new town corpora-tion established, many outsiders called in, and the prospects of their own authority shrinking.

Eventually some houses were produced at a snail's pace. The original plan presupposed that the new town would be built in about ten or fifteen years, after the designation order in March 1948. By the end of March 1951, twenty-six houses were built and 106 under construction.[24] During this period, the corporation was building under an agreement reached in June 1950 with the Coal Board. This provided that "land under which only two seams remained to be worked was available for residential areas of semi-detached houses grouped around a stabilised town centre area." [25] This arrangement, however, forced a piecemeal, fragmentary development of the site. It also limited building to a maxi-mum of 450 houses per annum and even this rate, it was discovered, couldn't be achieved. A new study was therefore requested of Mr. Whitaker, the Superintending Structural Engineer of the Ministry of Works. After reviewing the situation, he concluded "it was practicable to build upon areas in which three seams remained, provided building was limited to sites where mainly vertical movement was likely to oc-cur." [26] This view was accepted at a meeting between representatives of the corporation, the Coal Board, and the ministry. The decision, subject to review, appeared to make it "possible to build an average of 500 houses a year during the next fourteen years and achieve a population of not less than 21,000 by 1962 and about 25,000 by the end of 1965." [27] Since the agreement has been reached, progress has been more encouraging. By March 1952, 309 dwellings were completed.[28] A year later 819 houses were completed and 466 under construction.[29]

Meanwhile, other difficulties emerged. As the years passed, it seemed increasingly uncertain whether a sufficient number of industries would be attracted to provide more varied employment opportunities. The National Coal Board was from the outset perturbed by these aims. One of Britain's critical postwar problems has been to keep the miners in the mines. Premium wages, special rations, and other incentives have proved of limited value. If industry were attracted to the area, the board feared the miners would leave the pits. Probably the only satisfactory activities from the board's point of view would have been those employing women or unemployable miners; and such selectivity was not easy to ensure. In addition, there has been considerable local opposition to these industrial objectives. Representatives of nearby authorities, the Hartlepools, for example, have argued bitterly that any industry attracted to the area should go to the Northeastern Trading Estates. Because the estates, the regional agent of the Board of Trade, had

> failed to keep pace with the decline of employment in the region's older industries, to say nothing of the increase in its employable population, they and the local authorities have looked with disfavour on the rival claims of Peterlee.
>
> The Northeast Development Association, representing both employers and workers, at one stage demanded that industrial development in the New Town should be restricted to service trades. A particular bone of contention was the Corporation's desire to provide jobs in the New Town for the women and girls who now travel daily from their homes in the Peterlee district to work on the Hartlepool Trading Estate.[30]

Disturbed by this opposition, Peterlee thereupon sought recognition as an agent of the Board of Trade in this development area. The new town had many potential advantages. These included the assurance ultimately of better housing, more adequate community facilities, and more attractive surroundings than were available elsewhere within the region. It also was scheduled to have a technical college and a new business center; and it did have a considerable labor force within easy reach. Nonetheless the request was denied. But the board did acknowledge

> the corporation's interest in securing a balanced industrial structure for the new town and its right to lease sites direct to industrialists whose

103

applications for permission to build were approved. Eventually a standing joint committee of the board, the corporation and the N.E.T.E. (the North-eastern Trading Estates) was set up in 1950 to supervise the industrial development of the new town.[31]

Thus far the results have been rather paltry. By January 1953 only one industrial certificate had been granted, for a textile firm employing 335 persons. Negotiations were also started with Holyroyds, the Rochdale bearing manufacturers, Armour Laboratories of Chicago, and others. But except for the completion of a factory of 70,000 square feet for textile manufacture and the start on another smaller factory, nothing specific had materialized by January 1955. However, the corporation was determined to build its industrial estate. Originally planned to cover 65.8 acres, it was reduced to 42 acres and then approved by the ministry. The corporation hopes this estate will give the "desired impetus" to the program.[32] The issue, however, may well be decided on other grounds.

In 1950, the National Coal Board published a fifteen-year plan for the reorganization of the coal mining industry. According to this plan, the older uneconomic pits were to be abandoned and individual collieries reorganized. Far more coal is scheduled to be produced in half the number of pits operating in 1950, with 80,000 fewer miners.[33] Just how this program will ultimately affect Peterlee and Glenrothes, the new town for miners in Scotland, is still uncertain. Possibly the miners in Peterlee may be less than originally estimated. But the reduction of the number of workers in mining may release enough miners, primarily older and unemployable ones, to help man the industries which the towns have been seeking. Peterlee and Glenrothes could become areas to absorb miners relocated from the less efficient seams and to provide employment for those no longer required in the industry. If so, both the National Coal Board and the Board of Trade should prove more "cooperative" in the future.

The importance of the industrial development policy is underlined even more by a distressing attack which has come from still another quarter. Early in 1952, the Durham County Planning Office carefully restudied the statistical estimates on the basis of which the new town was planned. They claimed that the figures prepared in 1946 were based on erroneous or unrealized assumptions, all biased in the direction of a much larger population than could actually be anticipated.[34] Some of the points questioned were (1) whether property with a life up to twenty years ought to be demolished in ten years; (2) whether 5000 additional units could be demolished in ten to twenty years, despite higher standards; (3) whether all people needing new houses in twenty years would be rehoused in Peterlee. According to the county planning office, the economic problems of the postwar period made the first two conditions unlikely, at least for many years; and the need for development of existing villages plus difficulties in travel to work made the third unlikely. On the basis of more "realistic" assumptions, the report concluded that only a population of approximately 8000 could be counted upon; and even this drastically reduced estimate was judged to be contingent upon rent reductions and a considerable increase of industrial employment. If these estimates are more accurate and if the government makes no special effort at industrial promotion to augment the population, Peterlee, instead of turning out to be the focal center for the concentration of all the social facilities, may end up as another abortive mining village.

High costs also aggravated matters. Miners lived in the old company houses and paid almost no rent, or very little rent. Thirty-three per cent paid less than 10/- per week; about 62 per cent paid between 10/- and 15/-.[35] They were stunned to learn that the new three-bedroom houses with a total area of 895 square feet cost approximately 26/- or 27/- per week, this despite the fact that many of the miners could afford the housing. It was disquieting, especially to the miners' leaders, since other local authorities in the area were building new houses at a rent of 12/- to 15/- per week. The poorer families seemed unlikely to get into the projects, or to want to do so.[36]

Some of the miners' families who did come to Peterlee also became dissatisfied. There were many reasons. The miners' cronies were not nearby. At the outset there were few stores or social facilities. The costs were high, at least by comparison. These reactions tended to filter back. Many persons began to think of the new town as pie in the sky. Better a few new houses in the old villages, it seemed, than this new town. The miners' representatives got increasingly nervous and critical of developments. If this idea didn't work, the blame might well come to rest on them.

Still other snags imperiled the creation of a balanced community of varying social and economic groups. Long years of subjection to the fear of unemployment, pit disasters, and strikes had built up an extraordinary solidarity and comradeship among the miners. Paralleling this strong sense of status were the disdainful middle-class attitudes of the officials and tradesmen, still reflected in exclusive clubs and haughty postures. These relationships were further complicated by the low status of miners' wives, the result of slavish hours of household drudgery in houses with inadequate facilities, a dearth of employment opportunities for women, and a long history of low wages. Blunt's Dene, a huge gorge on the site, also threatened to split the town in half physically and probably socially unless ingenious site plans minimized the barrier. Clearly, painful readjustments had to be made. Success in achieving the "balanced" community may yet be possible. But much appears to depend on a frank recognition of the problems and a determined effort to break down the social and physical gulfs. To date, however, the middle classes are shying away from Peterlee and the poorest miners can't afford to live in the town.[37]

As for Peterlee's physical appearance, from the standpoint of contemporary design it is undistinguished. There is little variety of color. Uniform red brick is used to minimize the discoloration of the coal fumes. The site and house plans are quite conventional. In the past, two-story semi-detached houses were built. Subsidence presumably made flats out of the question (though Mr. Lubetkin denied this). Under the new three-seam rule, use is being made of detached two-bedroom house designs and "single block three story flats with foundation sizes sufficiently small to minimize any subsidence." [38] Nevertheless, the houses in Peterlee are far better than the miners have ever had before. They are better equipped and better planned. The Thorntree Gill area has even won a housing medal. They are the kind of houses the miners like, even if they are scarcely, if at all, better than those of most ordinary contemporary projects. The sanitary and kitchen equipment alone would set Peterlee off from the older mining villages. So would the increased social facilities. Plans are underway for two churches and a hospital of 300 beds; a primary school has been started; a junior high school is almost built; a regional technical college has begun. Despite delays, negotiations are being pressed for a health center, community buildings, and recreational facilities. Much work has also been done on the town center, which will accommodate 110 shops. In short, sophisticated criteria may be misleading. The better housing, the new equipment and superior standards, and the sharing of the many pangs and frustrations of the new town may well kindle strong loyalties to Peterlee. It is a miners' town; and their representatives will deserve much of the credit and blame for its ultimate character. The miners are tough-minded. They want what they like and no "fancy" experiments. They are getting it!

The Other London New Towns

The problems of the other new towns are not as dramatic as those of Stevenage and Peterlee. But with few exceptions they have had some trying experiences. Their lugubrious variety may be illustrated by capsule descriptions.

Basildon. Basildon, for example, serves a special purpose beyond the decentralization policy. Though it is located thirty-seven miles east of London in Essex and definitely in the London ring of new towns, its principal function is to repair the ravages of premature, shoddy, speculative fringe development. It was assumed that the techniques of building new towns could be used to transform this area into an integrated community. The idea was first broached by the local authorities: the County Council of Essex and the urban district council. They were later "joined by the County Boroughs of East and West Ham who regarded the area as a natural outlet for their own crowded inhabitants, large numbers of whom had already settled in it." [39] The minister hesitated at first. But a joint deputation of the four authorities helped to persuade him. It is a tribute to the imagination of Britain's planners that they did not shrink from such experimentation.

The decision to go ahead was made on January 4, 1949. About 25,000 persons were then living in this area. Originally a population of 50,000 was contemplated. But Basildon's site is the largest of all the new towns. It measures 7,834 acres. Because of its physical extent and the desire to achieve an urban focus, the population goal was raised to 80,000.

The present layout is haphazard and substandard: individual houses straggle throughout the area; roads are bad; there are no sewers. Most houses are not heated. They are generally satisfactory for summer, not winter, occupancy. Because of sparse development, large gardens are common. The owners, many of whom are simple folk, have very modest incomes. Most of these sites were purchased at so-called "champagne parties." Speculators purchased land at option, invited prospects to see the sites, provided entertainment and luncheons at Sunday gatherings, and secured down payments from would-be owners. Many families couldn't continue their payments; and properties were sold or foreclosed, often more than once and without acquiring satisfactory titles. The Basildon Corporation has developed special procedures to give existing owners firm legal titles; or in particularly difficult cases, to provide funds in escrow for unidentified potential owners. But at the outset, although the corporation had good intentions, resentment flared up against it because it paid only the existing site value, which, despite inflation, was often below the price the people had paid for their properties. The corporation couldn't pay more because development values had been purchased by the government under the Town and Country Planning Act of 1947; and the owners presumably were to be reimbursed for the development value by the Central Land Board. Unfortunately only a minority, about 40 per cent of the owners, were sufficiently sophisticated to have submitted applications. Recognizing this, the corporation is attempting to secure special consideration for the remaining families, with some hope of success. That they will be helped one way or another is all the more probable because the Conservative government has since abandoned the policy of purchasing development rights.[40]

Basildon's architects are particularly unhappy because of the peculiar difficulty of securing a semblance of architectural urbanity. Little development clusters are being planted in the gaps between the houses. Though the simple designs seem to have pleased most of the new occupants, many of the owners of older cottages with more conventional colors and traditional lines have been affronted and derisive. The conflict has been exacerbated because the corporation is responsible for checking and controlling all new development in the built-up areas. It must see that the development corresponds to the proposed plan for the new community and does not perpetuate the old patterns. Many of the older residents were not allowed to provide additions they had contemplated, although their neighbors may have done so before the corporation came on the scene. It is not surprising, therefore, that the existing residents were not quite enamored with the new town planners.[41]

Another of Basildon's major headaches is land costs, which are particularly high. There are numerous unusual complications, such as the need for clearing much waste and scrub land, the costs of demolition, and the extraordinary legal problems including title search, clearance, and the like. In addition, the sparse development imposes heavy costs. Not only are the houses built within the interstices of the developed area: the low density, large gardens, and lengthy roads also entail exceptional costs, especially for utilities. The corporation favors a special subsidy for the unusual land costs. Unfortunately, even if it is granted (and the issue has not yet been resolved), there would still be a large discrepancy in rents between the new and the old units.[42]

Full-scale development was also retarded by the proposed discharge of sewage and surface water drainage in the river Crouch. There were oyster beds in the river and some persons feared they would be harmed by the effluent and "the undue reduction of salinity." [43] The conflict of interests and the objections expressed by the Ministry of Agriculture and Fisheries produced the usual maddening delays. More than two years

108

elapsed before the permanent sewerage schemes were finally approved and the forebodings about the oyster beds laid to rest.

One might have supposed that the uniqueness and complexity of Basildon's problems would have encouraged an experiment in decentralization and administrative latitude. The former chairman, Sir Lancelot Keay, had a long and distinguished record behind him, including the well-known housing and industrial developments at Speke built under his direction while he was Chief Architect at Liverpool. But actually the budgetary controls and ministerial supervision have been exasperating in detail. Limited administrative powers only added to the difficulties. Basildon experienced the typical corporate anxieties because of insufficient industries, playing fields, and other community facilities. It was also "almost entirely a one class area." To correct this the corporation wanted to build more and larger houses.

> Bold steps are needed to attract the higher income groups to Basildon in early stages . . . a no risk policy will not suffice. It is the first tenants that are important; like attracts like, and once a beginning is made the rest will follow. The Corporation believes that a small act of faith may well produce rich dividends.[44]

But this goal, difficult enough to attain under more favorable circumstances, was even further handicapped by the inability to build adequate schools. Essex County, burdened by the growth in Harlow and elsewhere, was tardy in meeting its educational commitments. Families in Basildon have had to send their children twelve miles by bus to overcrowded classrooms; and meanwhile Basildon's planners, with their hands tied, fumed at the difficulties of attracting higher- and middle-income families until such services became available.[45]

By the end of 1955, however, there were some satisfying signs of progress. Cooperation was more in evidence. Basildon was no longer struggling to survive. Objections to land acquisitions were declining. There were actually a growing number of offers to sell to the corporation. A minor industrial boom was underway. Twenty-three factories with a floor space of approximately 900,000 square feet were completed; also twenty-nine shops, forming part of an undercover traffic free shopping area, plus four schools, a church, and a pub. Housing production too was rapidly increasing. To secure greater variety of design, the corporation had invited several outside architects to participate. In addition, it had accepted a proposal of the *Architectural Review* to study the planning and architectural opportunities of a compact town center; [46] and it was also experimenting with a novel form of competition for the complete development of the part or whole of a neighborhood unit of the new town. The selfishness of the speculator and the idealism of the planner have been the subject of scorn and ridicule, but it may well be that a combination of the skill of the architect and the experience of the developer could lead to more economic, if less orthodox, development without the loss of any essential standards.[47]

Harlow. One of the most experimental towns, Harlow has especially emphasized the use of different teams of architects, both consultant and staff, in designing housing areas within neighborhoods. Some attractive results have followed. They range from the consciously varied "street scenes," including Mr. Frederick Gibberd's solitary high-rise building and his medal-winning housing area "The Lawn," to the austere simplicity of Mr. Maxwell Fry's and Miss Jane Drew's houses, the more intimate designs of the corporation's staff architects, the modern sculpture, and the daring use of color.[48] Despite these efforts, some of Harlow's architects were dubious about whether they had created an urban setting. They also boggled at the rigid economies which forced the abandonment of many cherished details, including buildings which enrich the community's social life and "punctuate" their designs. But Harlow's major difficulties were not three-dimensional. There were other reasons why this new town, in the past at least, was deprecated as a white elephant.

Harlow was badly located. Though only twenty-three miles from London, it has no main electric railway line. Transportation to London is relatively slow and expensive. While these conditions exist, Harlow runs the danger of approximating what some garden city enthusiasts mistakenly advocated: an isolated, almost independent town. True, one of the leading personalities associated with the town claimed that this isolation was an advantage, that Harlow, unlike Crawley, would not end up as a London suburb. Perhaps! But during the first five years of its existence, the Harlow Corporation was quite apprehensive. They had far more houses than jobs, many complaints about travel, and serious problems in effecting speedy development.

Harlow's site had other unfortunate aspects. The existing water supply was inadequate. Because of the difficulties involved, the minister made the corporation at its own request a bulk water-supply authority. Pumping machinery has been acquired, and the corporation is now steadily exploring sites and searching for new sources of supply. To develop alternative sources many miles away has proved quite expensive.[49]

Sewage, however, was the really critical problem. At the outset of the new towns program, the ministry received warnings from the Metropolitan Water Board, the Lee Conservancy Board, and the Lee Conservancy Catchment Board that accelerated development of the new towns in Hertfordshire would be inadvisable, or at any rate costly, because of sewerage difficulties. It was made clear that the proposed discharge of effluent into the river Lee would probably result in the pollution of one of the chief sources of London's water supply.[50] The minister said that steps would be taken to deal with this problem, and a consultant was appointed. But the consultant pointed out that no easy solution was available, that the only right solution was for the water to be used either "as a conduit for treated sewage effluents . . . or as a source of a substantial proportion of the water supply of Greater London." [51]

Several short- and long-run schemes were considered, none without difficulties. But sooner or later a new sewerage system would have been necessary with the growth of the area. Therefore, the ministry favored "a central treatment works in the vicinity of Rye Meads, south of Ware, which would serve the Stevenage and Harlow New Towns as well as the New Towns of Welwyn Garden City and Hatfield and other towns in the middle reaches of the River Lee. 3,500,000 pounds was the estimated cost of this scheme." [52]

But the local authorities were disinclined to cooperate. The Hertfordshire County Council, disgruntled about the burgeoning of the new towns in their bailiwick, regarded this situation as a case of new towns chickens coming home to roost. They saw no reason to raise their rates, now or in the future, to support these developments. As a compromise, however, the council did propose that Stevenage should limit its size to a population of 18,000, i.e., the maximum possible if the local works were expanded, and that Welwyn and Hatfield should join the cheaper alternative system in the Colne Valley. The proposal was rejected. Since both Harlow and Stevenage were desperate and since development was sure to cease if prompt action were not taken, the decision was taken to build the Rye Meads works and worry about the finances later.[53] Contrary to expectations, the works were finished before building in Harlow or Stevenage was curtailed. But it was a close shave and hardly a creditable example of foresight in planning.

Now that the hurdle has been overcome, the proposed allocation of costs incites resentment. Both Welwyn and Hatfield were forced into the more expensive Rye Meads scheme against their wishes. The other local authorities adamantly insist upon a satisfactory formula before participating in the regional scheme.[54] Some sharing of the burden is necessary for the costs could not be loaded onto Harlow or Stevenage without imposing an impossible rent burden.

There have also been difficulties with the roads. The highway authority proved recalcitrant in shouldering part of the financial responsibility. To avoid delay, the corporation therefore constructed "only . . . housing estate roads and to a lower standard and specification than is considered really desirable for the heavy traffic which they will ultimately have to carry. The cost involved in improving and completing these highways later on will mean a significant increase in the total cost." [55] In addition, the deficit for building the roads must be met by the corporation since "the Ministry of Transport will not in any case make payment of highway grants retrospectively." [56]

Fortunately future prospects look far more encouraging. Under the canny leadership of the well-known British contractor, Mr. R. R. Costain, the pace of building has soared. A labor force of 2,000–2,500 has been amassed. By the start of 1955, 5,340 dwellings had been completed and another 2,150 were under construction. The corporation is geared to complete about "2,000 dwellings a year with industrial and other development in parallel." [57] Net density in the new neighborhoods is being increased to fifteen houses per acre. The object is to conserve land and reduce road and service costs, and probably also to produce a greater sense of urban enclosure. Flats, however, are being discontinued until there is greater evidence of demand.

Other building has also spurted. Approximately 788,825 square feet of factory accommodation, fifty-nine shops, five schools, twenty-six miles of road, and more than sixty miles of sewers (including two and one-half miles of trunk sewer) were built by 1955. Under construction were three schools and seventeen additional factories. Work has also commenced on the town center. In addition, the program has received an extra fillip by the decision of the Nuffield Provincial Hospital Trust to spend £60,000 in Harlow for three new permanent group practice centers with clinics attached. This was especially encouraging since the most serious deficiency is in community facilities. What is now available is determined "by the amount of expenditure which the Corporation is allowed to incur . . . since the local authority for the area . . . [is] not yet prepared to meet the costs." [58] Partly to correct this, the corporation is attempting to educate the community. Through the press and through the Tenants' and Residents' Association, it is steadfastly explaining the respective responsibilities and services of the corporation and the local authorities. School building, too, is now being spurred. The corporation wants to end "what has been perhaps the major complaint and fear of residents — that their children would be deprived of proper schooling." [59] Steps were taken to set up an urban district authority for the new town, and in April 1955 Harlow achieved this status. Undoubtedly local representation will help to check any undue propensity for delay.

Harlow has definitely passed the creeping stage, and considering the pitfalls already confronted, it is reassuring to learn that the corporation "is more than ever convinced of the successful development of the New Town." [60]

Welwyn and Hatfield. When Welwyn, the second garden city, was converted into a new town, many of the new towns proponents were dejected and resentful. Welwyn, it will be recalled, was built by the Garden City Association after World War I. Ebenezer Howard was irritated by the failure of the government to use the construction boom as an opportunity to build new towns. Boldly and without consulting anyone, he took an option on this site in Hertfordshire, about twenty-one miles north of London, and thereby forced his adherents to follow and support his lead.[61]

But Welwyn grew slowly, partly because of the depression of the thirties. By 1952 it had a population of less than 19,000. Nearby in Hatfield was the large booming de Havilland Aircraft works, where housing was badly needed. The ministry favored integrated planning of this area. It was sure that a new town corporation would speed up the building pace, serve housing and other development needs more efficiently, and eliminate company control of the town. A single new town corporation and executive staff was therefore established to serve both towns.[62]

However understandable the motive for this move, to the directors of the private company who had steered the town through many vicissitudes, and to the Town and Country Planning Association which represented the garden city movement, the decision seemed high-handed, arbitrary, outrageous. One reason for the irritated reaction was the reflection that the minister's decision appeared to cast, rightly or wrongly, on the past leadership and on the actual growth of the town. Appointment of Mr. Richard Reiss, one of the former directors of the company, as vice-chairman of the corporation only partially assuaged the wounded feelings.[63]

Others deplored the implications of this seemingly easy solution. For through this decision the recommendations to the minister by the earlier New Towns Committee to use local authorities and housing associations as well as development corporations had once again been overruled. Many persons regretted this narrow approach. It prevented desirable experimentation with alternative machinery for new town development at a time when there were serious questions whether the device of development corporations was the best expedient in all circumstances. It seemed almost irresponsible to do away with those alternatives that already had a historic claim to existence.

The pent-up bile affected the acquisition of the properties. The ministry, to its credit, tried to be generous. On the other hand, the company, understandably enough, took every occasion to maximize its profit.[64] It insisted on owning and was permitted to own Welwyn stores; it also retained considerable shop properties, 120 flats, and over 100 of the best houses. Many of the other better houses were also sold. "It was from these properties," the Committee on Public Accounts was advised, "that the bulk of the Company's dividends had been paid and what was left . . . contained very little that was profit making."[65] In addition, the company ceased to maintain the public greens and gardens when it realized that it would be bought out. The ministry therefore accepted this obligation even before entering into possession. It proved expensive, especially since some months were consumed in the process of settling the administrative and legal details. For a long time, maintenance, too, had been neglected by the company, perhaps because of the inability to get licenses. Whatever the reasons or justification, the government soon found that it had "to spend nearly three times as much on the repairs of the property as the Garden City Company had been spending."[66] Instead of the new development corporation obtaining, as anticipated, a property with a revenue surplus, it acquired one laden with liabilities that had to be added to "the usual expenses of management and overheads to meet."[67] So evident was this that the Treasury, which originally felt that the corporation needed no initial operating subsidies, changed its view and arranged for the same assistance allowed the other corporations.

These losses, however, were only temporary. Welwyn is expanding far more rapidly than in the past. New schools, shops, offices, factories, and a hospital are being built. The higher maintenance costs were disappointing, of course, since they added to the deficits even as late as the end of 1953. But they only transformed an investment with immediate prospects of a surplus into one which is expected to become profitable once the arrears are paid off and the income increased.[68]

Although both towns are under the same corporate leadership, they are in many ways dealt with as distinct entities. Thus in Welwyn, the intention is to retain the inheritance of a *garden* city with a net density of about twenty-nine persons per acre. Hatfield, on the other hand, with densities almost twice as high, is being designed as far as possible as a town with urban qualities and aspirations.

Since the corporation was established, both Welwyn and Hatfield encountered typical new town headaches. These included delays because of inadequate sewerage facilities, tardy approvals on road classifications and location, shortages of materials and labor, rising costs, and financial and administrative obstacles in providing for playing fields, community buildings, and similar requirements.[69] Hatfield, in addition, faces a special problem. Dominated by the de Havilland works, its economic base is not as diversified or stable as is considered desirable; but worse still, most of the works are located "just outside [the] designated area . . . It follows," says the corporation, "that the lack of income from industry and commerce through ground and rack rents prejudices the town being self-supporting." [70] The corporation, however, is undaunted. Diversification is being encouraged. One new factory has been completed and nine are under construction. Moreover, the corporation plans "to build as many houses in the main for the employees of Hatfield's major industry in the shortest possible time, yet at the same time creating a town with such facilities for shopping, education and recreation — as envisaged for the 'planned' New Town as circumstances permit." [71]

Hemel Hempstead. The new town of Hemel Hempstead illustrates what many persons, including responsible officials in the ministry, regard as a misplaced application of the corporate device. For Hemel Hempstead was an ancient borough in Hertfordshire, northwest of London, a borough with many hoary traditions and with a population exceeding 20,000 persons. By plumping a new town corporation into this area instead of relying on the local authority, the ministry had every reason to expect trouble; and trouble there was for many years.

The program started with a court case, the residents objecting that local views were not consulted. After a delay of six months, the ministry won the suit.[72] But the local authorities for a long time were sullen and protesting. According to one highly placed official, there was a period when scarcely a month went by when delegations did not arrive asking for the ejection of the corporation.

During the first five years, construction limped along slowly under typical handicaps. Even though Hemel Hempstead was the "furthest advanced of the New Towns . . . it [took] five years to produce 1,000

115

houses and a labor force of just under 2,000." [73] Mr. W. O. Hart reports that when he was asked whether he would be interested in new town work, he was told "that the program of decentralization was to be substantially completed in eight years," a reminder, he observes, of "how poor achievement has been compared with declared intentions." [74] A partial consolation, however, was that in 1951 the corporation and the chief architect "were awarded a housing medal — the first awarded to a New Town for its development." [75]

Construction has since surged ahead under a vigorous and able chairman. House building, for example, has now zoomed to approximately 1250 houses per annum. Eighty-two shops, seven schools, and nineteen factories were completed by the start of 1955. The basic services have been provided. Six factories and seven schools are under construction. The town center is underway. Community buildings, recreational areas, and other social facilities are also being provided despite limited cooperation from the local authorities and the ministry. Development generally has been quite successful.[76]

The borough council has pursued its own active housing program to meet the needs of the families on its housing lists. It has also started a slum clearance program in the old town. The corporation has aided by setting aside the northern half of its Highfield neighborhood for the purpose. A Joint Consultative Committee of the corporation and the council has been established to discuss questions of mutual interest, including general policies and specific subjects of disagreement, such as the maintenance of playing fields and the allocation of costs for main drainage.[77] Social activities have multiplied, and some of the new residents in Adeyfield neighborhood have already been elected members of the Hemel Hempstead Town Council. Slowly the animosities are subsiding. But friends of the new towns still have their misgivings and shake their heads sadly, deprecating the inflexible execution of the policy.

Bracknell and Crawley. The two remaining new towns in the London region, Bracknell to the west and Crawley to the south, on the whole have fared quite well. Probably their most serious problems resulted from the original site selection.

In Bracknell there were fierce protests from local farmers. To take account of these criticisms, the minister excluded 773 acres of the original tract. But the corporation later made a study of the area. It showed that existing development, subsoil conditions, and the lack of any greenbelt left "no margin to compensate for the loss of 30 per cent of the area" to accommodate a town of 25,000, a size that many persons regard as quite inadequate to sustain the necessary urban services and amenities.[78] Reacquisition of some of this land has been sought, thus far unsuccessfully.

Industrial development in Bracknell has kept pace with the rate of house building, and the corporation believes that the town will be completed "without a financial loss." [79] This view is held despite some costly obstacles now retarding speedy development. One of them is the need for a sewage treatment works. Another is the uncertainty of securing additional land for the enlargement of the industrial area. A third difficulty is the obligation either to relocate a "well established and well matured cricket ground" or to engage in "a considerable amount of demolition of existing residential property" before replanning of the town center can occur.[80] Regardless of the alternative pursued, a delay of at least two years is expected.

In Crawley, the designation order was challenged on the grounds "that the Minister had not given sufficient information about his proposal, had not properly consulted the local authorities concerned, had not held a proper public local inquiry, and had not fairly considered the objections." [81] Twelve months passed before the litigation ended in favor of the ministry.

Crawley has proved especially successful, if success may be measured by competent planning and design, steady, balanced physical development, and the absence of disheartening obstacles or dramatic blunders. At the beginning of 1955, the population had reached 23,500 and was increasing at a rate of 4,000–5,000 persons a year. Construction in every direction was proceeding vigorously. The building program included schools, churches, health centers, shops, factories, roads, and even a multistory college.[82] Most surprising of all has been Crawley's economic growth: 898,900 square feet of factory space is already occupied; and another 745,600 square feet, including additions, is under construction. This will create a total industrial employment of 7,000 persons, which is more than half of the industrial employment that it is considered will be needed.[83] Board of Trade economists, prompted by the knowledge that the major line of industrial growth and concentration lay in the north-northeast direction from London to Birmingham and the Midlands, voiced misgivings about the southerly location and its poor prospects for economic development.[84] Perversely enough, Crawley, with its good roads and railways and vigorous leadership, has enjoyed the most successful economic development of all the new towns.

The Scottish New Towns

Six new towns were proposed for Scotland. Of these, four were supposed to serve Glasgow, according to the Clyde Valley regional plan prepared by Sir Patrick Abercrombie. But during the first decade following passage of the act, only two new towns got underway. One of them, East Kilbride, serves Glasgow. The other, Glenrothes, is a mining town. A third, New Cumbernauld, was designated in 1955.

East Kilbride and New Cumbernauld. East Kilbride, established in August 1947, has an attractive site only six miles from Glasgow. Its chief industries have come from outside the area. Two of the more important are the Division of Industrial and Scientific Research and the Rolls Royce turbo prop and jet engine plants, which altogether employ 3,000 persons. The latter were obtained as a result of the defense program. Industrial development has proceeded so rapidly that population is not expected to catch up with jobs until 1962. The "jobs already secured are thought to be sufficient for a population of between 25,000 and 30,000. Already, about 4,600 people travel daily to work in East Kilbride from the rest of the Clyde Valley, and only 800 travel out." [85] By January 1955, 804,000 square feet of factory space had been built; 2,605 houses were completed; and another 1,400 were under construction. Fifteen miles of roads, one school, and nineteen shops were also constructed; and work was starting on two additional schools and the town center.[86] The corporation is reasonably sanguine about the future, although East Kilbride has experienced its share of problems, both typical and unique. The former include lukewarm relationships with the local authorities, difficulties in attracting a labor force, obstacles in decentralizing industry from Glasgow, high costs, delays in securing approvals, and not enough schools, cinemas, community buildings and facilities.[87]

East Kilbride also labors under a special disadvantage imposed by the peculiarities of the Scottish rating system. This requires that local rates be levied on the full amount of the rental. In England the properties are assessed on values that are much less than the actual rentals. The values are more comparable to similar properties erected before the war. As a result of the Scottish system, for each pound of rental received "approximately 12/- go in rates to the local authority and the balance of 8/- is left for all other charges including interest on loans, repairs, insurance, management, etc." [88] This has led to an absurd predicament. As explained by the corporation:

118

To obtain an increase of £1 of net rent to meet the higher costs of loan charges, repairs, etc. . . . [it has] to charge an increased rent of approximately 32/–, so that the gross outlay of rent and rates would amount to £4. 2s. in order to provide £1 of net rent to the Corporations. It is, therefore now well nigh impossible for the Corporation to obtain an economic return for any properties which are built for letting.[89]

At first the government was reluctant to tamper with the rating system. But in response to the persistent protests of the corporation, it has appointed a "Committee to investigate the Scottish valuation and rating systems with a view to recommending reforms." [90] Meanwhile, since full economic rents are not charged even after allowing for government housing subsidies, "there is a growing annual deficit on the housing account." [91]

But the principal issue overshadowing all the others confronting East Kilbride is the role it is destined to play vis-à-vis the Clydeside region. Key officials frankly admit that the new town has not served as a useful tool in dealing with Glasgow's slums and overcrowding or with the reorganization of physical development in the Clyde Valley region. East Kilbride has not significantly "decentralized" either the industry or the residents of Glasgow.

About a thousand families from Glasgow, East Kilbride, and other districts of Lanarkshire had been rehoused by the end of 1953. These are primarily employees of the industries, and not necessarily tenants on the housing lists of the local authorities. Moreover, as in London, new families have taken the places of those that have left. The experience is even more discouraging with industrial relocation. One hundred and ninety new factories were built with government aid in the region between 1945 and 1950. These factories received aid because the Clydeside is a development area. But since the location of industry within the region was largely ignored, the net result only added to the appalling congestion.[92] At the same time the East Kilbride Corporation complains that "although one of the underlying reasons for building the New Towns was the relief of industrial congestion in Glasgow, little assistance has been given to the Corporation in its endeavours to provide accommodation for industrial and commercial firms anxious to move from Glasgow to East Kilbride." [93]

Glasgow will face a housing crisis soon. At present, "one seventh of Scotland's population is crammed into three square miles of central Glasgow." [94] The area is made up predominantly of four-story tenements containing one- or two-row units. In some sections net densities approximate 730 persons per acre. Enough vacant sites existed in 1952 to serve a population of only 25,000–30,000. Limited water and drainage facilities are expected to cause difficulties even sooner. After all the vacant sites have been built upon, the Glasgow City Architect estimates that to achieve lower densities, land for 135,000 houses will be needed. In other words, improved standards imply an overspill population of 300,000–400,000, or almost half the present inhabitants of the city. Unfortunately,

> Clydeside's industry, . . . is predominantly of a heavy type — ship-building, marine engineering, general engineering, steel production, and coal mining (although the latter is declining rapidly through exhaustion of the central coal field) . . . the basin of the Clyde is surrounded on all sides by high hills, moorlands, and uplands, which rising as they do to heights of between 700 and 1,500 feet, forbid building on grounds of climatic severity, water catchment use, lack of communications, rocky or boggy foundations, etc. Further there are many factors within the basin which prohibit building, such as river flooding, mineral subsidence (existing or future), running sand, and the existence of tracts of really first class agricultural land. The Clyde Valley is a difficult place in which to build, and only its great industrial growth, due to the underlying coal-fields, forced the issue of much of its development in the past. Finally, since Glasgow is surrounded on every side by other built-up areas, it is impossible to meet her housing needs by ordinary expansion on the outskirts.[95]

Since Glasgow insists on retaining its "rateable values," annexation is undoubtedly contemplated but will be vigorously resisted; and considering the present hostile local attitudes, regional organization is unlikely. Given this context, how one town could have been expected to be more than an inconclusive foray for a region of approximately 2,000 is something of a mystery. But something had to be done. The tremendous pressures were bound to force a review of the situation. This occurred in 1955. It was announced that another new town, New Cumbernauld, twelve miles east of Glasgow, will be built either by Glasgow or by a development corporation. The target population is expected to be 50,000. Details have not yet been spelled out, but it is most probable that Glasgow will contribute to the cost of housing and thereby secure the right to "nominate" the bulk of the tenants.[96]

Glenrothes. Glenrothes, the Scottish equivalent of Peterlee, was the second town established. Miners leaving the old worn-out Lanarkshire pits went eastward to the mines in Fife County. Glenrothes was authorized in October 1948, about six months later than Peterlee, to provide for the anticipated shift. It is situated on the northern edge of the Fife coal field and fortunately is free "from the dread risk of subsidence." [97] Its progress has been somewhat slow, in fact about the same as Peterlee's. Only 1000 houses were built by January 1955. Another 660 were under construction. Nineteen shops, two schools and nine and one-half miles of new roads were also provided; and work is beginning on another school and the town center, including a cinema, public house, and public hall with a capacity of 700.[98]

Originally Glenrothes was to have all the new town trimmings, including varied industries and a balanced population with one miner for every eight or nine employees. This now seems unlikely. At the start the town had four industries: paper, whisky, plastics, and blankets, employing altogether more than 3000 persons. But, as with Peterlee, it was feared that if more industries were attracted, the policy of keeping and adding to the number of miners in the pits would be jeopardized. Indeed, some administrative officials say informally with some relief that unlike Peterlee, no attempt has been made even to advertise for industry. Some expansion of existing industry has occurred, however; and some employment can be expected in the shops and service trades. But no new factory space has been provided and the future prospects are somewhat bleak. The corporation has set aside some land for an industrial area. It has also submitted a memorandum to the Secretary of State for Scotland, underlining "the absence of financial advantages to be proffered to interested industrialists in comparison with the known advantages applying in other areas of industrial settlement in the country." [99]

These difficulties were at least temporarily compounded by the reluctance of some miners to go to the Fifeshire pits, oddly enough, because they were better seams on which to work. The old pits were so bad that the shared dangers produced a close camaraderie and a relatively free hand in the conduct of the mining operations. In the Fifeshire pits, the thick seams permit more mechanization and greater discipline, and a satisfactory adjustment had to be devised to quiet the miners' protests against regimentation.[100]

The corporation's progress has been held up by the usual shortages and restrictions, the difficulties of recruiting a labor force, and delays in securing approvals. Relationships with local authorities have also been soured by financial disagreements with the County of Fife. This has slowed up some matters, such as road building and the provision of recreational facilities.[101] Formerly an independent kingdom, the county is sensitive about its authority and has looked upon the new town as an intruder. Fortunately these attitudes are becoming less intransigent.

Glenrothes' population and characteristics depend largely on the manpower requirements and the industrial development policy. Though no ceiling was originally placed on the ultimate population of the new town, the corporation was instructed to make the present plan capable of accommodating 23,000 persons. However, the board expects a considerable increase in mining employment in East Fife over the next two decades. And on the basis of present decisions the total population "is unlikely to exceed 18,000 in the next 20 to 25 years." [102] Unless this policy is changed Glenrothes will therefore be a mining town. [103]

Much depends on these decisions, but if rumor is correct, much also depends on the owner of a large portion of the site. A figure reputed to have some influence in the Conservative Party, he has been violently opposed to the acquisition of his land. Apparently, after making a modest fortune he purchased several farms, improved the land, built a home, and then expected to retire peacefully. Along came the new towns program and the dispossession notice. Because of either underlying coal seams or other physical limitations, no alternative site in that area was satisfactory to the experts. To quell his furious opposition, the size of the designated area was cut drastically. However, the owner is fairly old, and the new town proponents comment blithely that in this case, at any rate, time is on the side of the new town development.

New Towns in the Provinces

Cwmbran. Since England and Scotland had their new towns, it was imperative that Wales should not be neglected. And so on November 4, 1949, Cwmbran was established as a new town in Monmouthshire, in the easternmost part of Wales.

Cwmbran's site, with an existing population of 13,000, was already highly developed. Industry had been attracted to the area because of the excellent road and rail communication. Twenty factories, employing 6,000 workers, mostly in metal and engineering industries, were already settled in the valley near the railroads. There were also steel, textile, and ordnance industries nearby, but outside the designated area. The main problems confronting the corporation were to provide housing for workers traveling five and more miles daily to work in the area; to cope effectively with the north-south routes that cut the area in two; to reclaim derelict land, primarily the sites of abandoned claypits of brickworks and colliery workings; to correct and forestall the "unsightly," obsolete, and scattered residential development up and down the valley; and to take into account the "fast flowing river liable to periodic flooding and pollution by industrial wastes." [104]

The area was otherwise physically attractive. In addition, it did not "impinge upon agricultural land of the highest quality." [105] It was close to employment. It was supplied with public services capable of expansion. It was also large enough to serve a town of 35,000 people.

Almost 1,100 corporation houses were built by January 1955, together with fourteen shops, one school, and nine miles of roads; and four schools and more than 700 houses were under construction. With the exception of service industries and the expansion of existing industry, new major industries in the area were barred by the Board of Trade. But these alone will soon provide some 300,000 square feet of additional factory space and employment for about 900 persons. Verily, "to him that hath shall be given."

The corporation has experienced no unusual difficulties. It was worried by a possible shortage of school facilities, partly because of its dependence on the Monmouthshire County Council for its building program. It was also concerned about the playing fields and allotments that were the responsibility of the urban district council. The rent schedules for three-bedroom dwellings, set at 36s. 6d. per week inclusive of rates, have shocked the corporation. It has also aroused the public, the press, and the tenants, who do "not always appreciate the factors which give rise to the higher rents charged by Development Corporations as compared with rents of Council houses." Nonetheless, "1483 applications for houses have been received; . . . and the waiting list continues to grow." [106]

Newton Aycliffe. Like Cwmbran, the selection of Aycliffe had some political overtones. Here a new war munitions factory was in danger of being abandoned. Rather than dismantle the facilities and let the workers lose their source of employment, a planned industrial district was established. Efforts were made to attract appropriate industries to use these plants, and housing was later sought for the employees.[107] Since the fate of Newton Aycliffe affected the jobs of many persons in the bailiwick of one of the members of the Cabinet, this is rumored to have influenced the decision.

The site's location is not too satisfactory. Set in a pass in the Pennine Chain, it is swept by heavy, bitter winds. A far greater problem, however, is the size of the town. Originally Aycliffe was limited to a maximum population of 10,000, which meant that it could not become a "balanced" town either in the range of its economic activities or community services. When pressure developed to permit expansion up to about 15,000 in size, if necessary, the ministry informally acquiesced, even though a town of this size also will probably not prove particularly economical or balanced.[108]

However, if further increases are allowed, intense opposition is expected. From the outset the surrounding authorities have been apprehensive. Bishop Auckland, which seats the important Labour Party leader, Hugh Dalton, fears it will lose its function as a shopping center for this area. It is now a town of 35,000. Aycliffe's expansion is considered a direct threat to Bishop Auckland's population, shops, and other economic activities. Similar fears disturb some of the other neighboring local authorities.[109]

On the other hand, if Aycliffe's size remains unchanged, it is certain to become a pleasant suburb of Darlington. Aycliffe is only eight miles away from Darlington, or about fifteen minutes by bus. With all the shopping facilities, services, and alternative opportunities afforded by a town of 85,000, there is not much reason to expect Aycliffe to become self-contained. The danger looms all the greater because of its lack of schools, places of entertainment, health centers, churches, and other community facilities. But the corporation considers itself virtually powerless. "It is mainly other authorities," it observed ruefully, "who are responsible for the provision of these amenity services and unfortunately [the Corporation] does not have it in its power to ensure that their provision keeps pace with the needs of the rapidly growing population." [110]

Aside from these problems and the high rents, the town's progress seems encouraging. By the beginning of 1955, it had about 60 per cent of its target population. Almost 1,900 houses were built; 450 more were under construction.[111] Few difficulties remained in securing the basic services. The trading estate was thriving. All existing space was taken up by new or expanding firms. The formerly complicated boundary jurisdiction was finally solved by an order of the Durham County Council approved by the ministry, which extended the parish of Great Aycliffe to include the new town site. The parish comprises two wards, one of which is the new town. Elections have been held and the town is now self-governing.[112] The danger of a population concentrated in the younger age groups with the familiar difficulties of a "bulge" was being partly corrected by leasing some accommodations to older service workers, some to miners in nearby collieries, and some to aged people, preferably relatives of existing tenants. And to cut site development cost per dwelling and allow for the possibility of an expanded population, higher densities of approximately thirteen houses to the acre were being adopted. These and other measures indicated how within certain limits the corporation was effectively taking advantage of its strategic function as a steering mechanism.

Corby. Unlike most of the other new towns, Corby's problems stem from sudden, rapid growth. In 1934 Stewarts and Lloyds' modern steel mill moved from Glasgow to a vast iron ore area in the Midlands, now expected to be a quarrying center for at least a century. Before the shift occurred, Corby was first a tranquil agricultural, then a quasi-industrial, village. The move generated a massive need for housing and community facilities for several thousand employees and their families.[113] Recognizing the scale of the problem and their own inadequacies, the firm sought the help of the local housing authorities and the Ministry of Health. But they found they had to handle the situation almost alone, "perhaps because the request was made at the end of the slump of 1929–32."[114] Yet in the first five years 2150 houses were built, plus a large social and sports club, churches, schools, a cinema, and thirty-three shops. "In general," Corby's consultants observe, "much more was done for new citizens of Corby than in comparable contemporary developments on the outskirts of large towns."[115]

Nonetheless what was done fell far short of what was required. It was a quick, expedient solution carried out largely without a plan. Corby just grew. In 1939 an urban district council was created. Aided by the customary housing subsidies, some additional houses were put up by the new authority, but not much else. Perhaps more might have been done had not the war and postwar restrictions ended further development. In the meantime, the old village of Corby went

> sadly to pieces. The majority of its stone houses have been either converted as shops or are in bad repair or ruinous. A few rows of new houses have been built where land was available, mostly on the south side. For the rest, land in and around the village carries a large number of shacks, sheds and temporary structures and enclosures, many of them in use by service industries which could obtain no better accommodation. There are also many patches of derelict land, and the whole village may be said to be under the shadow of the Works.[116]

The new landscape was like a dreary mining town, dominated by the blast furnaces and coke ovens of the company. In every direction there were digging and spoil heaps. There was little sense of community. Transport was poor. Social activity was inhibited. Serious overcrowding prevailed. There were inadequate "business and professional services, . . .

shops, cinemas, banks, libraries, laundries, parks, and other facilities and amenities, which are possessed by most well established towns." [117] For shopping and entertainment most persons traveled to Kettering, which had a population of 37,000, or to other towns more than twenty miles away.

At the end of the war the Northamptonshire County authorities favored a new town. But not the urban district council! Despite the company's vast expansion program, the council felt it could serve all needs by building 500 houses a year. Curiously enough, the company didn't particularly care. Despite extraordinarily high turnover and hence the sympathetic interest of the personnel officers, the company directors felt the local council could do the job. They also had misgivings about an outside agency intervening. Just what agency did the building seemed less important to the company than the possible loss of its mining land. Since the minister was uncertain whether the new town corporation should be established, no action was taken until April 1950, and by this time an ugly living pattern had mushroomed for about 15,000 persons.

The designation of the site resulted in further controversy. There were the familiar objections by the agricultural interests; by the local council, which claimed it could build all the necessary housing; and by the company, which protested that valuable mineral land was included in the designation. Indeed, "each acre of land saved for ironstone quarrying may yield 20,000 tons of limestone, worth in the ground, perhaps £12,000." [118] Much of the land in dispute was therefore eliminated by the ministry. Only 2,500 acres remained; and the ministry acknowledged that this area was probably inadequate for a town with a proposed size of 40,000. It was not surprising, therefore, that in September 1952 an additional 200 acres had to be added to the southern boundary. This represented "one-fifth of the land originally held. It contained land judged by the consultants to be indispensable for the complete development of the town and which could not have been used for quarrying operations for 35 years in any case." [119]

Because of this inauspicious beginning, relations between the corporation and the council were embittered. The fact that two of Britain's ablest planners were employed by the corporation was of little avail. Despite their great skill and tact, an unremitting campaign was waged by the council against the corporation. And, of course, the corporation's inability to start any construction during the first two years furnished an easy target for taunts and a field day for the local press.

But the program eventually did get underway. Like Peterlee, the plan called for the concentration of facilities in the town center, not neighborhood dispersion. The report accompanying the draft master plan declared that

> A new town centre . . . complete with shops and offices and a bus station, is just as urgent for Corby as new houses; and such a requirement cannot be expected to fall into line with either the national or the regional building programme. Moreover, the division of Corby — old and new — into conventional neighbourhoods, except for purposes of school building and the measurement of residential density, is unlikely to follow the usual pattern. The frontiers of Corby are restricted enough, and the distribution of places of public resort is already so wide that only the town as a whole should aim at being self-contained, and not an individual neighbourhood. While all sorts of subdivisions are likely to develop — housing groups, playground and school groups, town districts and parishes, the orbit of social activities, of further education, of opportunities for jobs and of the system of public transport can hardly be less than the complete area of the town. It may even extend to satellite villages when Corby itself becomes a real urban centre.[120]

To implement this objective, the corporation fought a drawn-out battle to get materials for community facilities. The minister, and then the interdepartmental authorities, had to be persuaded that an exception to the stringent limitations on materials was in order. The heavy turnover, the preference of most higher-paid employees for a home in more delightful but distant towns, and the insistence of some workers on commuting weekends as far as Glasgow where their families resided undoubtedly helped to win the case. Effective leadership also improved somewhat the reputation of the corporation. The latter was successful in getting an experimental college and technical hospital, in attracting industrial firms providing local employment for 300 persons, mostly women, in the commencement of schools, and in the provision of attractive shops, offices, and services in the town center. Now, too, the corporation's building rate is rising rapidly and will soon dwarf the activity of the local authorities.[121] However, there is a mounting rent problem. Prewar company houses are renting for approximately 10s. per week less than the local council houses; and the corporation houses cost about 10s. more per week.[122] The fact that Stewarts and Lloyds' expanding works lies outside the district boundaries adds to the difficulties, because it makes "no contribution towards the cost of the town's building and other programmes. The request of the council for an extension of boundaries to include these hereditaments was refused, and so the problem remains." [123]

Though the strained relationships between the corporation and council have been somewhat eased, evidence of discord still exists. Two local inquiries had to be held in 1952 and 1953 because of the urban district Council's insistence on providing shopping and other development in two areas contrary to the corporation's long-range plans; and the corporation has been seriously disturbed by the threatened overloading and delays that may be caused by the tardy expansion of the sewerage system by the urban district council. What has not been fully appreciated by the local authorities or the company is that ensuring development is really not the issue. That will certainly occur. Nor is it even a question of diversifying development, even though Corby is largely a one-industry town. Actually this industry is efficient, well located, and expanding, and is likely to grow for a long time to come. Corby's consultants have wisely recognized that

> although steel is the dominating employment in Corby, it comes well below clothing and footwear in the sub-region within 10 miles of Corby. This sub-region . . . is reasonably well diversified in employment. When one considers the demands upon building labour in Corby during the next decade for expansion of the Works, for houses and for service industries, the conclusion seems inescapable, that the best way to increase the variety of jobs available to Corby inhabitants would be to improve bus and train services to neighbouring towns.[124]

The future of Corby hinges on something else. That is whether it will be a "place where some workers stay if they get nothing better [or] a town to which people try to come when they have several choices." [125] At present, too many persons who can afford to live elsewhere do so.

Summary Observations

On the admittedly incomplete evidence before us, one may wonder whether the policy on the whole has "paid off." Suppose, however, there were no new towns. What would have happened instead in the dismal mining villages? In the boom towns induced by sudden expansion? In the dreary suburban extensions of the big city? What about the "normal" rape of agricultural and mineral land and the chaotic burgeoning of metropolitan areas? The answers to this group of questions will never be known. But if nineteenth- and early twentieth-century urban patterns are any indication, one might hesitate before dismissing the work of the new town corporations. After all, few responsible persons were satisfied with the old chestnuts.

Of course, there is also the possibility that the efforts poured into new towns might have been directed toward reconstruction of existing towns, or more economical planning of additions, or more effective use of the resources for other purposes. But there might have been difficulties and defects in the execution of such alternatives, too. These other possibilities, precisely because they are possibilities, are easier to believe or disbelieve than to estimate or weigh. For our purposes it is sufficient to remember that growth and urban reconstruction would have required much new building. New towns in some form or other would have been at least one of the ways of accommodating this development. Whatever the limitations of this tool may be, generally the choice is not of casting it aside, but rather of perfecting and using it more wisely.

However, to recognize the common-sense rationale of planned urban growth does not make the frustrations of the present program less vexatious. In these *planned* towns a bewildering variety of *unanticipated* problems have cropped up during the early years. They were not the physical problems, like subsidence, that are the raw materials with which planners must work. Instead they were problems that revealed the weaknesses of the broader economic policies and relationships, of the administrative machinery, and particularly of the corrective devices. The problems have appeared under many guises: in public understanding, in resolving conflicts of interests, in administrative flexibility, in coordination of inconsistent ministerial policies, in financial formulas, in technical studies on site selections and utilities requirements, in dealing with competing land uses, in timing of development, in setting or achieving objectives. As a consequence, the first model town became an example of bad practice. Towns that started with grass-roots support for a long time steadily lost that support. The garden city leaders, the most vigorous proponents of the program, have been outraged at the treatment of one of their experiments. The resort to a corporate device to achieve administrative flexibility has wound up with incessant protests against the Whitehall straitjacket. The planning mechanism has shown embarrassing failures in forethought. Comprehensive planning has not proved comprehensive; and to the extent that it has, equally comprehensive problems have been generated for which the planners were often unprepared. In short, there has been a deplorable amount of fumbling; and while the prospects for the future are generally more promising, not enough towns have developed sufficiently well for anyone to exude satisfaction in a job well done.

To concede these harsh conclusions, as many of those who are charged with the administration of the program do, is not easy. Many able and devoted men and women have spent their energies in this direction. Unfortunately, hindsight comes easier than insight or foresight. Blunders and leaps in the dark were generally inescapable. To have expected otherwise would have betrayed surprising naïveté. However, it would be tragic and far more disquieting than any of these defects have been if in the future some better corrective mechanism were not built into the administrative system, a mechanism which will spot the errors and minimize, if not preclude, the possibility of their repetition.

CHAPTER **8**

The Background of the Town Development Act

When the Conservative government took office in 1951, many town planners were anxious about the fate of the new towns. Drastic economies were anticipated. Undoing much of what the Labour government had done seemed likely. Prospects looked dim. But the fears proved to be exaggerated. The new minister decided to complete the new towns already under construction, a decision that was welcomed with relief. Unofficially, however, it was understood that no more towns would be started for some years, if at all. A new program, or rather an old neglected program, was supported instead. This took form as the Town Development Act of 1952. The main object of the legislation was similar to that of the New Towns Act, i.e., to relieve the congestion and overpopulation of central metropolitan areas. The means, however, were different. Under this program small towns were slated for rapid expansion and they were to be given aid to ease the process.

New Towns and Existing Towns

Sir Patrick Abercrombie's historic plans for London, it will be recalled, specified the need for seven to ten new satellite towns and helped to spur the new towns program into existence. Use of many existing small towns as reception areas for London's overflowing population was also counted on, in fact even more heavily; but this vital phase of town development had been neglected. Top administrators were worried about the inadequacies of the new towns program, and became increasingly sensitive to criticisms that the resources and interests of small and large local authorities were being slighted. This explains why the ideas behind this

131

legislation, hatched and developed in the ministry, would probably have been introduced even if the Labour government had stayed in power. Though sponsored by the Conservative government, the Town Development Act was conceived and formulated at least when Hugh Dalton was the Labour Minister, and perhaps even earlier. Hence the Conservative version of this measure received the support of the opposition, despite some derogatory comments by important Labour Party leaders.[1]

For somewhat similar reasons, the program was also accepted by the Conservative minister, Mr. Macmillan. But it received his vigorous support not only because it was in accord with his policy of placing more responsibility on local authorities; and because it might serve to silence the criticism of the opposition that housing must be built in the right places, that housing alone was not enough; but primarily because it meant more housing. It was a way of breaking a potentially dangerous jam threatening fulfillment of the pledge to build 300,000 houses made by the Conservative Party in the previous election campaign.[2] This fact is well illustrated by Mr. Macmillan's explanation of the term "congested area" in the committee discussions of his bill. "A local authority is congested," he explained, "if it cannot carry out the housing programme I am urging it to carry out because there is no more room left. Therefore it has to find somewhere else to carry out its housing programme."[3] The Town Development Act is designed to help make this possible.

Compared to past planning programs, the new towns policy seemed bold and exciting in its aims and scope. It went far beyond the traditional housing or trading estates program. Yet before long this policy too proved partial, limited, and dwarfed in scale. Only specially designated agencies, the development corporations, received assistance under the new towns legislation. Other forms of growth could and did occur with no special assistance from the central government. There was really no coherent or comprehensive policy of town development. There was only a program offering special assistance to the small number of towns undertaken by the development corporations. The other expanding areas, perhaps more numerous and at least equally significant on the basis of size and long-range prospects, were left to their own resources and expedients.

Unfortunately space for growth within existing boundaries was limited and dwindling. A crisis loomed ahead. London, Birmingham, Manchester, Glasgow, five of the six county boroughs of the Midlands, and many other cities were on the verge of exhausting their available building land. In the next twenty years it was expected that more than one million people must be accommodated outside the boundaries of con-

gested areas.[4] The usual improvised solutions meant either higher densities or the more typical uncoordinated expansion in peripheral areas.
Enough rankling and explosive issues were involved to make a new approach seem worth trying. The reasons will be clearer if the experiences
of the London and Lancashire county councils are examined.

The LCC and Neighboring Local Authorities

Impelled by political pressures and social idealism, the big and efficient building organization of the London County Council strained
every resource to overcome the postwar backlog in housing. Six years
after the passage of the New Towns Act, the LCC had a building record
of 10,000–12,000 dwellings a year, or more than three times the total housing provided by all the new town development corporations during this
period. From 1946 to 1955, more than 100,000 Londoners had been rehoused in thirteen new estates.[5]

There were no complaints about the LCC's rate of building. What
did cause concern was its manner and location. Less and less building
was done in the central areas. There was no space. There was also a limit
to the amount of vertical building that could be undertaken, given existing political, economic, and social attitudes. The new development plans
prepared under the 1947 Town and Country Planning Act set optimum,
or at any rate maximum, densities. Acceptance of these plans implied responsibility for rehousing a large surplus population outside of London's
boundaries. This amounted to approximately 316,000 of the county's residents and 511,000 residents of Greater London.[6]

In the early postwar period, as a temporary measure, some building
had been allowed in London's presumably sacrosanct greenbelt. But increasingly it proved necessary, if the building capacity were to be sustained and London's population housed, for the LCC to acquire sites and
build in other jurisdictions. This almost irresistible force overcame all
initial obstacles. But it also generated embittered and increasingly stub-
born opposition.

The housing estates were expensive dormitory areas, distant from the
jobs, available only at higher rent and transportation charges, and lacking
most of the customary community facilities.[7] The Hertfordshire Education Committee's report on Oxhey, one of the LCC's estates, notes a few
of the problems facing the tenants.

> Transfer to Oxhey presents many of them with an acute economic
> problem. The inevitable expenses of occupying a new home . . . are
> considerable, and to those must be added a normally much greater cost

133

of getting to work . . . This economic pressure has compelled a very high proportion of the mothers to find work in order to supplement the family income and, as there is very little work available for them in the locality, they also have to travel long distances . . . One Primary School Head has reported that three out of five mothers of children attending her school go out to work. Anyone visiting the railway station at Oxhey at 6 o'clock in the evening will observe the formidable number of men and women returning at this hour to their homes. As far as the mothers are concerned, their children have been without any supervision for at least two hours. The same parents very frequently leave home an hour before the children are due to go to school, and are therefore unable to ensure that they do so.

At one school alone 50 or 60 children have to be kept until 7 o'clock at night because their parents have not returned home to look after them.[8]

The absence of adequate facilities is also deplored:

Not only are the Oxhey tenants uprooted from their own background and moved to an Estate in which they are strangers, but there are no churches, no church halls, no public houses. After three years there is one small cafe. To enjoy these amenities the Oxhey citizens have to leave the Estate and visit neighbouring towns and this not only adds to their expenses of living, but prevents the growth of a sense of community.[9]

Aside from the character of the housing estates, most local authorities surrounding London didn't relish the prospect of another local authority owning land and building houses within their boundaries. They particularly didn't care for the London County Council in that role because of its power, its real or fancied arbitrariness, the potential dangers of annexation, and the difficulties inherent in large-scale, absentee, and public landlordism. The local authorities also, especially if wealthy or well-to-do, didn't like to see the character of their communities changed. They cherished their prestige, their political leanings, their socio-economic status. The thought of the LCC exporting its "slum dwellers" roused the most fervid emotions. Most enraging of all were the financial burdens imposed by such a "hit-and-run" invasion. Although the LCC built the houses and paid the local housing subsidy, the local authorities had to foot many of the additional costs of the schools, the hospitals, the expanded water, sewage, and road systems, and the like. It was indeed a grim irony for many of the residents of these communities that they were liable for the bills entailed in transforming their community into a type of place they preferred it not to be.

Though last-ditch battles were fought, opposition seemed to be in vain. The LCC would simply apply for a "CPO" (Compulsory Purchase

Order), and the minister, except in extraordinary circumstances, would generally acquiesce. For the LCC had a recognized responsibility toward London County residents. There was just not enough building space within the county's boundaries. Granted, zeal in developing their program might on occasion be indistinguishable from arbitrariness. Granted too, that the new areas might be only huge dormitories. Still, no minister would put himself in the position of even appearing to block or delay a vigorous building program.

Probably housing by the LCC outside its boundaries couldn't be stopped, regardless of the adverse effects on various private groups and communities.[10] Regional government or organization was deemed impossible by the ministry; improbable, and for the present not feasible, by the LCC; and most local authorities held it to be a device for entrenching London's administrative imperialism. Compromise was in order; and the best compromise local authorities could expect was some financial assistance for being obliged to help solve London's problems, and perhaps a stiffer ministry attitude toward the LCC's alleged arbitrary postures and ready inclinations for CPO's. Some satisfaction of these expectations, it was hoped, might encourage more reasonable negotiations to settle the ticklish problems of sharing building responsibilities and costs. The new legislation reflected these needs and possibilities. (See Map 4: London's Overspill.)

Lancashire's Experiments

The problems and experiences in the County of Lancashire, which includes the two large county boroughs of Liverpool and Manchester, also furnished some guidance for the town development policy. Indeed, the minister in the course of the committee discussions of the Town Development Bill declared:

> The arrangements made between Salford . . . and Worsley, assisted by the Lancashire County Council, is an example of the kind of scheme which I want to promote and assist under the Bill. That scheme is taking place through the voluntary unaided efforts of the three authorities working together. I believe that what Lancashire does today . . . England does tomorrow. This is a remarkable example. Lancashire is, on the whole, fairly well able to carry this but there are places where extensions of these schemes could not be done without some assistance, and that is the purpose of the bill.[11]

Let us, therefore, examine this Lancashire experience more closely. Like London, lack of space and overspill population called for a prompt solution. Manchester's satellite, Salford, couldn't build within its boundaries, yet housing was sorely needed for its population. Neighboring authorities were too crowded to receive any of these families. New housing could be provided only by "hopping" over Salford's adjacent areas to places like Worsley. Talk of wholesale annexation of intervening territory spurred Lancashire's active planning and government authorities into action. Lancashire County officials suggested that Salford negotiate with the Worsley Urban District Council for transfer of populations. Worsley was quite willing to expand, but had neither the resources nor the staff to cope with its desires. Financial and technical assistance had to be secured from some quarter to make the scheme work. To placate the conflicting authorities, to accept responsibility for orderly solution of problems of "regional" development and population distribution, and most important, to avoid encroachment on county boundaries and the absorption of existing local authorities, the Lancashire County authorities decided to give such assistance.[12]

This scheme, linked to a planned redistribution of industry, was considered ultimately self-liquidating and even profitable. But immediate costs of land acquisition and development, of sewerage and water supply, and of other services, were beyond the resources of any local or even county authority. Lancashire officials, therefore, took for granted at the very outset that the problem involved national issues and that assistance from the central government would be necessary. Financial assistance by the Lancashire County Council was presumed to be only temporary, and the central government was expected to introduce some legislation to shoulder most of the future burdens. The fact that the ministry provided special allocations for building licenses was held to be evidence of the acceptance of this view by the central government. Costs were allocated on an interesting formula. The county was to assist the smaller urban district councils to avoid financial loss arising out of development, including its assumption of the normal local housing subsidy. The assistance was to be extended as long as the returns from the rates did not equal outlays; and only if the local tax burden did not fall below the average for local authorities in the county.[13]

Technical assistance was necessary because the smaller authorities simply could not attract enough high-caliber personnel. Anticipating similar situations in other communities, the Lancashire County Planning Office recruited a varied and permanent staff of engineers, architects, and surveyors. Their functions included "site surveying, the preparation of detail layouts . . . , the preparation of design and contract documents

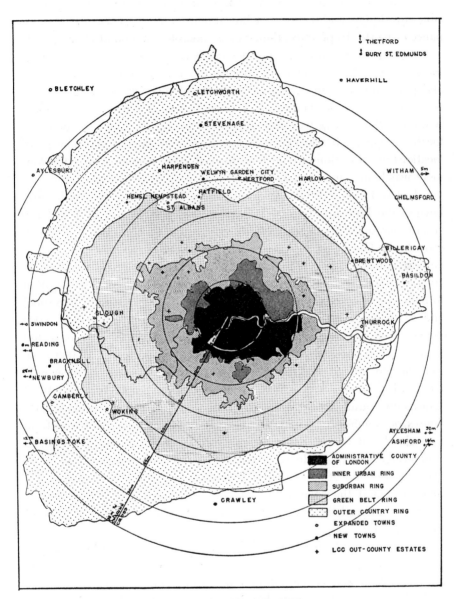

THETFORD
BURY ST. EDMUNDS

HAVERHILL

BLETCHLEY   LETCHWORTH

                   STEVENAGE

AYLESBURY   HARPENDEN   WITHAM   5m
                   WELWYN GARDEN CITY
                        HERTFORD   HARLOW
            HEMEL HEMPSTEAD HATFIELD   CHELMSFORD
                   ST. ALBANS

                                               BILLERICAY
                                          BRENTWOOD
                                               BASILDON
         SLOUGH
SWINDON   THURROCK
READING
   BRACKNELL
NEWBURY
    CAMBERLY
         WOKING
                                               AYLESHAM   32m
                                               ASHFORD   19m
BASINGSTOKE

                                ADMINISTRATIVE COUNTY
                                OF LONDON
                                INNER URBAN RING
                                SUBURBAN RING
                                GREEN BELT RING
                                OUTER COUNTRY RING
                          o   EXPANDED TOWNS
             CRAWLEY   •   NEW TOWNS
                          +   LCC OUT-COUNTY ESTATES

MAP 4. LONDON'S OVERSPILL

Source: London County Council, Administrative County of London Development Plan Analysis
(London: London County Council, 1951), p. 307; Town and Country Planning, vol. XXIII, no. 124
(August 1954), p. 382.

for estate roads and sewers and landscaping, the general programming and expediting of development." The county staff were largely responsible "for design, and the local technical officers for execution and maintenance of works. In practice, there is very complete liaison at all stages."[14]

A program of industrial resettlement was also devised. Its aims were to avoid dormitory settlements, to ensure a rational grouping of houses and jobs, and to secure additional sources of revenue. Resources of the region were surveyed. Suitable sites for industrial activities were mapped. A site-location service was also established for firms wishing or forced to locate elsewhere. It was expected, or at any rate hoped, that new plant locations or relocations would tend toward areas where orderly development was being encouraged.[15]

Unlike London or Glasgow, Lancashire County extends significantly beyond the built-up areas of Liverpool and Manchester, its two large county boroughs. Space for growth exists within its boundaries. For such growth, the Lancashire County Council can serve effectively as a regional authority. Lancashire's policy was framed with these prospects in view. Its tripartite program has been extended to other communities in addition to Salford and Worsley. (See Map 5: Movement of Overspill, Liverpool and Manchester Areas.) Whitefield has agreed to accommodate 5,000 persons from Manchester; Leyland, a major reception center, is expected to serve 6,600 persons from Preston, 3,000 from Wigan, and 23,000 from Manchester, Salford, and the surrounding district. In some instances only technical assistance is provided, as in the case of the Preston and West Lancashire rural district councils. Both have agreed to provide fifty houses per annum for population from Preston and Liverpool, and from Litherland and Bootle, respectively.[16] For all of the programs on which commitments were made, agreements have spelled out the amount of overspill, the allocation of specific reception areas, the time schedule for rehousing, and the specific agency for executing these responsibilities. Joint committees have also been formed to guide each major operation of the program.[17]

These tripartite programs are only one of four methods of implementing the more comprehensive plans for resettlement of population, *most of which will occur within Lancashire's jurisdiction.* Thus, large-scale development by county boroughs is also contemplated. Under this second method the plans are prepared or approved by the county planning authority, and the county council and county district provide the normal services.[18] The huge schemes in Bowlee and Kirkby, promoted by Manchester and Liverpool respectively, are notable examples of this ap-

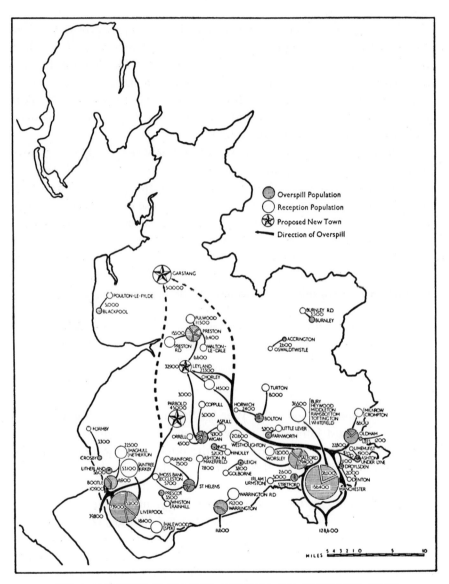

MAP 5. MOVEMENT OF OVERSPILL, LIVERPOOL AND MANCHESTER AREAS

Source: G. Sutton Brown, A Preliminary Plan for Lancashire (**Lancashire County Council, 1951**), p. 189.

proach; and the previous experiences of these county boroughs in the building of Wythenshawe and Speke evidence their capacity to build such communities.[19]

Tapping the resources of the smaller local councils provides a third string to the bow. If agreement, financially and otherwise, is reached, urban and rural district councils can build homes for overspill families nominated by county boroughs. Such arrangements have already been made by the "West Lancashire Rural District and Aintree and Maghull for tenants from central Merseyside, and Preston Rural District for overspill from Preston County Borough." [20]

There is also the possibility of building new towns. One such town was envisaged at Congleton, Cheshire, for the reception of overspill population from the Manchester district, but the proposal was subsequently rejected by the minister.[21] Indeed, because of the difficulties generally anticipated with such development, the new town approach did not rank as a major tool or as a tool of the first resort.

The Lancashire Development Plan made allowance for all four methods, and also for possible private activity.[22] The scale of the program for population redistribution is indicated by the following data.[23]

1.	In short-distance reception areas	201,500
2.	In long-distance reception areas	50,600
3.	In new towns	30,000
4.	Outside Lancashire	50,900

Of the four methods, the Worsley-Salford tripartite approach was "perhaps the most interesting innovation and . . . capable of very wide application." [24] This, at any rate was the opinion of the Lancashire authorities, who looked upon this approach as the really significant instrument in their kit of tools. Unfortunately some of the hopes for the execution of this policy in Lancashire were subsequently dampened. Loss of able leadership, conflicts with some of the neighboring authorities, and disagreements over the interpretations and decisions of the ministry were partly to blame. It is too early to tell whether the loss of impetus is only temporary. What is certain is that the ideas, having been broached and acted upon, exercised their catalytic effects. Ministry officials who had arrived at some of these ideas independently on the basis of London's problem examined carefully what was happening in Lancashire. Both experiences, plus a comparable program in Staffordshire,[25] helped to fashion the Town Development Act.[26]

The Town Development Act: Policy and Procedure

The new legislation converted these local experiences into a national policy for England and Wales. The object was to aid the expansion of conveniently situated country towns and rural districts if these towns provided substantial relief for congested cities.[27] To encourage this, the development powers of local authorities were augmented and the ministry was permitted to provide some financial assistance.

The act authorizes development agreements to be made between exporting and reception areas, subject to the approval of the ministry. The arrangements can be quite varied. Before a proposal is submitted, it is expected that there will be the customary prior consultation with the appropriate agencies, including the local planning authority and the government departments and public bodies concerned with development, such as the Ministry of Agriculture, the Ministry of Transport, and the joint sewerage and water boards. The agreements, as in the case of the Lancashire tripartite plan, will fix the amount and kind of development, the specific reception areas, whether the exporting or reception authority will do the building and subject to what conditions, the financial assistance that will be given by the exporting authority or authorities, by the county council, etc. When agreement in principle is reached, a preliminary scheme may be prepared and submitted to the ministry. It would describe the proposal, the physical plan, the probable costs, the assistance to be rendered by the other authorities, and the estimated effect of the program on local finances. On the basis of this information a preliminary commitment on the scale of the Exchequer contributions would be negotiated. These contributions can be made only to assist in the financing of the initial development costs, mainly water and sewerage services, land drainage, and site preparation. Save for the running expenses and debt charges associated with these items, it is believed that the costs of all additional local and county services (such as lighting, schools, health services, police, and libraries) can be offset by the additional income obtained from the development when it is completed. Rate-fund contributions (the normal local government housing subsidy) may also be made by the ministry. But this will only be done in exceptional cases. For example, this assistance may be made available for certain key employees needed by transferring industries even if these employees are not on housing lists.[28]

Exporting authorities too may contribute the normal rate-fund contributions for housing in return for the right to nominate tenants. Since

141

they would have to make such contributions for sixty years for rehousing these families, perhaps even at a higher rate if the rehousing took place in central areas, it is considered reasonable that the exporting authority should provide some assistance. For the present, ten years has been set as a fair period for assistance, with provision for further negotiation at the end of this period.[29] Uncertainty about what will happen afterwards has disturbed many potential or actual receiving authorities. But the size of the Exchequer grant has been deliberately left flexible. The aim is "to prime the pump," to help the receiving authorities over the early years when the burden will be heaviest.[30] Hence the amount is expected to vary with the circumstances, including the size and rate of the program, the resources of the reception authority, and the assistance rendered to the receiving authority.[31]

Reception authorities, including county councils, have secured development powers not ordinarily possessed, such as permission to build housing for families from other authorities. Similarly, exporting authorities may prepare the site, build housing, and provide other services for the families outside its jurisdiction, such as families in reception areas or other exporting authorities. The minister has indicated that he expects the receiving authority normally to do the building. However, the exporting authority or the county council of the receiving area may serve as a "participating" authority if the receiving authority is unable or unwilling to develop. The minister has the power to use force, though he has stated he hopes never to do so. The participating authority may either serve as an agent, in which case the receiving authority "would buy the land, pay the bills and own the houses and other buildings on completion";[32] or as a principal, in which case it would own the houses and other property although some agreement would be made for the eventual transfer of the property to the local authority.[33] Expansion on a large scale is most likely to take place under one of these arrangements.

The main purpose is to help congested or overcrowded areas. However, these terms are not defined. Presumably, if after a development plan is made and approved there are families that cannot be provided for by the local authority, congestion and overcrowding exist. Mr. W. A. Wood, one of the persons responsible for the drafting and policy-making aspects of the legislation, feels that for the present it is best to let the matter rest. "Like the elephant which is hard to define but easy to identify," he says, "we all know congestion and overpopulation when we see it." [34] This, of course, is a pleasant way of slipping over the controversial question of density.

The expansion must take place some distance from the congested area. No assistance will be provided for dormitory development. Subject to this limitation, the question of where the development will occur is a matter left to the local authorities. These decisions will as a rule be made by them during the preparation or revision of the development plans. It will also be spurred by the negotiating and prospecting abilities of the exporting authorities. Another factor limiting distance will be the ties of industries to the large cities, since the ministry has promised to encourage the relocation of industries *pari passu*, even though the act has conveyed no specific power to do so.[35]

Summary Observations

The shortage of space for housing sparked the adoption of the Town Development Act. Housing was a social service. The local authorities were legally obliged to provide accommodations for their inhabitants. They also had to prepare development plans based on some maximum density standards. Acceptance of these standards led to a surplus or overspill of families who had to be housed elsewhere. Strong political and moral pressures prompted the officials to discharge these responsibilities.

But the building of houses outside their boundaries, especially by the big local authorities, was causing bitter conflict between those spurred on by internal pressures and obvious needs and those threatened by invasion and its aftermath. The problem was widespread. But it attracted most attention in the London region, where the determined LCC was allegedly sweeping aside the opposition. A crisis was brewing. It threatened to upset the record output of houses sought by the minister to fulfill his party's election pledge.

New towns were bypassed. They were not available to some regions. Besides, the new towns in the London region were dealing primarily with some of the outer metropolitan boroughs, not with the county itself, and the corporations didn't particularly welcome the assistance of the LCC.

Some new arrangements were required to ensure more palatable agreements and patterns of development. Expansion of small existing towns had been recommended in the past by the Abercrombie plans and was under consideration for some time by the ministry. The tripartite experiment in Lancashire County (and also Staffordshire), involving fairly flexible agreements between exporting and importing authorities, coupled with financial and technical assistance provided by the county, seemed to point in the right direction. It became the basis for the Town Development Act.

143

In substance, the act does three things. It uses existing government machinery. Though no new agencies have been created, the powers of existing agencies were increased. It also offers incentives. However uncertain and perhaps ineffectual the bait may be, the act does try to entice a more balanced form of development. It tries to ensure this by insisting upon prior ministerial approval of the agreements as a condition for extending aid to receiving areas. And Exchequer assistance by reducing the financial burden may soften opposition to expansion or building by outside authorities. Finally, it provides a stronger club for the minister, entitling him to encourage county councils or county boroughs to participate if county districts prove recalcitrant in negotiating agreements.

CHAPTER 9

The Town Development Act: Problems and Implications

The Town Development Act was passed with the grudging acqui-
escence of the Labour opposition.[1] But historically it will be viewed as
another example of the long-range efforts of both parties to formulate a
comprehensive town-planning policy. Judging from the *possible* scale of
development and the *potential* effects on existing cities, this legislation
may some day far overshadow the earlier new town approach. Still, at
the outset it aroused no marked enthusiasm anywhere. Too many reservations existed about the meaning of the provisions, the way in which the
program would be executed, important gaps in the available powers, and
the possible accomplishments even under favorable circumstances. Most
of the doubts reflect a sophistication acquired from experience with the
new towns. They centered on the vagueness surrounding the amount of
financial assistance and the lack of power to coordinate industrial and
residential relocation. There were also misgivings about the neglect of
regional considerations and the limited exploitation of the building
capacity of the London County Council and the large county boroughs.

Financial Benefits and Interauthority Relationships

Despite repeated pleas and taunts from the opposition, no clear estimates of the possible scope and financial contributions of this program
were made by the minister during discussion of the legislation. Local authorities were uneasy. They preferred to know the financial burdens to be
assumed before undertaking their tasks. But local and national officials
realized that the costs would vary with different areas and periods, with
differences in the equalization grants, the local rates, the housing subsidies, the amount of industry and commercial development, and the like.

The framers of the legislation deliberately stipulated, therefore, that the grants would depend upon the circumstances.

Some cost approximations, however, have gained currency. Thus in the Lancashire County Council program for Worsley, the yearly deficit for county and district council services and the housing rate-fund contribution was about £10 per house.[2] This figure has been cited often. Similarly, Mr. W. L. Abernethy, Assistant Controller of the LCC, has estimated that the increased rate in the pound for the debt charges and the operating expenses for the sewerage expansion would in typical receiving areas range from 1s. to 2s. 6d.; and that the additional increase when the local housing rate contribution of the exporting authority ended would in four schemes under discussion be 2s., 2s., 3s., and 7s., respectively.[3] This burden is in most cases beyond the resources of the ordinary receiving authority even if some assistance is secured from the congested area. On a development of 5,000 dwellings, Mr. Abernethy reckons that the exporting authority's rate contribution for a ten-year period would be almost £450,000, plus more than £100,000 for interest charges. Even if only a few schemes were undertaken, the outlay would soon prove prohibitive. Because of the fairly limited and temporary assistance that can be expected from the exporting authority and possibly from the county council, the amount of the ministry's assistance must inescapably control the scale of the program. But it was precisely on the score of the ministry's intentions that the greatest uncertainty prevailed.

During the debate, Mr. Aneurin Bevan, the former Labour Minister of Health, contended

> If the amount of money were considerable, the Treasury would obviously insist on some figure being put in [the Financial Resolution]. The reason why the Treasury does not do so is because the Treasury knows it is a very small amount of money that is involved. From my own experience of the Treasury a very small amount of money indeed would be involved . . . so what we have here is a nice, charming piece of window-dressing that does not in fact deal with the problem at all.[4]

This charge was never countered. Later in the committee discussions, the minister, Mr. Macmillan, declared:

> What we have to do is what I keep coming back to, and that is to produce a Bill which will put some money at the disposal of the Minister, whoever he may be, to assist a very small number — and it will be quite a small number — of schemes by which authorities can help one another where there are not enough resources available to the local authorities themselves. That is all that this bill does.[5]

Of course, if the grants are too parsimonious, the number of participants may be drastically reduced. A good deal depends on how much the
community may want to expand and on its confidence in the intentions
of the ministry. The bargaining power of the local authorities is actually
quite limited. "Colonization" by the bigger authorities is still greatly
feared. All that was needed in the past was the minister's consent to a
Compulsory Purchase Order requested by the expanding authority.
Equal, if not greater, powers are now available in the new legislation.
The minister may instruct the LCC or some other authority to build if a
receiving authority is unable or unwilling to do so. He has said that he
hopes to use this power rarely; but it does exist. Presumably the same
weapon could be wielded to induce the London County authorities to
negotiate. For the minister can withhold his consent for a CPO if London acts too arbitrarily. This club may prompt "negotiated" agreements,
especially since there might be greater sharing of costs by the exporting authority and the ministry under this program. Also, the receiving
area may be able to insist upon more carefully coordinated development
than occurred in the traditional building patterns outside London.
Even Mr. Bevan termed past practices "an outrage against good local
government." [6]

The ministry is therefore cautiously hopeful. A few key officers believe that they have learned much from the experience with new towns.
They expect to learn even more by starting with friendly and cooperative local authorities. Their expectations have some justification. There
have been enough local authorities willing to become reception areas
under the present arrangements to avoid any compulsion. With the
possibility of financial assistance and better planning, still other local
authorities may be tempted by some of the other advantages. Thus the
program may quickly solve urgent local housing needs. There is also
the prospect of some added prestige. At a conference of country towns
officials, they were reminded by Mr. W. A. Wood that "some rural districts will become urban districts. . . , some urban districts will become
boroughs, and even some boroughs may become county boroughs." [7] Still
more important may be the opportunities which growth makes possible.
Greater variety of industries may be desired. Most of the expanded country towns will also acquire urban facilities and services that previously
they could not afford. Councillor Price pointed out that his town,
Bletchley, the first to build houses for London, looked forward to securing
an open-air swimming pool, a Woolworth's, a Marks and Spencer's, a new
cinema, better bus service, and more varied jobs and opportunities.[8]

147

The LCC, though officially on record in favor of the legislation, had considerable misgivings at the outset. They feared the increased competition for scarce building labor and materials. They were apprehensive lest their building organization might be raided or otherwise stymied by the newly created staffs of the receiving authorities. They were skeptical whether the Exchequer contributions would be adequate. They were worried about the time that might be consumed by negotiations. But they have nonetheless acted vigorously. They have decided to challenge the assumption that "England is to remain broken up into self-contained prohibited areas, and that London must remain an open rendezvous for all comers, mainly from the provinces, towns and villages in which people from London are to be barred." [9] Under the leadership of Mr. Reginald Stamp, the Chairman of the LCC Housing Committee, they have made a widespread effort to expand towns, as either principals or agents. Discussions have been started with more than sixty local authorities within a one hundred-mile radius of London. Close to 140,000 persons may be rehoused under these schemes if the plans materialize. Indeed, if the program does succeed, the LCC might emerge as the major regional building agency for communities with which mutually satisfactory agreements can be negotiated.

Unfortunately, progress has been somewhat slow. More than two years after the passage of the act there were complaints that "no town expansion scheme has been put in hand or even approved that was not already under way when the act was passed." [10] And in a special statement to the minister in March 1955, the Executive of the Town and Country Planning Association deplored the "slow progress," which was attributed to "the awkward complications of the local government finances together with the lack of that firm government leadership which alone can resolve them." [11] However, a more positive policy appears in the offing. On April 26, 1955, Mr. Duncan Sandys, the new Minister of Housing and Local Government, announced that fixed grants would be made to cover some of the increased costs of the receiving areas accommodating overspill population and industry. The grants will equal 50 per cent of the cost of approved water and sewerage extensions. In addition, exporting authorities were assured that they would be freed of responsibility for paying rate contributions (local subsidies) for housing in the receiving areas after a specified period, which is expected to average about ten years. The government expects to pay part or all of this grant, if the financial burden on the receiving authority warrants such assistance. Though some receiving areas may still have qualms about how the ministry will behave in the future, a large step has been taken in the direction of a fixed commitment. It remains to be seen whether the size of the grant will provide the leverage for the rate and scale of development desired.

Jobs and Homes

To build houses near jobs is one of the key aims of contemporary British planning. On this subject, however, the Town Development Act is silent. Nonetheless, Mr. Macmillan insisted that

> It is our firm intention that the new receiving authorities shall not merely be the recipients of a dormitory population from another authority. Those who go to them are not expected to travel daily backwards and forwards across the green fringe.[12]

Many workers, moreover, may not move to the new locations beyond the greenbelt unless jobs are nearby. Some persons assert that the present limits of travel have been reached. Existing transportation facilities are now serving peak loads. Further burdens will require costly extensions and improvements. If the jobs do not move with the workers, top ministry officials will consider the program a failure.

But to count on success requires much optimism. Town expansion, not industrial location, is the subject of the legislation, the minister said. That was his explanation of the absence of any powers affecting industrial location. He has also declared that the provision of houses, coupled with the powers and persuasiveness of the Board of Trade, should attract the desired economic activities. But the board has not proved altogether helpful in channeling industries to the new towns. Moreover, it has no control over offices or plant extensions. And in November 1955, licenses for building were abolished, with a corresponding reduction in the board's influence. These limitations, plus existing priorities favoring development and unemployment areas, may stymie even a cooperative board. As for the Ministry of Housing and Local Government, it has no explicit powers or subsidies in reserve to push or induce such relocation. So it is at least understandable why the opposition persistently questioned whether the powers were adequate for the goals, and whether there were enough jobs available for redistribution to expanded areas. The minister has promised that in the administration of the act, he will consider schemes submitted by local authorities "subject to . . . being satisfied that people moving out . . . will in general have work to go to." [13] The program has not advanced sufficiently to judge whether this promise can be kept.

However, another possibility for linking housing and employment is being pursued by the LCC. Since it plans to dispossess its nonconforming industries, it is attempting to negotiate for their transfer to those expanded towns with which agreements are concluded. According to Mr. Reginald Stamp, the "LCC alone has 1,500 acres occupied by nonconforming industry spoiling the character and amenities of many residential districts, apart from many industries unable to expand in industrial areas zoned for the purpose." [14] With these prospects in mind, Mr. Stamp has even issued a blunt threat to the new towns. Noting their problems in securing industry and their failure to give "metropolitan London the help expected of them, whatever relief they have given to the Greater London authorities," [15] he has declared:

> A fundamental flaw in the constitution of New Towns is the absence of any statutory function between them and the overspill authorities. The public pressure of need has been divorced from the means to fulfillment.
>
> There is a grave danger arising out of the present position that the powers now given to local authorities under the Town Development Act to make their own arrangements may slow down or even bring to a standstill the development of industry in New Towns. Now that local authorities have statutory rights they are more likely to seek to transfer unwanted industry to places where they have a function than by seeking the patronage of a New Town where they have no statutory rights. [16]

The LCC once offered to build a neighborhood unit in each of the new towns, an offer which *The Economist* observed "the Government Department, perhaps unfortunately, rejected." [17] It is this inability to help develop new towns, plus the LCC's very limited right to nominate tenants for housing in these towns, which has made Mr. Stamp so bitter.

But despite his pointed warnings and the measures taken by the ministry, the actual prospects of decentralizing the location of industry are still uncertain. Mr. Stamp, for example, knows that the ability to pay adequate compensation to the dislodged industry will be decisive. At present, he points out that "the government pays only 20 per cent and the local authority 80 per cent — too heavy a burden upon the rates." [18] Either a larger government grant or some form of levy has been urged by many persons who have studied the problem. Re-examination of the priorities governing the Board of Trade has also been recommended, because as Mr. Self emphasizes, "this is one field of planning policy where all is emphatically not well." [19]

In the ministry and elsewhere, however, the grounds for the assurance one encounters rest partly on the solid prosperity and industrial

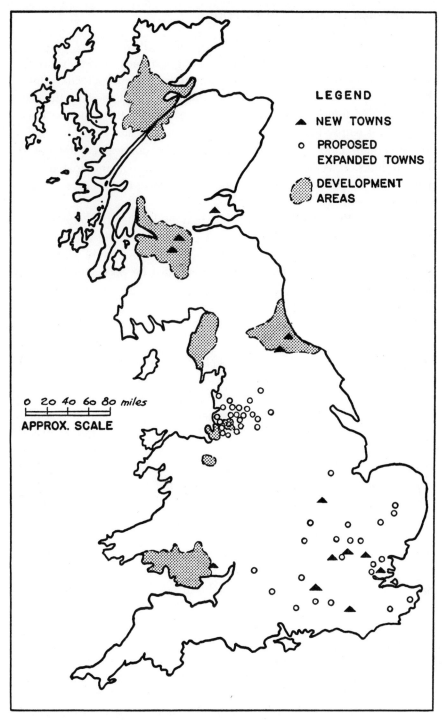

MAP 6. NEW TOWNS, PROPOSED EXPANDED TOWNS, AND DEVELOPMENT AREAS

Source: See Maps 1, 3, 4, and 5.

expansion that took the country by surprise in 1955. Others, less confident about this windfall, insist that the government must eventually coordinate and back up its varied commitments. Some officials want a definite proportion of the new plant construction assigned to the new and expanded towns. Sooner or later, it is reasoned, this must be done, especially if empty houses accumulate in both new and expanded towns and a vigilant labor opposition starts to make political capital out of these failures. It is argued that if this danger is not anticipated, new plants will be pushed there in short order once the failures become known.

However, this whistling in the dark may underrate other alternatives, perhaps equally likely. If there are not enough economic activities, development may proceed unevenly. Dormitory suburbs may be established and gradually accepted. The program may also be discredited and allowed to peter out. Or the results may prove sufficiently picayune to discourage active interest.

Regional and National Planning

Suppose, however, that these development difficulties are overcome. Will the locations of the expanded towns prove satisfactory for the new economic activities? Perhaps. But the present emphasis is largely on population resettlement where agreements can be negotiated. Efficient locations for industry and offices appear to be incidental. Granted Britain is a relatively small country generally well served by road and rail networks. Granted, too, that so many noneconomic factors affect the siting of plants and offices that the importance of some additional pressures can easily be overemphasized. Still, such comfortable assumptions may be dangerous for specific communities in an experimental program, during a period when Great Britain's economy is so dependent on increased efficiency for exports and for a higher standard of living.

At present, moreover, little account is taken by the town planners of the interregional patterns. It is assumed that overspill would be corrected in the general region where congestion exists. This may be advisable. But the program is headed toward serious conflicts with the policy of encouraging development areas or any regional redistribution of economic activity. (This problem can be appreciated better if the reader examines Map 6: New Towns, Proposed Expanded Towns, and Development Areas.) Though the issue has not yet been seriously faced administratively, questions are increasingly being raised as the consequences of the various policies are sensed. Professor Beacham has claimed that it is highly probable that some industries which would normally have gone to country towns have in part been diverted to Development areas . . . It is best to face the fact that part of the price paid for fostering the development or redevelopment of old centers of industry like South Wales or the North East is the starvation of the country town. I am not here debating which policy is right and which is wrong but simply pointing out that you cannot have your cake and eat it.[20]

Before long, the *ad hoc* corrective measures must yield to a more comprehensive approach if they are not to become increasingly inconsistent and self-defeating. Disturbing evidence of this trend already exists. Comparing the planners' policy for industry with the approach followed by the Board of Trade, Mr. Peter Self concluded that

The Board's approach is essentially static — to pump employment to idle labour wherever that labour exists. The planners' approach is dynamic — to influence the environment and conditions under which people do their work . . .

The Board's main interest is in inter-regional movements of industry and it is less concerned in securing a satisfactory distributon of industry within each region. For example, Merseyside, because of its employment record, has been made a development area. Mersyside, however, is also a badly congested area which is scheduled to lose a considerable amount of surplus population to other towns in Lancashire. . . It may possibly be desirable to introduce some new forms [of industry] in order to avoid too much dependence on the group of dockside industries. But if much new employment is created on Merseyside then its present overcrowding may be perpetuated and a modest program of decentralization will be made far more difficult.

The development area ought not to be Merseyside but the new parts of Lancashire to which its surplus population will move and where the provisions of work will be urgently needed.[21]

Mr. Self has also noted that the prospects for decongestion have been nullified in still another way. The Board of Trade had agreed to treat certain areas, particularly Greater London and Greater Birmingham, as "contraction areas." Presumably industrial growth in these areas was to be severely restricted. But exceptions were permitted for firms producing for exports or defense. As a result,

in the four years ended 30 June 1952, Greater London and Greater Birmingham accounted between them for 24.0% of all the industrial development certificates granted by the Board, while the combined total for the development areas was 15.6 per cent. . . These figures suggest that the exceptions have been so numerous as wholly to vitiate the principle of "contraction." [22]

More recent data published in 1955 confirm this trend. The employment statistics "show a slight increase over the last five years in the number of insured workers in Greater London, both absolutely and as a proportion of the national total . . . [and] the London and Southern region is the only one to have gained in the last three years a significant number of immigrants." [23] The net effect, therefore, of the board's carrying out its special responsibilities for promoting development areas and aiding the export and defense policies has been to augment growth in contracting areas. New branches and factory expansion account for this result, since the Board of Trade has rarely permitted new firms to enter the London region. To reverse this trend, therefore, the board must not only stop immigration of new factories but it must bar both new branch plants and plant expansions of existing firms unless they are undertaken in approved locations. Even this may not be enough if the secular expansion in tertiary or service activities continues, largely in response to rising income.[24] Indeed, with central office space at a premium, it would be ironical if such success as may ultimately be achieved in industrial decentralization were offset by increasing government and business activities, which have generally been overlooked in location policy. Indeed, nothing less than curbing expansion of offices as well as plants, plus a mechanism for synchronizing the present interregional and intraregional development policies, would seem to be capable of handling successfully the present policy commitments.

Two other weaknesses have further complicated intraregional development. Within the central government, there are defects in the regional departmental relationships. At present, coordination occurs in the ministry, particularly through the Regional Panels for Industry and Regional Committees for Physical Development. These committees, representing the relevant government departments, have served as decentralized centers for information and for interpreting local and national attitudes and policies. They have tried to reconcile obvious conflicts and to anticipate the effects of cumulative pressures that might have escaped the notice of individual authorities. But apparently "Whitehall" has too often failed to coordinate its departments satisfactorily. Mr. Reginald Stamp is simply echoing a widely held view when he declares that "to permit the present anarchy of each department of state developing its own programme, without relating it to other requirements on the same site, is to invite a slowing down and the maximum of problems in these new areas." [25] The fact is that enough bungling or near failures have occurred, such as Harlow's explosive sewage issue and Stevenage's dearth of economic activities, to prompt doubts about the relative efficiency of this regional coordination to date.

Another serious limitation is the administrative vacuum for carrying out regional plans within the larger metropolitan areas. The London Planning Administration Committee, appointed by the Minister of Town and Country Planning to advise on "the appropriate machinery for securing concerted action in the implementation of a Regional Plan for London," [26] agreed unanimously that the area must be treated as a whole. Problems of a greenbelt, water supply, sewage disposal, drainage, transport, power services, industry, housing and planning surveys and research, and adjustment of target population all require regional priorities and solutions, they declared. But, as might have been expected, there was disagreement on the specific agency to undertake the task. The over-all responsibility, to the extent that there is any, now falls by default on the regional panels, where the planning authorities have no representation. It is hardly surprising that there is often a serious divergence between the local development plans and regional departmental policies. The complications growing out of this situation led the London Planning Administration Committee to question whether

> the securing of concerted action in carrying through a plan ought to be the function of central government at all — except to the extent that it is for central government, in the exercise of its supervisory function, to see that concerted action can be, and is secured . . .

> Planning . . . is a local authority function; still more must, or ought to be, the carrying through of the Plan. Even if the machinery afforded by Departments were more effective and less cumbersome than it is, we should think it wrong to rely on it for doing something which ought properly to fall to the local authority to do. In common with a great many other people, we deplore the increasing central control of local administration which is steadily reducing the vitality of local government. Concerted action in implementation of the Plan is, we are convinced, a matter for local governments; and if the existing local authorities are not well designed for the purpose, it is in a modification of their design that we should look for the remedy, not in a diminution of their function.[27]

Unfortunately, creating adequate departmental and local machinery to secure coherent regional development is no easy task. Many proposals have been ventured. Professor Fogarty has urged that the better types of local and regional development councils would effectively represent various economic and social interests and serve as a counterweight to central government departments and even interdepartmental regional boards or committees. Others have urged the inclusion of local planning authorities

155

in the regional panels. The majority report of the London Planning Administration Committee favored a local joint advisory committee; and the minority argued for a stronger local joint planning board, assuming "the powers of the present planning authorities, the county councils and county borough councils." [28] But at present neither the LCC nor the ministry, nor almost any of the local authorities in the London region or elsewhere, are prepared to accept or press for some effective form of regional organization. Under the circumstances, comprehensive, consistent guidance of regional economic and town development can hardly be assured.

The Mechanism of Town Development

At the outset the legislative and administrative emphasis in town development was on encouraging "matchmaking" between the exporting and reception authorities. This was to take place under the benign auspices of the ministry and with the promise of a kind of dowry to reduce some of the forbidding costs resulting from the issue of the union. But before long it became obvious that in the London region at least there were a much larger number of exporting than receiving authorities. By May 1953, there were approximately twenty-seven receiving authorities, including new towns (more will be added), and eighty-seven housing authorities in the congested areas of London. With "direct arrangements" only a few authorities might benefit and not necessarily those most in need of assistance.[29] For under these arrangements, an exporting town could secure the right to nominate a large portion, perhaps even most, of the tenants by paying the local-authority housing subsidy; or by agreeing to accept responsibility for the development in whole or part on agreed-upon terms. Another complicating factor was the need for the residents to be selected on the basis of employment possibilities as well as housing need; and this might require a wider labor market for an industry than was available in any particular local authority. It was recognized too that these problems applied equally well to new towns: that as the building program of the new towns reached its stride, the limited agreements worked out with a few of the local metropolitan authorities benefited some at the expense of others; and that if these agreements continued, undue restraints might be placed on the selection of workers.[30]

As a remedy it was decided that some towns should expand without "direct arrangements." With a few exceptions, new towns also were to proceed without "direct arrangements." [31] In these towns persons were to be accepted from any of the potential exporting authorities. The ministry invited these authorities to form lists of eligible workers who might be interested in going to new or expanded towns, and the industries moving to these towns were asked to select their employees as far as possible from the lists. In short, the towns were to "draw their tenants through their industrialists and other employers of labor, who . . . recruit through the Ministry of Labor from lists prepared by the whole group of authorities." [32] London was divided into five sectors, with lists of exporting and reception authorities for each sector, in order to establish tentative channels for working purposes. [33]

Under this procedure it was no longer feasible for the financial arrangements to be negotiated by the local authorities if there were no "direct arrangements." The minister therefore proposed a standard agreement for all exporting authorities, namely that they pay the local-authority housing subsidy for a period of ten years for every family nominated by them that secured a house in an expanded town. The subsidy, moreover, is to be paid as long as the family occupies the house. [34] At the end of ten years, the situation was to be reviewed by the authorities. But, as noted earlier, according to a more recent directive the exporting authority will be relieved of further financial responsibility for the subsidy and the ministry will assume it, if the burden on the community warrants such assistance. If there is a dispute about the new arrangements, the matter is to be referred to the minister. Since the situation is identical in the new towns, the same rule is to be applied there. By this simple device, the burden of the local subsidy in new towns previously borne by the Treasury, has been shifted; and the large exporting cities have been induced to help finance their own growth or decentralization. [35]

But direct building of new towns by the county boroughs or the LCC is still shunned. Almost every other principal alternative has been explored, i.e., building by the new town corporations along with some building by existing local authorities; negotiated agreements between reception areas and the exporting authority or authorities, with either one or the other or both in combination doing the building; and self-expansion by the country towns. Despite the recognized building capacity of county boroughs and the LCC, they have not been encouraged to do more than erect housing estates or help expand existing towns under the postwar planning legislation.

Local Boundaries, National Interest, and Town Development

Fundamentally the problem confronting the policy of town development was how to facilitate large-scale expansion outside of the corporate jurisdiction of the metropolis, yet reconcile the interests of the satellite and central communities. Invasion and subsequent absorption was one possibility. Certainly it had often been practiced. But formidable obstacles lay in the way and the mood was against such an approach. Maintenance of the independence of local authorities had become a major premise. Both political parties conceded that the boundaries of local governments ought to be redrawn and local finances reorganized. That they will be appears unlikely. Aneurin Bevan may have twitted the minister with failing to tackle the basic question of local government reform and Procrustean local jurisdictions. But the Conservatives observed in turn that the Labour government did not show any avid inclination to tackle these problems when it was in office. The crux of the compromise was to shift the extra costs to the central government and thus provide a basis for negotiated settlement of other problems. Technical assistance is not provided; but it seems doubtful whether the government can grant funds and still avoid entanglements on questions of technical aid, standards, and supervision.

Associated with the boundary issue is a historically interesting shift in the financial responsibilities for urban expansion. In the nineteenth century, city growth was generally welcomed as a sign of health and prosperity. Local authorities did the building and financed the necessary services with revenues secured from all of their residents. Occasional defaults on debts could be dismissed as examples of unsound judgments or unfortunate incidents of the trade cycle. But sooner or later the resumption of growth on a still larger scale was expected.

This uncritical faith in the advantages of size has weakened. Gradually the central government has been assuming more and more obligations for financing many urban services through subsidies for special purposes, such as housing, and through general subsidies, such as the equalization grant. National financing of the building of new towns and the expansion of existing towns continues this trend. To encourage a preferred, nonautomatic, and independent form of urban expansion some distance from the boundaries of congested cities, the nation has accepted part of the costs ordinarily shouldered by an expanding metropolis.

Unless enough suitable vacant land exists within or adjacent to the overcrowded authorities, their boundaries will not be expanded. Neither is their population to overflow; nor are their existing densities to swell beyond a predetermined maximum. Instead the population is supposed to "hop" to agreed-upon receiving areas.[36] But since the receiving authority is no longer part of the expanding metropolis, it is scarcely able to foot all the costs alone. Neither can the local exporting authority or the county council. Hence the central government will make contributions, on the grounds that the pattern of urban development affects the national interest, and, in particular, such basic policies as industrial location, contemporary living standards, and defense. Finally, because many local receiving districts lack technical proficiency and staffs, and since technical aid is not being extended by the ministry, it is likely that outside authorities, probably the county or the exporting authority, may often have to aid and sometimes even execute the actual physical development.

Summary Observations

The Town Development Act has established another method of building towns. It retains some of the weaknesses of the new towns approach. Almost no change is involved so far as allocation of resources, over-all planning organization, location of industry, physical design, and research are concerned. Nor does the new legislation avert any more than the New Towns Act the treadmill tendency for new families and industries to reoccupy the places of those that leave.

But there are significant differences, advantageous because they add more leeway in the choice of methods for town building. There is also some possibility of more coordinated provision of basic services, more use of the machinery for town expansion in different regions, and perhaps even lower rents. But whether these possibilities will materialize is still a matter of speculation.

One difference is in origin and purpose. True, both expanded and new towns were intended to relieve congestion. Both also can trace their origins back to the prewar development patterns and the subsequent corrective forces channeling planning action. The new towns really evidenced a new threshold in the realm of more positive, comprehensive, physical development. When first introduced, they were to serve London primarily. They have since taken on other assignments, of which Corby, Aycliffe, Cwmbran, Basildon, Peterlee, and Glenrothes are examples. Since there was no policy for expanding existing towns, the new towns machinery was on occasion crudely twisted in this direction, although not without some anguished protests. Expanded towns, by contrast, were geared to a narrower objective. They were prompted by the lack of space for building in congested areas, a consequence largely of the development plans and the density decisions required by the Town and Country Planning Act of 1947. They were supposed to sustain the building programs of existing local authorities. Disputes that might block or retard

159

"balanced" development outside a local authority's jurisdiction were to be minimized or avoided by a judicious application of financial and technical assistance.

In a sense the New Towns Act, the Town and Country Planning Act of 1947, and other parallel legislation signalize the "breakthrough" of a certain approach to planning. The assumptions underlying this approach are persuasive to all major currents of opinion. Therefore, additional consolidating legislation can be expected to correct and to extend the policies now in force. The Town Development Act is an example. It is a ready adaptation of a ruling idea to the solution of a specific problem. Were it not for the existence of its pioneering predecessor, the New Towns Act, and of the new planning machinery established by the Town and Country Planning Act of 1947, it is improbable that there would have been a policy of "integrated" expansion of existing towns.

So much for the kinship between town development and new towns. There are also some interesting differences in administrative and operating characteristics. The most important is the reliance upon the local authorities. Instead of creating a new organization, as in the case of new towns, the Town Development Act taps to a greater extent than heretofore the building resources of the local authorities. The objective is to accommodate the overspill population, presumably with the reception authorities doing most of the building. So long as this legislation remains in force, it is unlikely that towns like Hemel Hempsted will be obliged to joust with a new town corporation.

However, the ministry's preference that the building be done by the reception authorities has not deterred the LCC, the principal exporting authority, from counting upon the extensive use of its resources in the form of participation agreements. There are reasonable prospects that the LCC may benefit from the legislation. But so, too, may some other cities, such as Birmingham, Liverpool, and Manchester, which the new towns program has slighted. Lancashire and Staffordshire, it will be recalled, pioneered the early town expansion programs.[37]

In comparison with the new towns, the financial arrangements appear to offer more latitude and advantages to the reception authorities. Like other local authorities they will be able to negotiate shorter-term loans and lower interest rates. Pressure, however, can be expected to equalize the situation for the new towns. Arrangements have already been made for the exporting authorities to provide the normal local rate-fund contributions that they previously escaped paying for families on their housing lists who received accommodations in new towns. As for the costs of drainage, sewerage, water, and site preparation, it is still too early to tell whether the arrangements favor either the expanded or the new towns. Local authorities are sharing their costs with the new towns, albeit after prolonged wrangling. Similarly, reception authorities will share these costs with the ministry and to some extent with other local authorities. An advantage for reception authorities compared to new towns, however, may be that fewer difficulties should ensue in the timing and provision of these services. This is because the participating exporting authorities have most of the necessary development powers.[38]

Both the expanded towns and the new towns are supposed to avoid becoming dormitories. Neither, however, is able to do much more than rely upon its powers of attraction. Much will depend on the Board of Trade, whose past record has hardly inspired confidence. Some faith is also being placed in the capacity of the exporting authority to channel its badly housed and nonconforming industries to the new locations. This neglected possibility has raised high hopes in some quarters. Even if these objectives are attained, no remedy seems yet to be in sight to ensure coherent distribution of development between different regions and more satisfactory coordination and execution of development within a region.

To widen the potential labor market for industries that locate in these towns, accommodations are to be provided for employees on housing lists regardless of where they live. Negotiated agreements between local authorities and expanded towns are being limited, therefore, to prevent only a few authorities, and possibly the wrong ones, from benefiting unduly from the program. Similar tendencies are in evidence for the new towns in the London region. Earlier agreements with some of the metropolitan boroughs surrounding London are now being extended to the other authorities and even to the LCC.

The ultimate scale of the program for expanded towns and new towns is uncertain. The same holds true for their relative importance. Though proposals for new towns may come from local authorities or the ministry, the ministry has made it clear that no new towns will be started unless Parliamentary approval is secured. If so, it may be easier in the future to expand new towns or country towns rather than to build new ones, since only ministerial approval is required. For the present, although no ceilings have been set for the expanded towns, and few, if any, new towns are yet in the offing, no major efforts are expected from either quarter.

Despite the uncertainties, it is clear that important modifications are still occurring, though many of their consequences have yet to be grasped. It is becoming distressingly evident that town development calls for more than adoption of a policy. Successful implementation presupposes a fairly coherent alignment of national, regional, and local programs and policies. These include basic services, housing, industrial location, transport, government boundaries, finance, education, and other matters, which, at present, are often geared to unrelated or partially related objectives. A few programs or policies significantly out of line can seriously hamper or frustrate attainment of the physical planning goals.

Only slowly is the essential interdependence of the components of urban areas dawning on the British planners and influencing their pioneering measures. New towns are one phase; expansion of towns another; reconstruction of existing towns still another; the organized settlement of existing vacant areas of cities, a fourth; and appropriate patterns of regional, national, and possibly even overseas development are yet to come.[39] Nor are these all-inclusive. Comprehensive town planning, in short, is still an unrealized ideal.

A PERSPECTIVE ON NEW TOWNS:
IMPLICATIONS AND PROSPECTS

PART | IV

CHAPTER **10**

Reflections on Newtopia

There is no single criterion by which the new towns policy can be judged. Success in decentralizing London is one measure; performance in planning, designing, and building is another; the cost of new towns is a third. Perhaps the most important of all is the diverse potentials of these ideas: their impact on planning; the deeper trends they exemplify; their positive contributions; the role they may play in the future. At the outset of this study the question was raised whether new towns made sense, considering the severest criticisms that could be leveled at the policy. The criticisms have been developed; they may now be re-examined in the light of these broader considerations, including the tangible experience of the past ten years.

New Towns: Basic Weaknesses

In retrospect two kinds of weaknesses appear to qualify the new towns achievements.

There was first of all the inability to reach the main objective. The British new towns policy was originally intended to curb the growth and perhaps reduce the size of London. These goals were to be accomplished by planned redistribution of jobs and population to more or less self-contained new communities. There was also the hope of arresting the movement of population from other regions to London and the home counties, and possibly of some transfer of population and activities to other regions of Britain. On the whole, these goals of the new towns policy were not realized. There was no effective way of stopping the replacement of the persons and activities drawn from the London region or the expansion of plants within the region. Naïve expectations or radical defects in the approach were to blame. The steady or increasing flow of new firms and inhabitants was misjudged. Somehow it was expected that the vacated plants and housing would be eliminated, when in point of fact they were valuable social capital — too expensive for owners to write off and too costly for local authorities to purchase. As a consequence, London, a decade after the new towns policy was adopted, seemed to be in no better position than the Red Queen.

Secondly, there were numerous shortcomings reflecting the human limitations on execution, skill, and insight. Although rectifiable, they detracted from the significance of the accomplishment. A few of the more important shortcomings were the failure to achieve balanced regional and national development; the errors of organization and administration; the inadequacies in dealing with financing and costs; and the neglect of applied research to guide or check fundamental policies.

Some of these difficulties can be discerned in Ebenezer Howard's original formulation. He could not foresee the auto period. His emphasis on new cities was misplaced. Ties between the new and old city were neglected. Many of Howard's assumptions needed questioning: for example, that the journey to work was evil, that industries might locate anywhere, that the flow of population to London would not equal or exceed the flow of population to the new towns. The problems, too, were oversimplified. This is most obvious in Howard's treatment of the costs and financial complications, the pace and ease of decentralization, and the possible solutions, especially his view that garden cities were *the* solution, not just one of perhaps several necessary tools.

Some of these notions were dropped or modified when the new towns policy was formulated. This was partly because of the lessons gleaned from earlier experiments, including Letchworth and Welwyn, and also because of the obstacles raised by shortages of materials and by urban reconstruction. But there was still the failure to think through, or at any rate to cope effectively with, the administrative tangles. The approach to the scope of the program was *ad hoc*. There was disproportionate emphasis on the self-contained towns. There was inadequate understanding of the necessary conditions for successful planned decentralization. There was a complacent assurance that the basic answers were known and that research was expendable.

The consequences soon became manifest in various ways: in the lack of coordination and consistency in the policies of the Board of Trade, the Coal Board, the Treasury, and the Ministries of Agriculture and

Transport; in the questionable relationship of the new towns to national and regional development; in the tenuous links between satellite new towns and the planning and building policies of large cities such as London and Glasgow; in the failure to mobilize the local authorities with development powers; in the absence of any provision for applied research on those matters where knowledge or technique were faulty and where substantial improvements were feasible.

As the new towns were built, these problems reappeared in another guise. The London and Glasgow towns did not alter the structure of the existing metropolis. Instead they provided one other channel for a small portion of the outward flow of firms and families. And since there were no new towns near the other large cities, growth elsewhere was wholly unaffected by the policy. In addition, the flimsy economic and population base of the self-contained towns resulted in harrying difficulties during the early years of development. These included the allocation of overhead and general development costs and the inability to set rents reasonably competitive with those of equivalent new housing of the local authorities, not simply with the older stock of housing. These dilemmas endangered other objectives because of the economies required, the higher income market served, and the fears, disillusionment, and opposition generated.

If the personal history of each of the new towns is scanned, variations of these common problems may be seen in a more individual and sometimes more aggravated form. In a class by themselves were the stormy conflicts between the National Coal Board and Peterlee and the complications of financing Harlow's sewage treatment plant. Equally vexatious have been the sour relationships in the case of East Kilbride and the London new towns and the local authorities in Glasgow and London whom the towns are presumably aiding. Almost as depressing were the many frustrations experienced by the new towns in dealing with the Board of Trade.

Other difficulties also obtruded. The austerity policy arrested and distorted development. The sudden resort to planning culminated in the sheer lack of enough skilled planners to handle the many new responsibilities dumped in their laps.[1] The egregious supervision by the ministry irritated and hampered the corporations so that some of the vaunted advantages of flexibility were lost. And the equivocal quality of new town design resulted in either passive acceptance or disappointment in some quarters, thus dampening part of the contagious enthusiasm necessary to nourish and strengthen the program.

The New Towns Hypothesis: Reformulation and Enrichment

But one must go beyond these limitations to estimate properly the possible success and the broader implications of this program. If, for example, Ebenezer Howard's proposals were considered as an hypothesis of urban organization and growth, they would probably rank among the most fruitful in town planning. This is so even though the hypothesis is in many ways false. For the effort to disprove or to defend it has eventually led to a clearer, more precise formulation, to an analysis of old and new data and ideas. Competing hypotheses are also likely to be explored, significant tests and procedures devised, and the results more carefully evaluated.

Consider, for example, the transformation of Ebenezer Howard's ideas into the subsequent new towns policy. Already the latter evidences some substantial modifications of the original thesis. The new towns are not expected to grow quickly and to develop their own satellites. They are either satellites to London or independent towns. Nor is the total population of London expected to drop substantially, though redistribution is intended. Even more important, the new towns idea has been pressed into service under many different circumstances. New towns are being built not only to channel the growth of large cities: they are also intended to foster a coherent growth pattern for an expanding basic industry and to establish efficient urban concentrations for straggling mining and even suburban settlements. These revised expectations and varied applications may more adequately represent the possible usefulness of the ideas.

It is unfortunately true that "the readings" are not being taken as they should be for such experiments. New towns have been treated too much as an accepted policy, as a program to be executed. They are in addition a series of significant experiments in public entrepreneurship on an impressive scale. They could profit from more controlled observations, more deliberate variations, more careful recording of their problems and progress.[2]

Even granting these defects, the significance of the new towns for research cannot be dismissed. The annual reports of the corporations, describing the plans, the experiences, the difficulties, and the costs of new towns, already constitute a mine of valuable information. We are getting and we probably shall continue to get valuable insights about development and overhead costs, problems of growth and industrial location, the provision of shopping centers, community and recreational facilities, and the difficulties of exploiting the economic and technical advantages of large-scale building of whole new towns. We ought to learn much about initial pioneering difficulties, the problems of social organization and participation, the handling and effects of large-scale civic design. Quite aside from any other considerations, this program is exciting because of the tremendous possibilities it opens as a field laboratory for research on these and many other questions.

The passage of the Town Development Act, regardless of its present inadequacies, is a good example of the progressive impact of the policy. It reflects a broadening conception of town development, a realization that national policies need more flexibility, that building new towns is only one tiny phase of a complex policy that includes the expansion of existing towns, the participation of local authorities, and the acceptance of financial responsibility on the part of the central government in realizing these objectives.

Similarly, there has been considerable rethinking of the educational requirements for planners.[3] Emphasis on the social sciences has increased. The planning curriculum has been opened to students of varied backgrounds. More research is being undertaken; and there is greater participation of social scientists in planning activities. These trends too are in part responses to the larger and more difficult issues and decisions that the policy commitments have thrust upon the planners.

In short, what is learned and what is done in trying to make this and similar programs work should teach planners everywhere to do their jobs better in the future.

New Towns in Perspective

The import of new towns also lies partly in the ideas they reflect as well as those they suggest. This may be clearer if we consider new towns in relation to some increasingly important issues, for instance, decentralization; standards of living and the trend toward public entrepreneurship; the contemporary preference for the suburban environment; the effect of urban form on vulnerability; and the growth of undeveloped areas. Each of these quite different aspects of new towns offers clues that may help us to weigh their contemporary meaning and historical significance.

New Towns and Decentralization. It is not surprising how little thought has been given to the circumstances under which planned decentralization could occur.[4] The issue is still fairly recent and has scarcely attracted adequate attention. Perhaps drawing a few tentative inferences and hypotheses from the new towns experience may help to make clear how many more pitfalls are involved than were originally suspected. For example:

1. Adoption of a policy of planned decentralization is of little consequence standing alone. Failure is being courted unless other important developers and strategic national and regional policies affecting development, particularly of industry and transportation, are geared in the same direction.

2. The best time for building new communities is during a period of growth; but, by a curious irony, cutting the size of giant cities or reducing their congestion is probably less likely in a period of growth. Such a period is generally characterized by a shortage of fixed capital. Vacated premises will be promptly occupied by newcomers or by those who are housed inadequately. Indeed, the availability of accommodations may induce a greater influx, as is often the case with highway improvements. Under the circumstances, one might be obliged to grind some satisfaction from the fact that because of what was done the situation has not gotten much worse.

3. If a policy of decentralization is pursued in a period of growth or shortage, then the investment must include the outlays for purchase and elimination of usable capital in central areas, i.e., factories, housing, and unused plant capacity of existing services. Assuming higher returns may be counted upon, it may make economic sense to scrap usable plants. Where this is not certain or agreed upon, there is considerable danger that the failure to eliminate this fixed capital may lead to intensified use and even renewal, and thus nullify the decentralization policy. There is, of course, a third possibility, namely to wait for the end of the period of growth. But this may take much time and involve the risk of building little or nothing.

4. New towns can serve as a method or as a specific pattern of decentralization. But their significance is a function of relative building volumes. In a period of growth, either of the entire metropolitan region or of the outer rings alone, they cannot exert a significant effect if their relative building volume is small compared to the total volume of building in metropolitan regions. Where this is the case, they may serve effectively as models, as research centers, as tools for dealing with especially difficult problems, and as a means of creating a greater range of choice of environment than is available under the existing pattern. These are perhaps more modest objectives, but they are achievable.

The new towns experience also underscores some critical gaps in our understanding of metropolitan decentralization. A major assumption of a planned decentralization policy is that there are optimum sizes for cities. As already noted, the available data and studies are meager and primitive. There is some evidence, not altogether consistent, that beyond a certain point costs mount with increasing scale. But in such studies there are serious difficulties in controlling the variables. This is particularly the case in establishing typical patterns, in measuring the quality of urban services, and in examining the cost threshholds of urban communities associated with presently unused capacity of the utility and service plant. There is also the question of the economies and diseconomies of urban scale for the family and firm. Because the economist has devoted so much attention to the firm and industry and has not dealt with other units, such as the metropolitan region, these subjects are virtually an unexplored frontier.

Another aspect of the optimum size of cities is the ideal urban network. Far more analyses of the functions, location, and economic relationships of cities are needed along lines developed by August Lösch and others.[5] To date, as one might have expected, expediency has played a large role in the selection of the new towns and the expanded country towns. The new town planners have placed emphasis more on balance *within* than *between* towns. Complaints about the effects and prospects of the new communities within the surrounding region should spur the search for more reliable criteria to guide the location of towns. Perhaps long-range considerations will be examined more carefully in the future in the various county development plans. Unfortunately there are almost no economists or social science analysts in these county planning offices at present; and it is even more probable that there is almost no one now interested in this range of problems. The same holds true for the ministry. In their new entrepreneurial capacities, the ministry, the counties, and the local authorities have tended to reflect the practical man's impatience with research that yields no immediate dividends. Universities, too, though less tainted by this attitude, have yet to evince any great interest in such studies.

Another basic assumption of a decentralization policy concerns appropriate densities, especially in central areas. The criteria that affect density decisions, the groups that make these decisions, the interaction of these decisions and costs, the appropriate accounting units, the effect of these decisions in creating an overspill population, and the problems of consumer preferences, efficiency, and social costs are obscure and controversial. At present the claims are contradictory, the evidence fragmentary, and the research underway negligible. Several fruitful hypotheses and methods for examining some of these issues have been suggested in

William H. Ludlow's excellent research monograph, but they have not yet been explored.[6]

A fourth strategic research area involves the concept of accessibility. We have had some able descriptive studies by Donald J. Bogue, Amos H. Hawley, Warren S. Thompson, and others, which explore statistically the spatial relationships of activities within metropolitan regions. These descriptive studies disclosed important empirical trends. But the mechanisms underlying these trends have not been explored and so we lack an adequate explanation of why they are occurring and how they might change in response to other forces. More analytical hypotheses by Robert M. Haig, Edward Chamberlin, and others have been suggestive about the role of demand and costs in influencing the competition for scarce locations. But the hypotheses are very general and have never been subjected to empirical tests. What we need and do not have are, first, a far more detailed understanding of how the functions of different types of firms and households dictate accessibility requirements; and, second, an understanding of the factors that determine the accessibility characteristics of vacant sites and existing structures.[7]

By examining locational processes through different types of firms and households, one may possibly observe the effects of both market and nonmarket forces at the point where decisions are made. Emphasis on the accessibility requirements draws attention to the spatial relationships; and it also provides a common denominator for the reinterpretation of all kinds of location studies: residential and nonresidential; economic, demographic, geographic, sociological, historical, political, and still other approaches. Factors such as convenience, prestige, transportation, speed, and the like would have to be translated into spatial and price relationships. Concepts of minimum and maximum accessibility may be developed for theoretical models. Practical problems, such as decentralization trends of retail, industrial, and residential location might be examined in these terms.

Though the idea of accessibility and even the term are not new, and in fact can be found in several different location studies such as those by Robert M. Haig, Donald J. Bogue, Amos H. Hawley, Richard U. Ratcliff, Chester Rapkin, and Harold M. Mayer, it has never been used as a tool for the systematic evaluation of the operational requirements of varying activities. This is what is being proposed using the convenient pegs of the market mechanism. We can examine under familiar categories the kind of accessibility required by different types of firms and households, the accessibility characteristics of different sites and improvements, the role and efficiency of the price mechanism for resolving accessibility problems, and the interaction of other phenomena, such as geographical factors, government policies, institutional channels, and technological changes, on accessibility characteristics and requirements. Research geared to this framework would have the further advantage of being additive and of contributing to a more basic understanding of these spatial relationships.

Standards of Living and the Trend Toward Public Entrepreneurship. Most discussions of British planning emphasize that until World War II planning was restricted to rules that curbed serious abuses and channeled private development. Bylaws imposed minimum standards on houses and streets. The Town Planning Acts of 1909, 1919, 1925, 1932, and 1935 successively extended the planning powers of local authorities almost up to the point of direct government action on a large scale. Fear of being forced to pay compensation, or of the loss of profitable activities, or of the probable outlays entailed in more positive measures inhibited bolder controls or policies. However, though this is the traditional view of British planning, it is not altogether accurate. Actually, the local authorities and central government can boast of considerable experience and examples in "constructive" activity during this period. Planners sometimes overlook this fact because they retrace planning history from the viewpoint of town-planning legislation narrowly construed.

Housing is one of the most important land uses of a community; and subsidies under Conservative and Labour governments have permitted local authorities to build housing since the end of World War I.[8] Manchester's development of Wythenshawe is possibly the most dramatic example. Less well known are the many experiments in building local and central government trading estates: for instance Speke by Liverpool, or Team Valley, Treforrest, and still others by the central government. Local authorities also purchased outlying land for greenbelts and for organizing the expansion of their cities. Liverpool is a particularly good example. More than 30 per cent of the land within its boundaries and almost 8000 acres outside the boundaries belong to the corporation.[9]

Looked at from this perspective, the new towns represent a more extreme point in the steady shift from a negative to a positive policy. With public leadership and social as well as economic objectives, the emphasis in town development has veered toward a more highly integrated approach, a clearer recognition of the interrelationships of housing, shops, industry, recreation, and the rest. Moreover, the pendulum has not yet

173

swung all the way. Awareness of the relationships between the new and the existing towns, and of the interdependence of new and expanded towns with nonurban land uses and with regional and national requirements is still inadequate. But whether the present efforts are satisfactory or go far enough may be of less importance than the direction of the change. The fact is that additional legal, administrative, and financial tools are being invented and improved to enable the government to guide urban growth, to build new towns, and to reconstruct old ones.

This trend is also influencing the form of economic progress. During the last century or two, the Western World has witnessed an impressive rise in real income. This advance has occurred in two ways. Possibly the more important in the past has been an increase in money income sufficiently significant in relation to prices to result in an increase of goods and services available to families in Western countries. Increasingly, however, collective purchases of goods and services are being substituted for family purchasing decisions. Education, parks, transportation facilities, and local authority housing illustrate ways in which government decisions have replaced private decisions in certain fields of consumption. These services, provided in whole or in part by the community, are financed by taxation. If the taxation is progressive, income redistribution in kind is also occurring.

Opinions differ on whether it may be wiser to let families make their own decisions on how to spend their money. This question is not an easy one to solve. It affects many basic policies and value judgments. But the community through its government has to make the decision for those goods and services that the community rather than the household or firm must purchase; and directly or indirectly, the government is tending to influence action or assume responsibility in cases where the decisions of private households and firms would otherwise entail excessive costs or problems for the public.

By the decision to build new towns or to expand existing towns, the central government has signified that the public has a large stake in community development. More decisive action is considered necessary to protect that stake. The national government will provide financial assistance; and the central or local government will serve as the principal fabricator of the urban physical environment. Private enterprise still operates in these towns, and with considerable scope, but largely as a contractor. The decisions on when, what, and how growth will take place will be made by the public. The public corporation as urban entrepreneur and innovator will take more of the risks, and if the program succeeds, may

garner more of the gains. If successful, these measures should either reduce the total of public and private costs of development or at least improve the community's environment and services. Faith in these prospects underlies much of the increasing government intervention today
and the shift in responsibility of many of the decisions on community development to a new group of experts. Whether this approach will be
successful is one of the great issues of this century.

The Contemporary Preference for Suburban Environments. Some
persons are content to rest the case for new towns on the way of life they
make available. Probably there are many people in Britain and elsewhere
who want to walk to work and to live in houses in a small community in
a country atmosphere, yet near a metropolis. Such towns might be desired even if it could be shown that they were not the most efficient use
of scarce capital resources. If there is a willingness to pay the price either
directly or in terms of the alternatives that this way of life precludes,
there is no reason why these desires should not be satisfied.

Some day, moreover, new towns may merit an accolade as suburbia
improved, or at any rate transformed. J. M. Richards has defended suburbs with great spirit and sophistication against sneers from "people of
taste." "Because [the theorists] make the mistake of assuming that what
is significant must bear the hall-mark of educated taste, they fail to observe that, not far beneath this chaotic surface, a common idiom of a kind
does lie hidden . . . the suburban style." [10]

Looked at as a social phenomenon, suburbia, according to Mr. Richards, is a remarkable adaptation of the contemporary mood to escape to a
more sympathetic world where personal creativity is possible. It finds expression in the emphasis on green verges and gardens, on curving streets
with romantic concealment and surprise, on the contrived picturesque
details and the scenic and sentimental rather than architectural effects.

> From Becontree to Wythenshawe, from Port Sunlight to Angmering-
> on-Sea, the startling consistency of suburban character — despite its no-
> torious vagaries in detail — indicates its origin in the living present. It
> could be the product of no other living age than ours. [11]

But suburbia also has its defects. It has been identified with snobbery
and self-deception, with poor location and unlimited expansion, with inadequate services and tedious, lengthy travel. [12] These and other failings
may be corrected directly and indirectly by the new towns. The quest for
balance, for self-contained communities, for provision nearby of jobs and

175

services, for recreation and social facilities for all kinds of persons may constitute the future extension and refinement of this vernacular.

Possibly, too, the nineteenth-century division between the men of taste and the men of power may also be narrowed in the new towns. In these huge enterprises one may expect the men of taste to acquire a more decisive and acceptable influence on the appearance of things. This at any rate is the promise, though some are skeptical of the consequences, judging from past versions of "improved" suburbs, model garden cities, and the present look of the new towns.[13]

Of course, there are many persons who will need or prefer different ways of living. The new and expanded towns can be one of the means for increasing the range of choice of living patterns, both in the central areas and elsewhere. By their existence they alter the form of the metropolis. By providing satisfactory alternatives for those who are displaced, they can facilitate the reconstruction of central areas. By experimentation they can also contribute to innovations adopted by others. Indirectly, therefore, they can make substantial contributions to greater variety in metropolitan form, density, and appearance.

New Towns and Urban Vulnerability. There are an increasing number of persons who have become interested in or supporters of new towns because of their potential significance for defense. As everyone knows, the prospects of nuclear warfare have made larger urban concentrations attractive targets. Even a highly efficient system of air defense, radar screens, and other devices is not expected to prevent terrific havoc resulting from a break-through of enemy planes. Understandably enough, many persons have considered decentralization to new towns as a possible means of minimizing vulnerability and loss of life.

What decentralization would accomplish has been vastly exaggerated in some quarters. With hydrogen and possibly cobalt bombs a reality, the rate of increased explosive power has already exceeded the feasible pace of urban decentralization. Though some satellite fringes of the metropolis might be spared obliteration, the devastation and impaired vital services would make life nightmarish for survivors. Moreover, considering the tremendous concentration of plants and equipment in existing cities, large-scale decentralization of these plants would be impossible. To the extent that present locations are efficient, such decentralization might even weaken the economy. If the time period within which such a shift is contemplated were short, few significant changes could be accomplished, and tremendous resistance could be expected from existing social, economic, and political forces. Meanwhile, overemphasis on the bombs might easily result in neglect of new and equally threatening forms of warfare.

These considerations suggest some of the limitations surrounding the easy, sweeping generalizations in favor of wholesale decentralization. But it is just as important not to be panicked

> by the awesome physical destruction to make occult predictions about the end of civilization. — Such prophecies are not only unscientific but actually harmful because they lead to apathy and ignorance in the area of civil defense. — Everyone is aware that atomic bombs exist and could be delivered against our cities, but most people fail to realize the consequences of such an event and practically nothing is being done to mitigate them.[14]

The fact is that neither complete decentralization nor complete security is attainable. But less congestion and less concentrated spatial distribution of activities may offer some protection against chemical and biological attacks as well as bombs, and possibly at a much smaller and more feasible cost than is realized.[15] The aim must be to achieve "relative security — to find a proper balance between the needs for programs of shelter, fire protection and dispersion and the fiscal abilities of the country." [16] Considerable movement out of central areas now occurs anyhow in response to the normal requirements of firms, families, and government agencies. This movement can be a starting point for action. Any program that provides more sensible channels for such relocation deserves careful scrutiny.

Most of the minimum steps urged by responsible persons are already in line with accepted planning policies, especially in Britain. Thus it has been suggested that a minimum program should include the following:

1. Definition of the dangerously congested areas from which dispersion is to be encouraged . . .
2. Adoption and application of standards the application of which will reduce density of industrial, commercial and residential development within these congested areas.
3. Coordination of . . . programs dealing with urban problems towards this goal . . .
4. Prevention of new target concentrations . . .
5. Planning this entire operation on a comprehensive basis.[17]

For all of these measures the availability of machinery to build new towns or to expand existing country towns would prove to be a valuable resource. What is perhaps astonishing in Britain, in contrast to the United

States where similar planning policies and machinery do not exist, is the almost total neglect by the present policy makers of the defense aspects of this machinery, this despite the original emphasis of the Barlow Commission in 1940 on the strategic significance of the program. Because this attitude prevails, the present piddling efforts are tolerated. Were this attitude toward defense ever to change significantly, so too would the attitudes toward the scale, coordination, and backing of these decentralization programs.

New Towns and Developing Areas. Growth in underdeveloped areas is another, less somber source of interest in a new towns policy. For wherever rapid economic development occurs, the same massive urbanization problems are generated that beset the Western world in the nineteenth century. Certainly anything that can be done to reduce the waste, ugliness, and misery bound to accompany this transformation deserves serious attention. Some version of a new towns policy offers such a possibility. It suggests at least a partial remedy: to conduct some of the growth away from one or a few large cities and to encourage the expansion of existing small cities and in some cases the building of new towns.

True, with the meager evidence now available it is not easy to say how applicable these possibilities may be in different types of countries, or whether more or less resources would be required for implementation. Also, considering offhand the modest resources available under any circumstances, one is almost driven to dismiss the significance of any of the potential economic and social effects. "In a very, very poor area," Professor Millikan has observed, "you simply cannot afford to devote very much to the manufacture of assets to be used to provide future consumption because it is all you can do to keep alive." [18] Professor Millikan drives home his point by making rough, albeit somewhat generous, estimates for the case of India. His estimates show that the total amount available for investment in housing alone would probably be less than $250 million per year, or about 250,000 houses, if one figures on a minimum standard house costing approximately $1000. But this "outside" total of new housing must serve a population of approximately 350 million and an annual increase in population of about 4 million persons. Even if allowance is made for mobilizing, through self-help and other devices, a large share of the existing idle resources in India (or countries with similar problems), it is still unlikely that the dimensions of the problem would be significantly changed.

Nor are these the only discouraging obstacles. The current is actually moving in the direction of concentration in big centers in many of these developing countries. One would have to be optimistic, to say the least, to believe that the probable efforts to avoid congestion of these larger towns would offset the attractive force of more income, or the prospects, real or apparent, which such towns offer of more social and economic opportunities. One must also couple this 'pull' with the extraordinary capacity and relentless readiness in these countries to carve up existing housing resources still more and more intensively, and with the pathetic adaptability of human beings to the most makeshift and terrible shelters. Moreover, a policy geared to redirect this flow would in most cases not be able to count on adequate financial and administrative powers, or on an efficient, vigorous civil service, or on more than lethargic public understanding and support. It is probable that the sheer lack of skilled experts may leave no alternative but a highly centralized administration with its inflexibility and its insensitivity to local requirements.

Formidable, indeed, are the difficulties! Nonetheless, there is much that can be done, and there may still be solid satisfaction in ensuring far better results and far more sensible long-run physical patterns than otherwise would have been the case. Thus, in any rationally planned program, it is likely that available resources will be allocated to the most productive activities. Which activities so qualify may be difficult to determine in specific cases; but on the whole, ports, power installations, certain light and heavy industries, and similar avenues of investment would tend to receive high priorities compared to consumer durables such as housing or 'luxuries' such as new towns. However, this would not hold true for situations where the housing or the new towns constituted indispensable 'overhead' for the continuance of high-priority activities. In these circumstances, housing and new towns would be treated as complementary productive activities, and they would be entitled to somewhat similar priority ratings. In other words, within the "ground rules" which might be expected generally to govern any effective program of economic development, there would still be a strategic role for the new towns and for the planned expansion of existing towns. In fact, even within such a restricted framework, and not counting such developments as may be stimulated through self-help, the scale of the problem may be much greater than the availability of skilled personnel. For it is increasingly evident that a redistribution, as well as an increase, of population can scarcely be avoided in most of these areas. Sooner or later the basic questions must be faced: in what locations, on what scale, and using what administrative tools, standards, and physical patterns will these resources for new development prove most efficient and most satisfying? In addition, there will be the responsibility of avoiding the inefficiency resulting from the location of high-priority activities where other physical and human resources may be wasted in whole or part. The compelling need for optimum use of these resources will provide powerful incentives for coherent regional programing and for a carefully considered policy of urban growth.

Perhaps the chief advantage of a new towns policy is that it would create a mechanism to grapple with the problems of growth, decentralization, and new development; to raise some of the relevant questions concerning scale, location, and procedure; to anticipate and correct disorders when they are perceived, if possible before they become too serious; and to steer development, whenever feasible, to the most advantageous locations with minimum stress placed on existing resources. Before long such a policy may be expected to orient thinking toward significant issues such as the skilled technical and managerial personnel required, the importance of adequate administrative machinery for resolving conflicting government policies, the most effective means of coordinating development programs between and within different regions, and the feasibility of applied research to improve existing practices.

Beyond the technical measures of efficiency, there is the possibility that some urban developments may be designed to popularize what is contemplated and to illustrate other ways of doing things. Albert Mayer, in helping to guide village development in India, recognized that for many reasons few of the things undertaken could be carried out either as well as they might be or as he wished. But he always tried to have a few projects point up something different and something better, that could serve as an example, as a contrast, as a form of practical experimentation without risking large resources. Rising income, rising standards of demand, more rapid growth, and large-scale urbanization in these undeveloped areas are bound to place terrific pressures on existing resources and to produce unavoidable slums, congestion, exploitation, and misery. Nonetheless, there can be some varied and successful solutions, some evidence of the right direction, some dramatic and popularized symbols of improvement and better prospects ahead. The reward of success may be a disproportionately favorable impact on the morale, the incentives, and the energies of the people.

New Towns and the Campaign of History

When the new towns policy was introduced in Britain, it was welcomed with exceptional good will. Even those who had misgivings were moved by the goal and the challenge. This good will was coupled with an extraordinary mixture of admiration and envy, which the program understandably excited among planners in other countries. The reasons are still vivid in our minds.

The world saw Britain emerging from a second terrible war. Her sources of income were sharply cut. Investments abroad were liquidated. Submarine warfare had inflicted grievous losses on her shipping. Her richest colonial possession secured its freedom. Competition for foreign trade was becoming more difficult, especially against countries like the United States, which during the war had captured abandoned British markets in places like South America, or against old competitors like Japan and Germany emerging from the war with new plants and equipment. To set the sights so high, to provide for various social services, to build new towns — projects that other countries with more resources still shrink from undertaking — required, after all, great courage. The fact that the programs revealed flaws and that the burdens were perhaps excessive may be of minor significance historically compared to their ultimate impact on the enthusiasm and imagination of the British people and on the vision of town planners all over the globe.

Whatever the failings and shortcomings, consider for a moment some of the extenuating circumstances; and also some of the lessons learned and progress already made. London is still overflowing; but this is not the fault of the new towns, even if one were to assume that the process could be arrested. Conflicts still mar the various government policies; but it is easier to talk of an ideal consistency than to hew such a program out of the rough and tumble of pressure groups, private interests, and democratic politics. Regional considerations may have been neglected; but as the program unfolds this is becoming clearer and corrective measures can still be taken. Deciding between agricultural, commercial, and residential claims on the land is difficult; at present the criteria for policy making are vague or nonexistent; but the problem is being faced more directly, whereas in the past such decisions were made in the market with many social costs ignored. Planners may have acquired responsibilities beyond their present training and capacities; but this is in the process of being remedied. Meanwhile social scientists have been prompted to take note of the plans and the need for participation in their preparation and execution.[19] Disproportionate emphasis may have been placed on new towns. But some of the limitations have already been perceived; and more attention is being given to expanding small towns and still other possibilities.[20] Ministerial supervision may have been excessive; but the insistent protests as well as the greater experience of the corporations should lead to more flexibility. Local authorities in the past were barred from direct building activity; but now the Town Development Act is encouraging the harnessing of their resources. New towns may not be as heterogeneous as originally envisioned; but efforts are being made to correct imbalance and to prevent excessive distortions. The over-all physical plan and design of new towns may leave much to be desired; but in many ways they constitute a vast improvement on past patterns; and the possibility of further improvement still exists. Research is limited, almost negligible; but so too are resources of money and personnel. Moreover, the studies, though few in number, are increasing and may continue to do so.

In other words, because the ministry must wrestle with the problems, the policy tends to be self-correcting. Once the machinery is established, the assumptions and purposes may be altered as experience suggests. Mistakes, of course, have been made and still more can be expected; but is no price to be paid for pioneering social experiments? Often we must act first and decide afterwards whether we have acted wisely. We do not always have the time or evidence to tell in advance. To some extent that has been true of the British new towns policy. Its advisability could have been argued for another generation or two. The fact that Britain has embarked on this program has put planners all over the world in her debt. Britain has taken great risks in the hope of equally great dividends. Today when more and more of our entrepreneurial decisions are being made by government officials, we must expect, and respect, the boldness and determination that we once admired in the great "captains of industry" of the past. "Nothing ventured, nothing gained" is a truism that we should remember in the future in government operations. The bureaucrat is notoriously identified with timidity and reluctance to act. That the government has decided to move decisively may be a stirring example for other ventures in other parts of the world. The fact that fifteen new towns will be built despite the many trying obstacles and mistakes is no mean accomplishment.

Behind the deed, however, is the word; and here one is reminded of one of the greatest and most influential of Britain's economists: John M. Keynes. Unlike Howard, Keynes had a sophisticated, brilliant mind, backed up by a solid education, the prestige of a university position, and considerable experience in government and business affairs. Yet the Keynesian thesis, after almost two decades of controversy, has proved to be another example of the false but brilliantly suggestive hypothesis. It has swept the world and changed the thinking of economists. A prominent economist has said:

> this theory did, and does, have something which supplements what our thinking would otherwise have been. It does not make us Keynesians, it makes us better economists.[21]

And Schumpeter, another great economist, observed in turn:

> Whether we agree or not, this expresses the essential point about Keynes' achievement extremely well. In particular, it explains why hostile criticism, even if successful in its attack upon individual assumptions or propositions, is yet powerless to inflict fatal injury upon the structure as a whole. As with Marx, it is possible to admire Keynes, even though one may consider his social vision to be wrong and every one of his propositions to be misleading.[22]

Substitute Howard for Keynes and the observations are equally apropos!

APPENDICES

The Achilles Heel of British Town Planning

When the difficulties which have harassed the new towns are considered, one wonders how much the town planners themselves are implicated. Have they perhaps been too successful? Do they now constitute a potential Achilles heel of contemporary town planning? Certainly their position is vulnerable. They are watched by foe and friend alike. Advantage will be taken of their mistakes. If care is not exercised their adherents, still full of expectancy, may drift away. The fact is that the town planners' intellectual lines have been overextended: their base needs strengthening; their supplies are limited; they are operating in unknown terrain; and their key personnel are not well enough equipped for many of the problems that lie ahead.

Two of the most glaring weaknesses are in planning education and planning research. At present the stock of intellectual capital of all town planners is meager. What exists is subject to rapid depreciation. Replenishment is long overdue. At the same time, British town planners have acquired almost all the tasks and legislative tools they sought. Their increased powers have brought them to grips with new, complex problems. But these problems and decisions go far beyond the technical. They are social, economic, and political; and the background of the town planners is extremely limited in these directions. They possess little knowledge of the social sciences. They have only modest understanding of or capacity to do research.

These observations imply no invidious comparisons. Similar problems confront town planners in America and elsewhere. But there is one vital difference. More faith has been placed in and more duties given to the planner in Britain; and so the responsibilities are far more grave.

Faultfinding would be presumptuous. The ability, imagination, and great traditions of British planners are admired throughout the world. But each generation of planners must shoulder new burdens and advance the work of its predecessors. It seems doubtful whether the British planner today can adequately discharge his new responsibilities without correcting the deficiencies of his own background.

The Planner's Background

In the past, British planners have been recruited primarily from three professions: engineering, architecture, and surveying (real estate). The reason, as the *Report of the Committee on the Qualifications of Planners* (Schuster Report) states, is that the profession was founded when the conception of planning was mainly local and restrictive, and when the main skills required were those of the architect, engineer, and surveyor.[1] The report also records the findings of a recent survey of 153 planning authorities of all types. It was pointed out that "senior planning responsibility was held in 81 cases by engineers, in 34 by architects, in 32 by surveyors, and in 6 by members of the Town Planning Institute who have qualified through the examinations of the Institute without having the basic professional qualifications."[2]

The composition of the Ministry of Town and Country Planning is not markedly different. Most of the planning officers are qualified planners who were originally educated as architects, engineers, and surveyors. Most of the research staff were admittedly not conducting research. They gathered the operating physical, economic, and social data. This group comprised primarily planners, geographers, and geologists. There are very few, if any, economists or sociologists now on the staff.[3]

The London County Council has the largest local planning organization in England. More than 260 persons were employed in June 1952. Twenty-four persons were on the "research" staff. Almost all these persons gathered facts for informational purposes or current administrative assignments. The chief of research was trained as a surveyor. The research staff comprised surveyors, geographers, architects, one or two statisticians, and "perhaps" a sociologist. There were no economists on the staff.[4]

Manchester prepared its development plan with a staff of approximately forty-six persons. The top positions were held by engineers. No social scientists were employed. According to the chief engineer, his staff learned the necessary social science on the job. Birmingham, Glasgow, and other large cities were not significantly different. Occasionally exceptions might be encountered, as in the case of the Lancashire County Planning Office. There the chief of research had training in economics.[5] But even in Lancashire the chief planning officer felt then that the top positions, except in unusual circumstances, belonged to the architects and engineers.[6]

Until very recently planning curricula in the universities provided almost no training in the social sciences. Consider, for example, the Department of Civic Design of the University of Liverpool, the oldest in this field. Until 1950 the chief subjects were outlines of town and country planning, law of housing and town and country planning, civic engineering, valuation and hygiene, landscape design, civic architecture, and civic design. The program was inspired and developed by two distinguished planners in Great Britain: first by Stanley D. Adshead, and then even more by Patrick Abercrombie. It influenced other university programs, particularly those of London, Leeds, Edinburgh, and Manchester. Similar requirements held for subjects in the qualifying examination for membership in the Town Planning Institute. Until 1950, the chief subjects in which the institute tested applicants or required equivalents in the universities were the history of town planning, town-planning practice, town planning in its relation to architecture and amenities, town planning in its relation to surveying, and the law relating to town and country planning.

In short, the emphasis was on physical planning or practical professional routines. The planner was taught to think physically, visually, technically. He still does. He was only crudely, if at all, familiar with the nature and use of research and scientific method. He knew little of the thinking or of the applicability of the social sciences, particularly economics and sociology. These observations may not apply to the rare individuals who personally educated themselves to overcome these deficiencies. But there is no question that the few statistics presented above accurately depict the present formal training and qualifications of most British planners.

Why this was so is easy to explain. The town planner's duties were formerly quite circumscribed. At best, they involved the layout of streets, roads, utilities, squares, and parks. Technical knowledge and three-dimensional expression were required. In the past, moreover, architects and engineers were not so highly specialized: they were broad-gauge men familiar with design, engineering, and developments in other fields.

Social sciences didn't exist as separate disciplines. Ignorance of the scattered fragments could not really constitute a dangerous gap in knowledge. When the first school of civic design was established, sociology was hardly known. Economics was considered a "dismal" and highly abstract science which still had to develop meaningful empirical tests and analyses of significant propositions. It never occurred to most economists, sociologists, or students of the social sciences that the problems of city planning were and would increasingly become problems of applied social science.[7] Most development decisions were made by private entrepreneurs. Government activity was relatively minor. The market, through the price mechanism, guided activities, instead of the planners. To most planners of the period, with rare exceptions, research in social science was considered scarcely relevant or necessary.[8]

This technical approach was perpetuated by the town-planning schools, guided largely by architects and engineers, and by the Town Planning Institute, the professional organization that set the seal on technical qualifications. It was also aided and abetted by the traditional distinction in the British civil service between policy makers and administrators, and the technical staff. In the ministry, policy was presumably set by the minister and his immediate administrative subordinates. The town planners gave technical advice. In the local authorities, policy was set by the council committee on housing and planning. There, too, the chief architect or planner or engineer gave technical advice. Rarely was there any recognition that there were problems in social science and issues in town planning that required "technical" advice and research which the policy makers needed and did not obtain. When such recognition occurred, it was often difficult to interest the social scientists as well as the policy makers.

Consequences of the Planner's Background

Few universities with schools of architecture in the United States and Great Britain have adequate research facilities or research training. Many staff members are employed part time, with the remaining time generally spent in professional practice. While there is deep interest on the part of students and staff alike in new designs, new materials, new construction techniques, more efficient utility and heating systems, and the like, these researches are generally conducted by other departments or outside organizations. Direct university research by architects has been quite limited.

When the architect becomes interested in planning, some of this approach and these habits of thinking are carried over. Many town-planning faculty members are also part-time practitioners. When they teach, the work on the drafting board commands major attention. Most of the other aspects tend to be side issues. In general, the same holds true for engineers and surveyors in the field.[9] This emphasis in education, thinking, and teaching, coupled with very limited financial resources, largely explains why university planning departments have not engaged in much research.

Universities, however, ought to make a major contribution to the advancement of knowledge. Actually, few contributions are made in this field. Discussion and general thinking there are aplenty: look at any journal of town planning. Deepening and broadening of insights from professional practice also occur, and indeed are quite valuable. Teaching without such experience would soon go stale. There is also some penetrating historical research. But none of these activities are substitutes for careful and sustained inquiries into the problems, including the social and economic problems, confronting the profession.

Ministry officials and organization reflect these attitudes. Their planners don't press for research. The top policy-making officials are bluntly skeptical about the results.[10] With limited financial resources, there is little inclination to devote staff and money to discover either what they think they know or what they don't care to know. They want immediate returns. Universities could not be of much assistance. Their town-planning departments have neither the facilities nor the staff. Social science departments have scarcely any persons interested in these problems. For most social scientists, rewards lie in more traditional directions of inquiry. Consequently, little research of any significance has been sponsored or conducted by the ministry.[11]

As yet most local authorities do not see this need either. Their resources are limited. Their staff were only recently recruited and from the same sources. Their policy-making committees want to save money. They look with jaundiced eyes on any long-term research programs that could offer no firm commitments or specific returns.

Private or quasi-public research organizations do not exist in this field. There are some specific research programs for special purposes, as, for example, in the building research stations which are an important unit of the Department of Scientific and Industrial Research. These inquiries are largely geared to technical building problems, such as materials, structures, techniques of building, site operations, and requirements of users. But no significant aspects of planning have as yet been systematically investigated by any well-established research organization. Certainly the professional organizations that might have taken the lead in this direction never did so, and probably for the same reasons.

No vigorous endorsement or call for a systematic planning research program by the universities or the ministry has ever been pressed by the Town Planning Institute, though it does have a standing committee with instructions to coordinate or stimulate such research.

This approach to urban planning in the past probably discouraged many social science students, unwittingly perhaps, from entering the field of planning. Of course, town planning until recently was scarcely more than bylaw housing regulations. But it was commonly accepted as a technical field. To pass the institute examination, a specialized background was required; and in the universities the programs were not open to social science students.

Social scientists, on the other hand, were concentrating on the development of the concepts, methodology, and core problems of their disciplines. Urban, regional, and national land-planning problems were specialized peripheral issues, and they neglected them. Occasional stray researchers might get absorbed in questions like the location of industry, the urban neighborhood, and the history of cities. But there the matter ended. As a consequence, there was scarcely any recognition of common denominators. Interdisciplinary studies were unusual. Collaboration between departments rarely occurred. Each department and school went its own way.

New Trends

Signs of a change are evident and not unexpected. Even before the war, the School of Planning and Research for Regional Development, which was not associated with a university, attempted to provide a broader educational program than the traditional schools or the Town Planning Institute. Its courses were also open to students of varied backgrounds. It has since gone out of existence. Durham University too has pioneered. In 1945 it added to the traditional graduate program a five-year undergraduate degree in town and country planning. This was "the first recognized course which did not require the preliminary qualification of the architect, engineer, or surveyor. It attempts to teach those parts of each of the three basic qualifications which are related to planning but to mingle them with the subjects taught in the town planning diploma courses elsewhere." [12] The objective was to produce planners with an education geared to the larger problems of land use in town and country that now confront the profession. Starting in 1949, a similar undergraduate program was initiated at the University of Manchester.

The University of Liverpool also introduced significant innovations

192

under Professor Stephenson, formerly Chief Planning Officer of the Ministry of Town and Country Planning. Initiated in 1950, the new graduate program provides, in addition to studio work, a fairly comprehensive group of courses. Greater emphasis is placed on the social sciences, including land economics, social survey, statistics, geography, law, and sociology. The courses are open to university graduates from almost any department of any faculty of an approved university in any country. Similar changes are occurring in other universities.

The Town Planning Institute has also revised and expanded the scope of its examination. The new subjects are the historical development of planning; outlines of social and economic organization; town-planning practice; architectural design and amenities in relation to planning; civic engineering in relation to planning; surveying in relation to planning; law in relation to planning; elements of applied geology and economic geography.[13]

Some progress in planning analysis and research has also been made. Liverpool reactivated the *Town Planning Review*, which has published papers by economists, historians, geographers, sociologists, and others. Durham, too, has established a journal, entitled *Planning Outlook*, to encourage research over a wide field. More contributions from writers in different professions are also appearing in the *Journal of the Town Planning Institute*.

The Liverpool Department of Civic Design has also introduced a housing research program in collaboration with the economics and social science departments. At the University of London, a social research unit has been temporarily established under a Nuffield Foundation grant. Planning organization and problems and the potential contributions of social research are being studied.

There is even evidence of interest on the part of social scientists. More of them now participate at the sessions of the Town and Country Planning Summer School. There is also an increasing output of studies by social scientists on planning subjects. Professor M. P. Fogarty has been bold enough to observe in his survey of town planning that he is "conscious of having played down the most obvious and spectacular part of planning, its three-dimensional approach to the problems of architecture, engineering or landscaping." And he adds: "Perhaps at this point in planning history, that is not such a bad thing to have done. The architects have had their innings; and, watching the new order in planning as it comes to birth, it is obvious that more limelight is now needed elsewhere." [14]

Another key influence has been the report of the Schuster Committee on the qualifications of planners. This committee, appointed jointly by the Minister of Town and Country Planning and the Secretary of State for Scotland, received much oral and written testimony. Their report reviewed the history of planning, its nature, scope, and objectives, the place of design, the planning process, and the posts to be filled. These are some of its "radical" conclusions:

> The Town Planning Institute provides an obvious foundation on which to build, but the basis of membership must be substantially widened. . .
> The Council of the Institute should also be changed. The provision that nine out of the fifteen members of the Council must be architects, engineers, or surveyors should be rescinded. The Council should be empowered to co-opt at least one third of its members and in doing so should bring in persons representing the economic and social sciences.[15]

Many persons have disagreed with some of the specific findings. But few will question that the report is a major landmark in the thinking about town and country planning education in Great Britain.

Some Unsolved Problems

How can the social sciences best be incorporated into planning education? Besides his "technical" tools, the planner must be reasonably familiar with political, economic, and social organization and processes. He should have intimate appreciation of the political process, local and central governmental organization and administration; some grasp of statistics, economics, and industrial location and organization; and of that group of studies in human relations identified with cultural anthropology, sociology, and social psychology. He also requires training in logical analysis and techniques of social research; and he needs some of the insights and vision of philosophy and the humanities. Obviously the list can be broadened and extended.

To become an expert in any one of these fields would involve a lifetime devoted to formal education. The problems of choice have resulted in many sonorous and witty observations on both sides of the Atlantic. The former dean of the Harvard University School of Design has called attention to the 120 required and 75 desirable courses to equip the planner for his task.[16] *The Economist* of August 14, 1948 has asserted in a widely quoted article that

> The ideal town planner considered as an individual would need to be a superman. He should be a good economist — for only a profound and practical knowledge can serve as a basis for estimating loss and gain in

the siting of industry and agriculture. He should know a great deal about geology and the limits it imposes on engineering; about water supplies, subsidence, soils and gradients. He should have an artist's eye for landscape and layout and an architect's sense of the possible. He should have a profound sense of history combining respect for the past with an abiding recollection that the greatest numbers are still unborn, and above all he must be capable through experience and imagination of putting himself in the shoes of those who are to live and work in the community for whose physical framework he may be responsible.

What is the solution? The planner can't hope to master all of these fields. All agree he must work with other specialists. But there is still strong disagreement whether he should be educated first in architecture, engineering, surveying, or in almost any other field; or whether he should start earlier his undergraduate work in planning. The latter possibility, either as an undergraduate major in planning or simply as more under-graduate specialization in planning, at present is the minority point of view.[17] Yet perhaps it deserves more sympathetic consideration. Why?

If there is no undergraduate education in planning, it means that persons who wish to become town planners must study some other sub-ject first even though they have scant resources or negligible interest in doing so. Granted it may be useful to have some planners educated first as architects, engineers, or surveyors or in any of the social or physi-cal sciences; but if this is the sole or principal channel of professional education there are also some serious disadvantages. Earlier entry into the field is precluded, and the method is expensive and wasteful. Many of the persons educated in these other fields who then serve as planners will forget the bulk of their undergraduate specialization: the facts, the techniques, the concepts, possibly even the point of view. At best, most of them will be superficial architects, surveyors, engineers, or whatever they happen to have studied. After all, an undergraduate major provides only limited orientation and tools. Much of the refined technical and professional education occurs in the more advanced programs and in outside professional practice. If further graduate work and direct experi-ence in the original professional field do not occur, is not the educational result half-baked architects, engineers, and social scientists with a thin veneer of planning education, who gradually, as they acquire experience, become more expert as planners?

The same men may take their graduate education in town planning and work in planning agencies, but not as planners. They are *specialists in the field of planning*, not *planning specialists*. They are attorneys or geographers or architects or engineers in the field of planning, not planners with specialized training or experience. This distinction may seem unimportant. But actually it can help us to understand the role of planning education for these persons and their possible contributions to planning. A program of education to create town planners should be quite different from a program for providing specialization in planning for those whose tools, perspectives, and contributions to planning will come from another profession.

But is town planning a separate discipline? Does it have special techniques, concepts, and perspectives? Or can one only practice and make a contribution as a specialist planner? What, indeed, could such a nonspecialist planner do? Persons educated in an undergraduate program as town planners would specialize in making and helping to put into effect comprehensive land-use plans for neighborhoods, towns, and regions. The core function would be to organize transportation, utilities, housing, playgrounds, schools, shops, industrial areas, and other land uses into an efficient physical whole. To do so involves intimate understanding of the tools, concepts, and potential contributions of other disciplines. It also presupposes collaboration with many specialists, such as geographers, economists, sociologists, political scientists, architects, engineers, and surveyors.[18] But the town planner also has distinctive tools and approaches that can exercise crucial influence on the process and the final product of town planning.

Properly taught, this discipline should deepen insight and develop humility concerning the limits and potential contributions of the town-planning profession and the equally vital contributions of others; and it should above all encourage the fundamental team attitude that would help to produce economically efficient, socially desirable, and visually satisfying streets, neighborhoods, and towns. A person might well be able to master this profession without going through the whole of an architectural, engineering, or surveying course.

Is a planning course too narrow? Does it represent too specialized a perspective? Ought it to be preceded by a more general education, as is the case with law and medicine? Certainly not at present; nor in the future if present trends continue. On the contrary, education in town planning will stimulate interdisciplinary perspectives and collaboration. Aside from such specialized tool courses as land-use planning, civic design,[19] drawing, and transportation, the town planner, like the physicist and biologist, will also take courses in related fields, particularly the social sciences and the humanities. For example, he may find it helpful to have a working knowledge of geography, land economics, economic history,

196

sociology, political science, philosophy, logic, and scientific method. Undergraduate education in planning will be at least as broad as the education for a historian, sociologist, economist, physicist, administrator, or an architect.

Important advantages might follow from undergraduate specialization in planning. Students with an undergraduate major in other fields serve effectively in business and government. Certainly this is true for physicists, biologists, and economists, to take specific examples. The abler students often rise to high positions by dint of their ability. And those who receive further graduate education should be able to handle more complicated or more specialized assignments. They are also better equipped to handle the ordinary jobs that are available. It is from this group that the men who do research, contribute to professional journals, and work in the universities generally come. We don't ask a physicist to study first the classics or to take a liberal arts degree. Take away his undergraduate specialization, and his training and professional development would be impoverished.

The same advantages should hold for town planning; and perhaps even more so because there is less danger of overspecialization. Men with a rigorous undergraduate education in planning ought to be able to handle the junior assignments in town-planning agencies. Those of equal ability with both undergraduate and graduate education in planning should be able to perform more competently, or to handle more difficult or specialized assignments. The top positions will probably go to men of this or any of the related professions who have proven their ability and leadership qualities on the job.

Recognition of the emergence and independent stature of town planning may help us to understand better why architecture, engineering, surveying, and much later the social sciences, have been the important background professions in planning, and why they will continue to play a key role in the future. Each of these fields provides training and insights in appreciating either the functions or the physical and visual organization of land uses. Architects, engineers, surveyors, and social scientists who later worked in planning or became planners possessed important assets. They already had acquired facts, tools, and ideas that were useful in planning. To recognize that the planning function has acquired sufficient stature to allow a direct education in planning does not imply that each of these professions will not continue to contribute its share of recruits to the field. This contribution will come in any of the three traditional ways. The professions are still sufficiently interrelated

197

so that some persons may be able to practice in both, if they are fortunate enough to secure the right education, experience, and opportunities. Others will find it desirable to work as *specialists in the field of planning*, and still others may actually decide to do their major work as planners.

But is the graduate program to serve all of these educational functions equally? Is it to provide the same training for planners, planning specialists, and specialists in the field of planning? Will it continue to transform relatively inexperienced architects, engineers, surveyors, and social scientists into hyphenated planners? If so, graduate education in planning will have to assume responsibilities for undergraduate subjects or introductory approaches to planning, starting on the base of whatever nondescript degree a student happens to acquire.

Experimentation in other directions is also evident. For the advanced degree needs to be and is being converted into a more effective instrument for graduate education and research. At present the faculty in planning schools are under constant pressure to expand the number and detail of their courses; and the student has very limited time to deal adequately with the courses presently required. This problem of squeezing the subject matter into the program of graduate education can be eased by providing courses and methodology earlier in the undergraduate's career, or by extending the time required for a graduate degree, or by developing a still higher or research degree.

In Britain, a higher graduate degree is less common than in the United States and certainly not necessary if some undergraduate planning specialization occurs prior to the professional courses; or if the time required for a graduate degree is extended. The graduate program could then better provide more intensive education and research. Pioneer experimentation with the first of these possibilities is already under way at Liverpool, initiated originally under the collaborative guidance of Professors Stephenson and Gardner-Medwin. Planning courses and ideas are now being introduced earlier in the undergraduate architectural curriculum. Graduate education in civic design will be correspondingly more advanced and intensive.

Such experimentation is fruitful and promising. If this innovation fares well, it would not be surprising if additional departments explored similar possibilities. For if graduate planning education is open to others besides architects, perhaps the advantages of this innovation may also apply to these additional fields as well. Moreover, if the master's degree program became more intensive, nonarchitectural students might require preliminary courses to do the advanced work. Were such programs to develop, the master's degree might eventually be limited as a rule to candidates who have had or were willing to acquire some prerequisite undergraduate planning subjects. If so, the master's program would be able to develop more rapidly, and not be forced to spend valuable time in providing introductory materials.

Such changes offer many advantages; but they also involve some disadvantages that may be minimized, perhaps, if not avoided. One of the major obstacles confronting undergraduate planning schools at present is the lack of a market. Town planning is not one of the more well-known and traditional professions. It still lacks adequate prestige and financial rewards. Its career possibilities are generally not recognized until the student has completed or nearly completed his studies in some other field. Planning schools at the graduate level therefore have the opportunity to secure more and better students; and some of these students may well come from disciplines with high prestige, which have forged powerful tools and fruitful concepts and points of view. Attracting these students, with their varied skills and habits of thought, is one effective way of stimulating and enriching the field of planning.

These arguments have force; and there is therefore some point in encouraging entry into planning at the graduate and undergraduate level. It will also take time in any case before the stiffening of the graduate entry requirements will prove seriously discouraging to many candidates. But we must not forget that at present, top-notch students are lost to the field because earlier entry is not possible. Also, one of the surest means of enticing high-caliber students is to raise the intellectual and financial standards of the field. As this is achieved, more mature persons would be attracted from outside activities to the university to explore problems of special interest. These persons could also use this period to ponder many of the fundamental issues of theory and policy. More mixing of undergraduate and graduate students in planning would also occur, thereby contributing further to a healthy ferment. That at any rate was the experience when the older men returned to their studies after their war service. Finally, more research would be encouraged in a field which needs it.

Cumulative benefits would flow from these research activities. Students would receive more rigorous training; graduate students would participate as research assistants, and would conduct some of the research in fulfillment of dissertation requirements. Additional staff would be available for teaching or occasional lectures and consultation. Improvements might be expected in planning techniques, concepts, and knowledge. Not least would be the excitement and contagious enthusiasm that every university should beget in being close to the research frontiers. The end product ought to be better and accelerated solutions of those problems that in the past have been subject to discussion rather than to analysis and empirical tests.

Financing may be managed through endowment funds, through contract grants with private, quasi-public, and public agencies, and through government grants. Such sponsorship, particularly by the government, has been said to be long overdue. Tremendous sums, relatively, have been provided for research in the physical and biological sciences. Professor Fogarty has pointed out that the Ministry of Town and Country Planning has at least a research staff, but that

> the universities are, if anything, worse off. The number of senior members or university staff who take part in anything classifiable as town planning research can almost be counted on the fingers of one hand. That is partly due to neglect of the subject; but it is also, and even more, due to the general lack of staff and funds for research in the social sciences. The official departmental committee on the Provision for Social and Economic Research pointed out that in 1938–1939 universities other than Oxford and Cambridge spent £1,873,000 on teaching and research in science and medicine (not, it is only fair to say, that even this sum was remotely within reach of adequacy) as compared with a miserly £116,000 for economics, economic history, anthropology, industrial relations, social science, social psychology, demography, economic statistics, commerce, sociology and political science. Even with a small addition for architecture, the butter was clearly spread thin. Of this miserly sum, a bare £7,600 (again plus an addition for architecture) was spent for purposes other than salaries of teaching staff, that is, there was almost negligible provision for secretarial assistance, computing or field work, all of them obviously of vital importance in the type of sociological or demographic research needed in connection with town planning. The committee asked for a further £250–300,000 a year, in terms of post-war prices, and the Government has granted this. The butter is still to be rationed, but may at least become a little easier to observe with the naked eye.[20]

Considering the tremendous government stake in the new town-planning programs, it would seem wise to invest in research and education to help secure better talent and more fundamental knowledge.[21] Would any other measures provide more effective insurance of the larger investment; or a surer way of obtaining efficient and attractive towns?

Summary Observations

Education and research are still weak points in contemporary British planning. The new planning responsibilities require, first, advanced planning education, and particularly strengthening in the social sciences; and, second, research and research mindedness to develop the concepts, methods, and knowledge of the profession.

Present experimentation in planning education already foreshadows some basic changes. Town planning has emerged as an independent discipline, despite close ties to architecture, engineering, surveying, and the social sciences. Planning education is also becoming more intensive as well as broader. Some evidence of these changes are the new undergraduate degrees in planning and the undergraduate planning courses introduced to strengthen and advance the graduate education.

Still to be solved is how graduate education in planning will serve the varying requirements of planning education, namely education for planners, for planning specialists, and for specialists in planning. Possibly the more advanced courses in planning may eventually be limited to those who receive some prerequisite education in planning.

These changes appear to be only the initial adaptations to the heavy responsibilities placed on the British planner. Much will depend on the outcome of these efforts. For there is a basic and often unavowed assumption of contemporary planning. It is that key errors, distortions, and imperfections of the market mechanism can and will be corrected by the planners. But even those who have staked their professional careers on this article of faith sometimes become uneasy when the deficiencies of the planners and their tools are examined. For the new machinery, like the market system it is intended to supplant, is not without its limitations. One is reminded of Freud's sage observation that the problems of adolescence may be solved by marriage, but this does not solve the problems of marriage. If these limitations are not soon recognized, the results of planning policies may not be significantly better than those of the free market; and the reaction against planning may be as decisive as that against *laissez faire*.

British Local Government Organization and Functions

The powers and duties of local authorities in England and Wales are derived from royal charters in the case of boroughs, or from an act of Parliament for the other local authorities.

Some of their duties and powers are obligatory, such as the preparation of development plans and the provision of education and housing. Others are permissive, such as the erection of official buildings to conduct local business. The powers also depend upon the nature of the authority, that is, whether it is a county council, a county borough, an urban or rural district council, and the like. For instance, there used to be 1441 local planning authorities in England and Wales. Now there are only 145, since planning powers may be exercised only by the counties and county boroughs as a result of the passage of the 1947 Town and Country Planning Act.

The local authority may perform some functions under an adoption act that permits the exercise of certain powers for authorities of a certain class. Additional special powers may also be conferred on local authorities by Parliament in private or local acts. Liverpool, for example, received some additional powers for the development of its satellite, Speke.

Certain local powers may be delegated. Every county council outside of London may delegate some of its powers. Permitting control of development by a local council within the county is an example. Joint committees and boards may also be formed to carry out jointly one or more functions as, for instance, the provision of medical services. Such joint committees or boards have been proposed as temporary or permanent solutions for coordinated planning of the London region and the Clyde Valley.

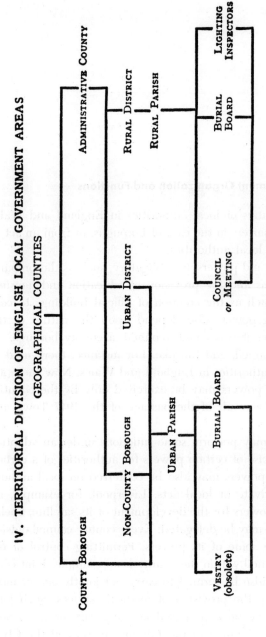

IV. TERRITORIAL DIVISION OF ENGLISH LOCAL GOVERNMENT AREAS

GEOGRAPHICAL COUNTIES

NOTE. Each Local Authority, with the exception of the County Borough and County Council, administers, broadly speaking, a Unit forming a component part of another Authority's Area.—
Thus: The Administrative County contains the Areas of Non-County Boroughs, Urban Districts, and Rural Districts;
The Non-County Borough and Urban District contain the Area of one or more Urban Parishes;
The Urban Parish may have a Burial Board;
The Rural District contains the Area of one or more Rural Parishes;
The Rural Parish possesses a Parish Council or a Parish Meeting, and may possess a Burial Board and Lighting Inspector.
Source: J. J. Clarke, *The Local Government of the United Kingdom* (London: Isaac Pitman & Sons, Limited, 1948), p. 905.

204

V. LOCAL GOVERNMENT IN ENGLAND AND WALES

FUNCTIONS, CONTROL, ADMINISTRATION AND FINANCE

Function	Central Controlling Authority	Local Administrative Authority	Finance	Remarks
Public Health . . .	Ministry of Health	County, County Borough, Borough, and District Councils		Rural District Council may delegate functions to Parish Council. County District Councils may relinquish to County Council. County Councils may delegate to District Councils
Housing . . . Town and Country Planning .	Ministry of Health Ministry of Town and Country Planning		Rates: No Statutory Limitation	
Highways, Streets, and Bridges	Ministry of Transport	County, County Borough, Borough or U.D.C.		
Public Undertakings . . .	Board of Trade Ministry of Health Ministry of Transport Ministry of Fuel and Power	County, County Borough, Borough, and District Councils	Limitation of Charges in certain cases	Special restrictions as to Adoption of Acts
Adoptive Acts . . .	Ministry of Health	C.C., C.B.C., B.C., also Urban District and Parish Councils, Burial Boards, Lighting Inspectors	Rates: Statutory Limitations in some cases	Electors may make representations C.C. must appoint Small Holdings Sub-Committee
Small Holdings and Allotments	Ministry of Agriculture and Fisheries	C.C., C.B.C., B.C., U.D.C, R.D.C. P.C.	Rates: No Statutory Limitations	Any Six Electors or Ratepayers may make representations
Public Protection, viz. Police and Civil Defence	Home Office and Ministry of Home Security	County Councils, also Borough Councils: 10,000 Population	One-half net approved cost of police refunded from Government Grants on satisfactory Report	Parish Councils may appoint Parish Constables. Application to Quarter Sessions or Home Office
Education – (1) Further . . (2) Primary . . (3) Secondary .	Ministry of Education Ministry of Health for Audit	C.C. & C.B. Councils	Rates: No Statutory Limit. Gov. Grants	(1) Divisional Educational Executives (2) P.C., U.D.C., or B.C. may be Minor Education Authority

Source: J. J. Clarke, *The Local Government of the United Kingdom* (London: Isaac Pitman & Sons, Limited, 1948), p. 906.

There are a vast number of permutations and combinations of the few simple patterns noted here. There are also differences in administrative organization and detail for Scotland. For these reasons, any list of the "distribution of functions between the various classes of local authority" must be "incomplete . . . [and] subject to considerable local variation." * With these reservations, Tables IV and V, prepared by Mr. J. J. Clarke, provide a helpful bird's-eye view of the control, administration, finance, and functions of local government in England and Wales.

* For a brief lucid description of what local authorities do, how they do it and where the money comes from, see W. Eric Jackson, *Local Government in England and Wales* (Harmondsworth: Middlesex, 1945), chaps. iv, v, vii. For the most comprehensive compendium of information on this subject in a single volume, see J. J. Clarke, *The Local Government of the United Kingdom* (14th edition; London: Sir Isaac Pitman and Sons, Limited, 1948).

APPENDIX C

The Look of the New Towns

Three different aspects of the new towns are shown in the following photographs. Group I is an exploration in detail of Harlow, one of the most attractive of the new towns. The aerial photographs were taken by the Harlow Development Corporation; the others belong to Mr. Frederick Gibberd, the corporation's architect planner. They provide a sympathetic interpretation of the town's development. They also illustrate some of the principal features of one new town. (Further descriptive detail with plans and photographs can be found in Gibberd, "Harlow New Town," *Architectural Review*, vol. 117, no. 701, May 1955, pp. 310–329.)

Group II provides a brief photographic survey of some of the other new towns. The aim is to give a somewhat more varied description than is possible by studying one town in detail. Most of the prints were obtained from the chief architects of the various development corporations and from Dame Evelyn Sharp and the Public Relations Officer of the Ministry of Housing and Local Government.

Group III offers a less sympathetic evaluation. The photographs are a sample of some of the street scenes reproduced by the British journal, *Architectural Review* (vol. 114, no. 679, July 1953), in its corrosive criticism of "prairie planning" of the new towns.

Within a narrow range, the three groups of photographs can give some inkling of the quality and appearance of the new towns. But adept or inadept use of the camera can easily mislead. By recognizing this danger, the reader may be able to sensitize himself to the possible direction of the bias, if not the range of error.

THE LOOK OF THE NEW TOWNS

1. HARLOW NEW TOWN. View looking north. The neighborhood Mark Hall South is in the foreground, and the neighborhood Mark Hall North and the Eastern Industrial Estate are in the background. (Aerial Photograph by Photoflight Limited.)

GROUP I

Harlow New Town

3. THE STOW. Sub-shopping center for the Mark Hall and Netteswell neighborhoods, showing recreational ground. Behind the center are residential neighborhoods and the county primary school.

5. ORCHARD CROFT AREA. Architects: Harlow Design Group.

6. ORCHARD CROFT AREA. Architects: Harlow Design Group.

7. "THE LAWNS," MARK HALL NORTH. The south and east facades of the flat blocks are seen across the landscape way, with two-story houses at the rear, enclosing the space Architect: Mr. Frederick Gibberd.

8. CHURCHFIELD. Architects: Richard Sheppard and Partners.

9. PENNYMEAD. Two-story two-bedroom maisonettes, and bed-sitting room flats. Architects: Norman and Dawbarn.

10. WARD HATCH. Mark Hall North sub-shopping center, consisting of four shops and a small public house. Architects for shops: Harlow Design Group.

11. VIEWS WHEN WALKING THROUGH THE STOW SHOPPING CENTER. Mark Hall and Netteswell neighborhoods.

12. VIEWS WHEN WALKING THROUGH THE STOW SHOPPING CENTER. Mark Hall and Netteswell neighborhoods.

13. MARKET SQUARE. Photograph of a model.

14. EDINBURGH WAY. The main industrial road of the Eastern Industrial Estate.

15. EASTERN INDUSTRIAL ESTATE.

1. CRAWLEY NEW TOWN. Aerial view of the northern part of Crawley New Town. This shows the industrial area lying near the main London Road (top left) close to the residential areas but with space for expansion northwards. The industrial area is separated from the residential areas by a broad greenbelt, and in the center can be seen one of the cycle tracks that link the factories and houses. The neighborhoods have large playing areas. (Aerial Photograph by Aerofilms Limited.)

GROUP II

Views of Other New Towns

2. WEST GREEN, CRAWLEY NEW TOWN. Bungalows and terraced housing face a green area where children can play.

3. VANNERS, NORTHGATE, CRAWLEY NEW TOWN. A group of seventeen houses planned at fifteen to the acre. This is the most compact development undertaken by the Crawley Development Corporation. It is on a site near the center of the town.

4. THREE-STORY FLATS IN CRAWLEY NEW TOWN. The flats are built on a star pattern. Every building contains nine flats, each provided with a living room, kitchen, two bedrooms, and a bathroom.

5. THE DRIFTWAY, CRAWLEY NEW TOWN. An old cattle track, retained as a footpath.

6. TOWN CENTER, CRAWLEY NEW TOWN. This area is the first stage of the developing town center. Broad Walk, a pedestrian street of twenty-five shops, will lead from the old Crawley High Street to the new Queen's Square. Maisonettes form the upper story on the north side, while on the south, set back to let sunshine into the street, the buildings in the rear consist of one-story offices or storerooms, with single-story flats above. Frames for the display of posters by local organizations form an attractive feature at the entrance.

7. INDUSTRIAL AREA, CRAWLEY NEW TOWN. View from Manor Royal Road.

8. INTERIOR OF STANDARD FACTORY, CRAWLEY. This was designed and built by the Crawley Development Corporation to be leased to industry. The roof is of shell concrete construction and has top lighting. The building can be let as one unit of 20,000 sq. ft. or divided into units of 5,000 sq. ft. Toilets and office accommodation are provided for each unit.

9. **RECONSTRUCTED TOWN CENTER IN HEMEL HEMPSTEAD.** This aerial photograph shows the new town center at Hemel Hempstead in its present state of reconstruction. Reading from the top of the picture downwards along the main spine street known as "Marlowes," the reader will note just below St. Mary's Church (with the spire) an area of existing buildings which is to be the new administration center. Only one side of this area shows any present indication of development. This is the new central police station. Below this and separated by a back service road, there is an area as yet undeveloped. This is for the cinema. Below this site is the new town square with Scotch pines bordering it; below that a new block of shops with maisonettes above them, and below that a large block of new shops under construction, with offices above them. The portion in the center of this block furthest developed is known as the "Bank Court" and will be an enclosed court in which the banks will be situated. The development terminates with the public house at the bottom of the picture, which is already completed. The other side of the street is to be developed similarly. Architect: H. Kellett Ablett. (Aerial Photograph by Photoflight Limited.)

10. QUEEN'S SQUARE, ADEYFIELD NEIGHBORHOOD, HEMEL HEMPSTEAD. This neighborhood shopping center has shops with maisonettes around the square. At the bottom right of the square may be seen the New Venture Public House, and in the center, the Adeyfield Hall. The open area to the left of the picture is for service industry. In the background one may see the relationship of the neighborhood center and the Junior Modern and Infants School, one of the two primary schools in this neighborhood. In the distant background one may see the industrial area, which is separated from the neighborhood by a belt of trees. Architect: H. Kellett Ablett.

11. ADEYFIELD HALL, COMMUNITY CENTER, HEMEL HEMPSTEAD. Architect: H. Kellett Ablett.

12. INDUSTRIAL AREA, HEMEL HEMPSTEAD.   Architect:
H. Kellett Ablett.

13. TERRACE HOUSING IN HATFIELD.   Architect: Lionel Brett.

14. FLATS IN HATFIELD.   Architect: Lionel Brett.

15. GARDENS IN THE REAR OF HOUSES IN
HATFIELD.

16. AERIAL VIEW OF BASILDON NEW TOWN. The Basildon Development Corporation is attempting to fill in an area of scattered residential development and create an integrated community. This aerial view illustrates the difficulty of "in-filling." In the foreground the reader can observe the preexisting development. In the center and upper left of the photograph are examples of relatively large-scale open-land developments. Small groups of houses are also being built within the existing built-up area. In the upper right-hand corner beyond the residential development is one of Basildon's industrial areas. (Aerial Photograph by Photoflight Limited.)

17. PLANTING AND PRESERVATION OF TREES IN RESIDENTIAL AREAS IN BASILDON NEW TOWN.

18. NEWTON AYCLIFFE. Three-bedroom houses in pairs, with garages attached, for middle-income tenants. On the left and in the background are bungalows for old people.

19. BUNGALOWS FOR AGED PERSONS IN PETERLEE. Each house has a living room, bedroom, kitchen and bathroom.

20. TYRIE CRESCENT, GLENROTHES, SCOTLAND. Three terraced apartment houses form a crescent, terminating with a three-apartment block. Each unit of the terraced block is straight. The curving effect is obtained by pilasters between each unit.

21. LOCAL SHOPPING CENTER, WOODSIDE RESIDENTIAL PRECINCT, GLENROTHES. There are twelve shop units with flats or maisonettes above, all grouped around a pedestrian court. In the foreground is a community hall which seats 240 persons. There is a parking lot in the rear. (Photograph by James R. Smith.)

22. EAST KILBRIDE FROM THE NORTHEAST. This view shows the general architectural effect aimed at in East Kilbride. Architect: Donald Reay.

23.   TYPICAL BLOCK OF FLATS, EAST KILBRIDE.

24.   ENTRANCE TO THE BARCLAY SECONDARY MODERN SCHOOL, STEVENAGE.   Sculpture by Henry Moore

25. ST. ANDREW'S CHURCH HALL, BEDWELL NEIGHBORHOOD CENTER, STEVENAGE. This is a dual-purpose building for religious and social activities. It includes an altar at one end that can be closed off and a stage at the other.

26. THREE-BEDROOM TERRACE-TYPE HOUSES, BEDWELL, STEVENAGE.

27. THREE-BEDROOM SEMIDETACHED HOUSES, MARYMEAD, STEVENAGE.

28. BRITISH VISQUEEN, LTD., FACTORY IN STEVENAGE INDUSTRIAL AREA.

1. STEVENAGE.

The following pages contain some of the photographs printed in *The Architectural Review* to support the charge that the new towns are a failure, at least on architectural grounds (Gordon Cullen, "Prairie Planning in the New Towns," vol. 114, no. 679, July 1953). The criticisms are focused particularly on the "vast" open spaces, the low densities, the "dreary" townscape, and the absence of architectural urbanity.

The photographs are obviously strong statements, and no further comments are provided.

GROUP III

Visual Criticisms of the New Towns

2. STEVENAGE.

3. STEVENAGE.

4. HEMEL HEMPSTEAD.

5. HEMEL HEMPSTEAD.

6. HEMEL HEMPSTEAD.

Notes

LIST OF ABBREVIATIONS

HMSO: His Majesty's Stationery Office

Cmd.: Command Papers

RDC: Reports of the Development Corporations, London HMSO

RDC Scotland: Reports of the East Kilbride and Glenrothes Development Corporations, Edinburgh, HMSO

CHAPTER 2

Ebenezer Howard and the Campaign of History

1. E. Howard, *Tomorrow: A Peaceful Path to Real Reform.* This book was originally printed in 1898 and then reissued with slight revisions in 1902 under the title *Garden Cities of Tomorrow.* A more recent edition has been printed in London, 1945 by Faber and Faber, Limited, with introductory essays by F. J. Osborn and Lewis Mumford. All page citations are from the 1945 edition.

2. F. J. Osborn, "Sir Ebenezer Howard – The Evolution of His Ideas," *The Town Planning Review,* vol. XXI, no. 3 (October 1950), p. 222.

3. Osborn's comments, cited above, provide the best short summary of Howard's early life. This resume leans heavily on Osborn's article. For other descriptions see Osborn's preface to *Garden Cities of Tomorrow* and his *Green-belt Cities* (London: Faber and Faber, Limited, 1946); C. B. Purdom, *The Building of Satellite Towns* (London: J. M. Dent and Sons, Limited, rev. ed. 1949), pp. 26–28; also E. B. Carter, "Sir Ebenezer Howard" in *Dictionary of National Biography* (London: Oxford University Press, 1922–1930), pp. 434–437.

4. For a discussion of Howard's views and their reflection of the ideas of the age, see W. A. Eden, "Ebenezer Howard and the Garden City Movement," *The Town Planning Review,* vol. XIX, nos. 3, 4 (Summer, 1947), pp. 123–143.

5. Osborn, *The Town Planning Review,* vol. XXI, no. 3, p. 225.

6. *Ibid.,* p. 225.

NOTES TO CHAPTER 2

7. *Ibid.*, p. 226.

8. *Ibid.*, p. 231.

9. Eden, p. 134.

10. *Ibid.*, p. 134.

11. Howard, p. 42.

12. Mumford, "The Garden City Idea and Modern Planning," introductory essay in Howard, p. 36.

13. *Ibid.*, p. 29.

14. Purdom, pt. II, chaps. vii, viii.

15. *Ibid.*, p. 175.

16. Osborn, *Greenbelt Cities*, p. 107. The best short descriptions of the financial problems encountered by Letchworth and Welwyn may be found in this section. For further details see Purdom, pt. II, chaps. vii, viii, especially pp. 158–159; and pt. III, chaps. vii, viii.

17. For a personal description of this incident see Osborn, *New Towns After the War* (London: J. M. Dent and Sons, Limited, 1918, reissued 1942), pp. 8–9.

18. Purdom, pt. III, chaps. vii, viii; and Osborn, *Greenbelt Cities*, chap. v.

19. *Ibid.*, p. 321.

20. Purdom asserts: "It may justly be said to be a wonderful testimony to the promoters of the first garden city that they succeeded in sustaining their scheme intact. Was there ever a first attempt that was so successful? How many models of a great invention have to be made and scrapped before a satisfactory result is reached? In town building such prodigality cannot be practised; but it would have been strange, or contrary to human experience, if a number of attempts at building garden cities had to be made before anything worth having was reached" (p. 178). Osborn notes that "Letchworth and Welwyn certainly did not yield a full commercial return to their equity shareholders; but they came near enough to doing so to show that with adequate initial capital and a greater pace of growth they would have been financial successes in this sense . . . If the two companies had not been stinted of capital, or if fashion in industrial location had changed a little sooner, or if there had been some measure of canalisation of development towards dispersal centres under a national planning policy the financial success of the garden cities would have required no qualification at all" (*Greenbelt Cities*, p. 112).

21. *The Building of Satellite Towns.* See also Osborn, *New Towns After the War*, p. 7.

22. *Town and Country Planning* is the journal of the Town and Country Planning Association, formerly the Garden Cities and Town Planning Association, founded in 1899.

23. See M. Bowley, *Housing and the State: 1919–1944* (London: George Allen and Unwin, Limited, 1945). For a more popular review with greater emphasis on the planning problems, see G. D. H. Cole, *Building and Planning* (London: Cassell and Company, Limited, 1945), chaps. i–iv; see also L. E. White, *Community or Chaos: New Housing Estates and Their Social Problems* (London: The National Council of Social Service, 1950); R. Durant, *Watling, a Survey of Social Life on a New Housing Estate* (London: P. S. King

and Son, Limited, 1939); T. Young, *Becontree and Dagenham* (London: The National Council of Social Service, 1934).

24. A good review of these problems may be found in S. R. Dennison, *Location of Industry and Depressed Areas* (London: Oxford University Press, 1939).

25. A more detailed review of the problems discussed in this and the preceding two paragraphs may be found in the *Report of the Royal Commission on the Distribution of the Industrial Population*, Cmd. 6153 (henceforth referred to as the Barlow Report; London: HMSO, 1940), pts. I and II. There is also a wealth of detail in the 26 volumes of testimony gathered in the *Minutes of Evidence* taken by this commission in 1938. A more recent summary account is available in W. Ashworth, *The Genesis of Modern British Town Planning* (London: Routledge and Kegan Paul, Limited, 1954), chap. viii.

26. Ministry of Local Government and Planning, *Town and Country Planning, 1943–1951*, Cmd. 8204 (London: HMSO, 1951), p. 4. For a brief description of the powers and structure of local government in England and Wales, see Appendix B and Tables IV and V.

27. Barlow Report, p. 1.

28. *Ibid.*, p. 8.

29. *Report of the Committee on Land Utilization in Rural Areas*, Cmd. 6378 (London: HMSO, 1942).

30. *Report of the Expert Committee on Compensation and Betterment*, Cmd. 6386 (London: HMSO, 1942).

31. Ministry of Health, *Interim Report of the Committee to Consider and Advise on the Principles to be followed in Dealing with Unhealthy Areas* (London: HMSO, 1920); *Garden Cities and Satellite Towns: Report of the Departmental Committee* (London: HMSO, 1935).

32. P. Abercrombie, *Greater London Plan 1944: A Report Prepared on Behalf of the Standing Conference on London Regional Planning* (London: HMSO, 1945).

33. Cited in *Town and Country Planning, 1943–1951*, p. 1. Note also that "Planning in Scotland is administered by the Department of Health for Scotland under separate Acts corresponding closely to the English ones" (*ibid.*).

34. C. M. Haar, *Land Planning Law in a Free Society* (Cambridge: Harvard University Press, 1951); cf. also W. Wood, *Planning and the Law* (London: P. Marshall and Co., Limited, 1949). For short summaries of the basic planning legislation, see J. J. Clarke, *Social Welfare* (London: Sir Isaac Pitman and Sons, Limited, 1953); Town and Country Planning Bill, 1947, *Explanatory Memorandum*, Cmd. 7006 (London: HMSO, January 1947); D. Heap, "Legal and Administrative Aspects of the Town and Country Planning Act, 1947, and its Regulations and Orders," *Report of Proceedings, Town and Country Planning Summer School, Cambridge University, 1948* (London: Town Planning Institute), pp. 15–32; The Royal Institution of Chartered Surveyors, *The Town and Country Planning Act, Defects of the Act and Its Remedies* (Surrey: The Press at Coombelands, Limited, no date).

35. Clarke, p. 207.

36. New Towns Committee, *Interim Report*, Cmd. 6759 (London: HMSO, 1946), p. 3.

NOTES TO CHAPTER 2

37. Lord Reith had a long record of distinguished service. He has been the Director General of the British Broadcasting Corporation (1927–1938); Chairman of the Imperial Airways (1938–1939); first Chairman of the British Overseas Airways Corporation (1939–1940); Minister of Information (1940); Minister of Transport (1940); first Minister of Works and Buildings (1940–1942); Director of Combined Operations, Material Department, Admiralty (1943–1945); and Chairman of the Commonwealth Telecommunications Board (1946–1950). These are only a few of the posts Lord Reith held before he was made Chairman of the New Towns Committee in 1946.

38. *Interim Report*, Cmd. 6759, p. 4.

39. Howard, chap. x.

40. O. W. Holmes, "John Marshall," *Collected Legal Papers* (New York: Harcourt, Brace & Company, 1920), pp. 267–268.

CHAPTER 3

Newtopia versus Megalopolis

1. C. Stein, *Toward New Towns for America* (Liverpool: The University Press of Liverpool, 1951), p. 207.

2. Howard, p. 146.

3. *Ibid.*, p. 159.

4. General Register Office, Census 1951, *England and Wales, Preliminary Report* (London: HMSO, 1951), Appendix A.

5. Howard, p. 146.

6. General Register Office, *Census 1951, England and Wales, Preliminary Report*, Table G. On the size of the housing program, see New Towns Committee, *Second Interim Report*, Cmd. 6794 (London: HMSO, 1946), p. 11.

7. Howard, chap. vi.

8. See the sections of Chap. 9 dealing with regional and national planning, and local boundaries, national interest, and town development (pp. 152–159).

9. *Ibid.*, p. 142.

10. *Town and Country Planning*, Vol. IV, No. LXXXII (June 1936); see also *ibid.*, Vol. IV, No. CXIV (September 1936).

11. Thomas Sharp, *Town and Countryside* (London: Oxford University Press, 1933), pp. 171–172. It should be noted, however, that population pressures continue to play a key role in urban growth in other countries, such as India and the United States.

12. Barlow Report, p. 3.

13. "Planning: Location of Employment," *Political and Economic Planning*, no. 224 (August 25, 1944), p. 13. Political and Economic Planning is an independent, nonparty research group in England, which prepares a fortnightly broadsheet on planning as well as occasional full-scale reports on a variety of economic and social problems.

14. "The group who started Letchworth in 1904," Osborn said, "were so confident of the essential soundness of the idea, that in selecting the site, they gave the enterprise no adventitious advantages of any kind. Indeed,

they may be said to have carried the scientific temper of their experiment so far as to load the dice against it. They chose what was then a remote site where there was no tendency whatever to spontaneous development" (*Minutes of Evidence Taken Before the Royal Commission on the Geographical Distribution of the Industrial Population, 20th Day,* May 5, 1938, p. 620). See also G. and E. McAllister, *Town and Country Planning* (London: Faber and Faber, Limited, 1941), p. 137.

15. C. Goodrich, *Migration and Economic Opportunity* (Philadelphia: University of Pennsylvania Press, 1936), chaps. vi, vii. See also S. Helburn, "Location of Industry," *Journal of Land and Public Utility Economics,* vol. XIX, no. 3 (August 1943), pp. 253–263; and D. L. Munby, *Industry and Planning in Stepney* (London: Oxford University Press, 1951), chap. viii and Table 37. Some additional studies with conclusions pointing in this direction are E. M. Hoover, *The Location of Economic Activity* (New York: McGraw-Hill Book Co., Inc., 1948), chap. viii; D. J. Bogue, *The Structure of the Metropolitan Community: A Study of Dominance and Subdominance* (Ann Arbor: University of Michigan Press, 1949); R. M. Haig, "Toward an Understanding of the Metropolis," *Quarterly Journal of Economics,* vol. XL, pt. 1 in no. 2, pt. 2 in no. 3 (February and May 1926); Dennison, *Location of Industry and Depressed Areas;* P. Self, *The Planning of Industrial Location* (London: University of London Press, 1953). See also the reports on industrial location by the National Resources Planning Board, Political and Economic Planning, and the Barlow Commission.

16. *Town and Country Planning,* Vol. IV, No. XCVII (June 1936).

17. *Minutes of Evidence,* p. 646.

18. *Ibid.,* pp. 646, 649–655 (italics by the author). The New Towns Committee observed in its *Final Report,* Cmd. 6876 (London: HMSO, 1946), p. 12: "To locate new towns far away from existing great cities in regions with a relatively sparse population but with good communications and other facilities available, might be very advantageous both in providing a new centre of cultural life and a more substantial economic foundation for local government services in the area selected. Whether it would be possible to induce industrialists and workers to move far from the centres to which they are accustomed we cannot be sure." A more recent statement sponsored by the Town and Country Planning Association reaffirms these views. Peter Self concludes in his able study *The Planning of Industrial Location,* p. 41, that "Both the new towns being built around London and those proposed for central Lancashire will flourish only on the basis of close industrial linkage and good communications with the big urban centres. The result may disappoint those planners who cherish the ideal of creating fully self contained communities. But if the new towns can achieve a reasonable autonomy and can provide work locally for a high proportion of their residents, they may fairly be accounted a success. They will offer an improved way of life and help to solve urban congestion as part of a scheme that is economically workable."

19. This was partly due to the fact that daily transportation was a relatively new phenomenon with causes and implications that were quite unclear. J. Crane has pointed out that "since Ebenezer Howard first formulated the

English Garden City principles — transit and automobile developments have freed residential settlements from the earlier necessity of immediate proximity to industry" ("Location Factors in Housing Programs" in *Housing — the Continuing Problem*, Washington, D.C.: National Resources Planning Board, December 1940, p. 125). This is cited by Mr. Crane as an argument for departing somewhat from the original garden city principles tying residential settlement close to industry.

20. K. Liepmann's study, *The Journey to Work* (New York: Oxford University Press, 1944), still represents one of the most illuminating contributions to the subject.

21. *Political and Economic Planning*, no. 224 (August 25, 1944), p. 7.

22. Liepmann, chap. v; for parallel views, see Sharp, *Town and Countryside*, pp. 171–172, and *Town Planning* (London: Penguin Books, Limited, 1940), pp. 50–52, 66–67; also Sir G. Gibbon, *Problems of Town and Country Planning* (London: G. Allen and Unwin, Limited, 1937), chaps. vii, viii, ix.

23. Purdom, pt. II, chap. vii, pt. III, chap. vii; Osborn, *Greenbelt Cities*, pp. 106–108, 153. The new towns, as indicated here in Chapter 6, also experienced many difficulties because of the long development period before the capital assets could fructify. For an able discussion of the intricacies of the analysis of comparative benefits, see A. Smithies, *The Budgetary Process in the United States*, A Research Study for the Committee on Economic Development (New York: McGraw-Hill Book Co., 1955), chaps. xiii, xiv, xvi.

24. *Ibid.* These claims are often made in the pages of *Town and Country Planning*, or by garden city proponents.

25. The scale and significance of the loss of good agricultural land because of low-density development has occasioned much controversy. More emphasis is now being put on the cost of creating new farm land rather than on the value of the output of land which is absorbed by other land uses. For some brief summary discussions, see R. W. Dale, "The Garden versus Farm Controversy," *Journal of the Town Planning Institute*, vol. XI, no. 1 (December 1953), pp. 8–9; G. D. M. Block, *The Spread of Towns* (London: The Conservative Political Centre, 1954), chaps. i and ii; and especially G. P. Wibberly, "Rural Land Policies in an Urban Britain" in *Report of Proceedings, Town and Country Planning Summer School, St. Andrew's University, 1954*, pp. 66–84. For other analyses of the problem see Osborn, "Housing Density in England," *Town and Country Planning*, vol. XXIII, no. 128 (December 1954), pp. 634–645; "The Scare About Food Growing Trends," *ibid.*, pp. 607–610; C. D. Buchanan and D. H. Crompton, "Residential Density," *Report of Proceedings, Town and Country Planning Summer School, Nottingham University, 1950* (London: Town Planning Institute, 1950), pp. 7–34; J. L. Womersley, "Economic Housing Layout," *Report of Proceedings, Town and Country Planning Summer School, University of Bristol, 1953*, pp. 20–42; D. Senior, "Gardens and Food Production," *Town and Country Planning*, vol. XXIII, no. 131 (March 1955), pp. 124–128; Wibberly, "The Challenge of Rural Land Losses," *Journal of the Royal Society of Arts* (July 9, 1954); and D. T. W. Price, "What Constitutes a Successful Marginal Farm Policy?" *The Farm Economist*, vol. vii, no. 5 (1953).

26. I am indebted for this definition to my colleague Professor Kevin Lynch.

27. The most thorough examination of the problem of urban size has been made by Otis Dudley Duncan, "An Examination of the Problem of Optimum City-Size," Ph.D. Dissertation, Department of Sociology, University of Chicago (March 1949). An abstract is provided by Duncan, "Optimum Size of Cities" in *Reader in Urban Sociology*, edited by Paul Hatt and Albert Reiss (Glencoe: Free Press, 1951), pp. 632–645. For a useful appraisal of the literature, see R. M. Lillibridge, "Urban Size: An Assessment," *Land Economics*, vol. XXVIII, no. 4 (November 1952), pp. 341–352. See also Sir William Holford, "Central Areas: Some Aspects of Size, Function and Design," *Report of Proceedings, Town and Country Planning Summer School, University of Bristol, 1953* (London: Town Planning Institute, 1953), pp. 6–10. See also R. Unwin, "The Town at the Best Size for Good Social Life," chap. iii in Purdom, *Town Theory and Practice* (London: Benn Bros., 1921).

28. R. Glass, "Observations in Lansbury," *Journal of the Town Planning Institute*, vol. XXXVIII, no. 1 (November 1951), pp. 9–11; and A. G. Sheppard Fidler, "Lansbury's Problems compared with those of a New Town," *ibid.*, pp. 12–13. See also K. Lynch, "The Form of Cities," *Scientific American*, vol. 190 (April 1954), pp. 55–63.

29. S. Anderson, *Winesburg, Ohio* (New York: The Modern Library, 1919), pp. 11–12. Used by permission of The Viking Press, the copyright holder.

30. National Resources Committee, *Our Cities* (Washington, D. C.: Government Printing Office, 1937), p. 53.

The New Towns Act and the New Towns

1. New Towns Act, 1946, 9 & 10 Geo. 6, c. 68, p.l.
2. *Ibid.* For convenience, future references will be made only to the ministry as the over-all authority.
3. New Towns Committee, *Interim Report*, Cmd. 6759 (London: HMSO, 1946), pp. 9–10.
4. Ministry of Local Government and Planning, *Town and Country Planning, 1943–1951*, Cmd. 8204, p. 123. The description in the next few paragraphs leans heavily on the account provided in this publication and is supplemented by knowledge gleaned fom field investigations.
5. New Towns Committee, *Final Report*, Cmd. 6876 (London: HMSO, 1946), pp. 11–13. See also *Interim Report*, Cmd. 6759, p. 5; and *Town and Country Planning, 1943–1951*, pp. 124–125.
6. *Ibid.*
7. New Towns Act, 1946, p. 2.
8. W. O. Hart, "The Development of New Towns," *Report of Proceedings, Town and Country Planning Summer School, Bangor, 1952* (London: Town Planning Institute, 1952), p. 65.
9. *Ibid.*

10. Aycliffe is an exception since it has its own "Direct Labour Department." See *Reports of the Development Corporations* (henceforth referred to as *RDC*; London: HMSO, March 31, 1953), pp. 6–7; *ibid.* (March 31, 1954), pp. 14–15.

11. The Reith Committee supported this approach because of the view that in the early years the undertaking would not be self-supporting and because no other sources of funds were available. For a fuller statement of these reasons, see New Towns Committee, *Second Interim Report*, Cmd. 6794, pp. 14–17.

12. New Towns Act, 1946, p. 13.

13. *Town and Country Planning, 1943–1951*, pp. 133–134. The New Towns Act empowers the Treasury to issue to the minister sums from the Consolidated Fund for him to advance to corporations for their capital requirements, and it empowers the minister to make grants out of his vote toward the expenditure of corporations on other than capital account.

14. *RDC* (March 31, 1953), p. 88; *ibid.* (March 31, 1952), pp. 87–88.

15. *Town and Country Planning, 1943–1951*, p. 134.

16. *Ibid.*, p. 19.

17. Block, pp. 32–33.

18. *Capital Investment in 1948, Presented by the Chancellor of the Exchequer to Parliament, December 1947*, Cmd. 7268 (London: HMSO, 1947), pp. 4, 10.

19. RDC (March 31, 1953), pp. 15–16, 153, 242, 282.

20. Block, p. 36.

21. See Lynch, *Scientific American* (April 1954), pp. 57–58.

22. The amount of public space "varies widely from town to town: from 1.25 acres a thousand in Peterlee to 8.3 in Crawley. More important the standards of public open space arrived at in the plans seem to be extraordinarily different:

	Per 1,000 population
Basildon	2
Bracknell	7
Crawley	4.4
Harlow	5
Hatfield	10
Hemel Hempstead	11
Stevenage	3.22
Welwyn	9.5
Cwmbran	12.4
East Kilbride	5.2
Glenrothes	7
Newton Aycliffe	8

But these figures may not all be comparable" ("New Towns in 1953," *Town and Country Planning*, vol. XXII, no. 117, January 1954, pp. 18–19). See also Holford, "British New Town Planning," *Journal of the American Institute of Architects*, vol. XV, no. 1 (January 1951), pp. 46–50.

23. *RDC* (March 31, 1953), p. 232; *ibid.* (March 31, 1952), p. 239.

24. H. F. Lydall, "Rents, Rates and Family Income," *The Manchester Guardian Weekly*, July 29, 1954, p. 12. See the section on rents in Chap. 6; and for a complete description of the methods and results of this survey, see H. F. Lydall and R. F. F. Dawson, "Household Income, Rents and Rates," *Bulletin of the Oxford University Institute of Statistics*, vol. 16, no. 4 (April 1954), pp. 97–129. See also *Town and Country Planning*, vol. XXII, no. 17 (January 1954), p. 49.

25. These and the previous percentages are rough estimates to give some indication of the relative emphasis on the different kinds of housing.

26. *RDC* (March 31, 1953), p. 233. For a more detailed discussion of the policies, see *First, Second and Third Reports From the Committee of Public Accounts, together with the Proceedings of the Committee, Minutes of Evidence, Appendices and Index* (*Session 1951–1952*) (London: HMSO, 1952), pp. 238, 240–241, 247–256.

27. *First, Second and Third Reports From the Committee of Public Accounts 1951–1952*, pp. 238, 240–241, 247–256; Self, "The New Town's Industrial Boom," *Town and Country Planning*, vol. XXIII, no. 129 (January 1955), pp. 14–18.

28. The attitude is neatly summed up in the reply of Sir Thomas Sheepshanks, Accounting Officer of the Ministry of Town and Country Planning, in response to a query from the Committee of Public Accounts about rents charged to government departments. He said, "I am afraid it is a very sore point with our English Corporations that Crown departments stoutly refuse to pay a penny more than we have to pay under the law. They say, 'We are entitled to existing use value, and we do not pay a development charge, and we want your good sites.' The result in one or two cases has been that the corporations have said 'Rather than that, we would rather not have you . . . If we dispose of this to an outside industrialist we shall get a handsome rent, and we can make a very nice profit, and although we should very much like to have this government factory, rather than let them have it on those terms we would rather find somebody else'" (*First, Second, Third and Fourth Reports from The Committee of Public Accounts, together with the Proceedings of the Committee, Minutes of Evidence, Appendices, and Index*, 1950–1951, London: HMSO, p. 1503). Sir Thomas Bennett, Chairman of the Crawley Corporation, has contended that, in effect, the attitude of the government departments would result in a direct capital loss for the corporations if they transferred it on the basis of existing use value instead of development value. He insisted that "if we buy land at prices varying between £70 and £134 an acre, which is the variation of existing use agricultural land in Crawley, and on the constructive competitive tendering we put in roads and services, and make proper calculations, our resulting developed land costs us today, at 1952 prices, something over £4,000 an acre, and there is no question of profit, it is purely a reimbursement of developed value, and that is the figure which is being discussed for the basis of local authority purposes where charges are allowed" (*First, Second and Third Reports from The Committee of Accounts*, 1951–1952, p. 244).

29. *RDC* (March 31, 1952), p. 238.

30. For a characteristic statement on this subject, see *RDC* (March 31, 1953), p. 390.

31. *Town and Country Planning*, vol. XXIII, no. 219 (January 1955), pp. 6–7.

CHAPTER 5

New Towns: National Policy Issues

1. The board, under the 1934, 1936, and 1937 legislation for special areas, is attempting to minimize unemployment in depressed areas. Their powers include grants for water, gas, and other services, and for clearance and conversion to new uses. They also include the building of planned industrial estates, sectional factories, and housing for key workers. Under the 1945 and 1950 legislation, the board is responsible for industrial location policy with special responsibilities for areas of unemployment. Also, under the 1950 act contributions can be made to the costs of transfer of firms and their workers to these areas. These general powers were supplemented in the past by the government's control over building licenses, which ended on November 11, 1955, and by the general priorities for building materials and raw materials for production. The 1947 Town and Country Planning Act gave a further strategic power, namely the responsibility of seeing that new industrial development with floor space of 5000 square feet or more was consistent with the government's policy of industrial distribution. For an excellent review of these powers, see Self, *The Planning of Industrial Location*.

2. White, *New Towns: Their Challenge and Opportunity* (London: The National Council of Social Service, 1951), p. 87.

3. Unemployment areas are smaller localized areas of unemployment. Development areas may include part of the whole of a metropolis or region.

4. Hart, p. 63.

5. *Ibid.*

6. Ministry of Local Government and Planning, *Town and Country Planning, 1943–1951*, Cmd. 8204, p. 135.

7. *Ibid.*, p. 136.

8. For further information see the discussion in the *First, Second, Third and Fourth Reports of the Committee of Public Accounts* (1950–1951), pp. 499–502; and also the memorandum in Appendix 15, submitted by Sir Thomas Sheepshanks, estimating the cost of housing each person and family in new towns (pp. 629–630). In this memorandum, Sheepshanks assumed an "average cost of working class dwellings 'of about £2,800.' In each case the estimate included provision for the cost of land and site development, e.g., estate sewers and roads, the cost of building and of expenditure it was expected would be incurred in bringing civil engineering and building labour from a distance to the new town, more particularly in the earlier years . . .

"In a new town for 50,000 persons corporations providing housing for 47,500, the cost of housing to the development corporation would on these basic figures be nearly £20 million out of the total estimated expenditure by the corporation of about £25 million. Housing accounted for nearly £132 million, an average cost per person of about £416, out of the total estimated potential Exchequer liability of from £165 million to £190 million. The remaining provision was for other development by the development corporation, e.g., main services, industrial and commercial buildings.

"The cost of the two Scottish new towns was estimated at £35 million which added to the estimate of the eleven new towns in England and Wales, makes up the United Kingdom estimate of £200 million to £225 million."

Block notes that the cost is expected to be higher than that estimated above — probably close to £500 million, a figure cited by H. Macmillan, the former minister, when he spoke to the 1952 Conservative Conference (*The Spread of Towns*, p. 32).

9. Block, p. 33.

10. The Reith (New Towns) Committee stated that "To a large extent, the nation will be spending outside congested areas money otherwise spent, possibly to less good purpose, within them. The task is to allocate in the most efficient and socially useful manner an investment which is, in one way or another, inevitable" (*Second Interim Report*, Cmd. 6794, p. 13). Cf. *First, Second, Third and Fourth Reports from the Committee of Public Accounts* (1950–1951), pp. 499–500.

11. J. Dean, "Measuring the Productivity of Capital," *Harvard Business Review*, vol. 32, no. 1 (January–February 1954), pp. 120–121. For some of the analytical problems involved on the national level, see Smithies, chap. xiii.

12. Questions and protests about this emphasis have already been voiced. For instance, G. Stephenson notes that "All the New Towns . . . instead of . . . being elements in a decentralization policy, . . . are becoming additional capital expenditure, underwritten by the Government, in the very part of the country which the Barlow Commission recommended should be restrained in growth" ("Design in Its Relation to Economic Factors," *Report of Proceedings, Town and Country Planning Summer School, University College of North Wales, Bangor, 1952*, p. 47). Cf. E. H. Ford, "Presidential Address," *Journal of the Town Planning Institute*, vol. XXXVIII, no. 1 (November 1951), p. 4.

13. Ministry of Local Government and Planning, *Town and Country Planning 1943–1951*, Cmd. 8204, pp. 25–26. Self says, "The extent to which the 1947 Town and Country Planning Act has revolutionized the scope of planning is still not appreciated. Planning today seeks to mould the size and character of communities, and their distribution throughout the country, as well as performing its older functions, of controlling lay-out and visual design. The key to this sort of planning is control over the volume and distribution of employment. . . The planning Ministry not only lacks the authority to control the distribution of industry, it has not yet evolved a policy in this matter. If it did have the powers, it would not (at present) know how to use them . . . It would be less than fair to criticize the Board of Trade too harshly for its indifference to planning aims, when these aims have not been properly stated or advocated by the responsible Ministry" (*The Planning of Industrial Location*, p. 36).

14. R. B. Black, "Town and Country Planning in England's Northeast Sec-

tion," *Journal of the American Institute of Planners*, vol. 15, no. 3 (Fall, 1949), p. 31.

15. Ministry of Town and Country Planning, *Report of the London Planning Administration Committee* (London: HMSO, 1949), p. 10. There is a fairly large literature on the problems of regional organization. For an excellent brief review, see Self, *Regionalism: A Report on Local Government* (London: Fabian Publications, and Allen and Unwin, 1949).

16. R. Vance Presthus, "A Note on British Town Planning Coordination," *Journal of Politics*, vol. 14 (1952), p. 487.

17. There were no legal impediments to prevent the minister from allowing approved authorities to participate. Indeed, the New Towns Committee specifically recommended that "the rehousing of people displaced on the redevelopment of congested areas . . . might be provided by a dispersing authority, as part of its rehousing programme, on land leased from the Corporation; or by the Corporation itself; or by a housing association under agreement with the Corporation or with the dispersing authority" (*Second Interim Report*, Cmd. 6794, p. 16). For one of the few evaluations of the pros and cons of the local authority development on the basis of Speke's experience, see G. Mercer, "Speke as a New Town," *Town Planning Review*, vol. XXIV, no. 3 (1953), pp. 215–238.

18. The *Report of the London Planning Administration Committee* was unanimous on the need for regional organization.

19. These authorities will most probably be the urban district councils. But if a council is large enough, it can proceed in the ordinary way to become a municipal borough. The new town corporations, of course, have no governmental powers. They are public development agencies. For a discussion of the present plans for the windup of the corporations, see *Hansard*, vol. 422, no. 134, col. 1083, May 7, 1946; *ibid.*, vol. 424, no. 169, cols. 2379–2401, July 4, 1946. Cf. also *Second Interim Report*, Cmd. 6794, pp. 19–21.

20. For example, note the views expressed by Reginald Stamp, Chairman of the LCC Housing Committee, concerning the redistribution of nonconforming industries in London County ("New Towns for Old," *Town and Country Planning*, vol. XXI, no. 108, April 1953, p. 162). See also Mercer, p. 233.

21. For further details see the section on rents in Chap. 6.

22. Osborn, "Public Influences on Planning," *Report of Proceedings, Town and Country Planning Summer School, Oxford University, 1951* (London: Town Planning Institute), p. 81.

23. This is a well-known difficulty, and Osborn observed that "Certainly 10,000 houses a year in new towns cannot solve the London dispersal problems. The expansion of many existing towns, and a few more new ones will also be required. Industrial dispersal must be speeded up, reoccupation of factories checked, and schemes for more office space in the City (and South Bank and Berkeley Square) looked at critically in the light of London's planning as a whole. London has not yet turned off the tap that makes the sink spill over. But the new towns, almost alone so far, have done something both to direct the inflow and catch the outflow" ("Success of the New Towns," *Town and Country Planning*, vol. XXII, no. 117, January 1954, p. 10). See also Self, *The Plan-*

ning of Industrial Location, pp. 28–32; anon., "Hands Across the Greenbelt," *Town and Country Planning,* vol. XXIII, no. 130 (February 1955), pp. 69–70.

24. *Advisory Committee for London Regional Planning Report to the Minister of Town and Country Planning* (London: HMSO, 1946), p. 11.

25. *Greater London Plan Memorandum by the Ministry of Town and Country Planning on the Report of the Advisory Committee for London Regional Planning* (London: HMSO, 1947), p. 5.

26. See Chaps. 8 and 9.

27. B. Hutchinson, *Willesden and the New Towns: An Inquiry Carried Out by The Social Survey for the Ministry of Town and Country Planning* (December 1947). New town corporations are not restricted to a forecast of the economic activities that will locate and thrive in the town and of the characteristics of the future residents. Their assignment is to build a town of specified size with a variety of jobs and population, within the limits of their capacity to attract population and industry; they can and should attempt to steer in certain directions. The corporations also have some flexibility in their building program, since a few reasonable ranges of income, family sizes, and types of commercial and industrial activity can be established as first approximations. Additional facilities can be established later in response to felt needs. But steering is generally surer if the direction of the current is understood.

28. Ministry of Local Government and Planning, *Town and Country Planning 1943–1951,* pp. 165–166.

29. See Appendix A, "The Achilles Heel of British Town Planning"; also M. P. Fogarty, *Town and Country Planning* (London: Hutchinson's University Library, 1948), pp. 194–200; Sir William G. Holford, "Presidential Address," *Journal of the Town Planning Institute,* vol. XI, no. 1 (December 1953), pp. 5–16.

30. One might have thought that, at least in the building programs, the brilliant forays in operational research would have been exploited by the corporations or by the ministry in behalf of the corporations, if not for housing policy generally. Dr. J. Bronowski has presented convincing evidence that the studies were able to provide valuable cost data in a form usable to the builder. Some examples are the variations in output associated with bonus payments, the size and number of houses, the type of site, and the like. But this effort also miscarried. Though inexpensive and "practical," the work languished and disappeared. For a short description of the achievements of these research studies, see Bronowski, "The Application of Statistical Techniques to Building Research," *Proceedings of the Conference on Building Research,* E/ECE/122, E/ECE/ — IM/HOU/BR/2 (Geneva: United Nations Economic Commission for Europe, 1950), pp. 137–151; "Operational and Statistical Research in Building," *Architects' Journal,* vol. 113 (March 29, 1951), pp. 403–406.

31. R. K. Merton, *Social Theory and Social Structure* (Glencoe: Free Press, 1949), p. 195.

32. "Planning Problems of Town, City and Region," *Papers and Discussions at the International City and Regional Planning Conference, New York City* (Baltimore: Norman Remington Co., 1925), p. 8.

CHAPTER 6

Problems of New Town Development

1. See Chap. 7.

2. Ministry of Local Government and Planning, *Town and Country Planning 1943–1951*, Cmd. 8204, p. 125. Basildon, for example, was in two urban district councils. Crawley dealt with three county councils, three rural district councils, and five parish councils; Aycliffe had three urban district councils. Aycliffe's corporation complained strenuously about the administrative difficulties, and was finally able to secure readjustment of boundaries by a county order. The whole site now lies in the Darlington District. Crawley's problem was also complicated. Originally it had three county councils. The Local Government Boundary Commission was expected to effect reorganization, since the task of securing necessary services such as schools, highways, sewage facilities, police, and fire protection was proving slow and cumbersome. These hopes were dashed when the Local Government Boundary Act was repealed in 1948. However, the West Sussex County Council in 1952 applied for an order under the Local Government Act of 1933 to extend the county boundary to include the parts of the designated area in East Sussex. This was approved by the minister, and as a consequence "practically the whole of the designated area will be in the County of Sussex" (*RDC*, March 31, 1953, p. 153; *ibid.*, March 31, 1951, pp. 7–8; *ibid.*, March 31, 1952, pp. 7–8). See also *First, Second and Third Reports From the Committee of Public Accounts* (1951–1952), p. 238; also Block, p. 40. There are also some other boundary questions. Aycliffe, for example, was built to serve its trading estate but is outside the administrative area of the estate. Corby, too, is outside the boundaries of the steel works which is the *raison d'être* of the town (K. C. Edwards, "Corby — a New Town in the Midlands," *The Town Planning Review*, vol. XXII, no. 2, July 1951, pp. 123–131).

3. *RDC* (March 31, 1949), pp. 58–59. See also Appendix B and Tables IV and V.

4. *RDC* (March 31, 1950), pp. 103–104.

5. *Ibid.*

6. *First, Third and Fourth Reports From the Committee of Public Accounts* (1950), pp. 56–57.

7. See Chap. 4, p. 42.

8. Hart, p. 9.

9. *Ibid.*

10. *RDC* (March 31, 1949), pp. 12, 35, 99, 134; *ibid.* (March 31, 1953), pp. 18, 51, 236, 278. L. W. G. T. Kirk points out that the minister said that local rates would not rise because of new towns; but that the county authorities are expected to provide schools, police stations, classified roads, public libraries, and health services; and that district councils are expected to collect garbage and refuse, take over and maintain streets and light them, provide open spaces and public conveniences, improve existing roads and sometimes facilities for

sewerage and sewage disposal ("Local Authorities and Development Corpora tions," *Town and Country Planning*, vol. XXI, no. 105, January 1953, pp. 23–26).

11. The problem was studied by a working party under the chairmanship of the former Deputy Secretary, now permanent Undersecretary of the Ministry, Dame Evelyn Sharp.

12. This question warrants more research. I am assuming that possibly higher administration, road, and utility costs for new towns were offset by other efficiencies and economies.

13. For example, the Stevenage Corporation complained that "The ban on capital expenditure is still preventing the construction of a Water Pollution Laboratory for the Department of Scientific and Industrial Research. The site for this building has been developed for some time and the ban is therefore causing an appreciable loss of interest on the capital invested in the roads" (*RDC*, March 31, 1952, p. 338). The amount of capital invested per acre of land has been estimated to be over £4,000; cf. *First, Second and Third Reports From the Committee of Public Accounts* (1951–1952), p. 244. For a lower estimate, ranging between £1,200 and £3,000 per acre, see Block, p. 42.

14. Most of the corporations believe that ultimately the new towns will prove self-liquidating, largely because of the revenues obtained from their shopping and commercial centers, their industries, the pubs, and other income-producing activities such as housing for higher income groups. For a few expressions of these views, see *RDC* (March 31, 1953), pp. 88, 154–155, 243; also Block, pp. 40–42; *First, Second, Third and Fourth Reports From the Committee of Public Accounts* (1950–1951), p. 517. However, R. L. Reiss, formerly Vice-Chairman of the Welwyn Garden City and Hatfield development corporations, and of Welwyn Garden City, Limited, seems to think there may be large losses because of the high interest charges, the inability to profit from gas and electricity undertakings, and the inflated costs during the period when the towns were built ("Finances of New Towns," *Town and Country Planning*, vol. XXI, no. 105, January 1953, pp. 13–17).

15. This practice would even be a questionable way of judging the comparative profitability of alternative investments. Professor Dean suggests that it is better not to deduct interest from project earnings but rather "to use cost of capital as a cut-off rate to select acceptably profitable projects." He also notes that for private corporations the more appropriate interest charge would be the high-cost equity capital rate (Dean, pp. 126–127). See also *RDC* (March 31, 1954), pp. 16, 169, 306.

16. Both the central government and the local government contribute subsidies to reduce the rent of housing. The central government's assistance is usually known as the exchequer grant, and the local authorities' grant is referred to as the rate fund contribution. The money for the local grants comes from the local rates or taxes.

17. Lydall, *The Manchester Guardian Weekly*, July 29, 1954. For the rent estimates in the new towns, Crawley's costs have been assumed to be about average. See *Town and Country Planning*, vol. XXII, no. 117 (January 1954), p. 49. Gross rents include rates, i.e., taxes for local government services. Evi-

dence that rents in new towns approximate those paid by the "middle classes" may be found in R. Lewis and A. Maude, *The English Middle Classes* (London: Phoenix House, 1949), chap. xii, pp. 206–208. The study by Lydall and Dawson indicates that "On the average, tenants who are salaried or self-employed pay over £1 a week in gross rent while manual workers pay less than 15s. a week" (p. 124).

18. *RDC* (March 31, 1953), p. 88; *ibid.* (March 31, 1954), p. 169. See also *First, Second and Third Reports From the Committee of Public Accounts* (1951–1952), pp. 242–243.

19. *RDC* (March 31, 1950), pp. 56–57, 94. Crawley Corporation asserts that flats cost approximately £100 more than houses. The word "claim" is used advisedly because the whole issue and technique of analyzing these costs is rife with controversy. See also *RDC* (March 31, 1949), p. 46.

20. *RDC* (March 31, 1951), pp. 11, 231. Sir Thomas Bennett, who has contended that Crawley has been able to serve workers without difficulty, has asserted, however, that "we are very close to the stage at which we shall have difficulties. . . We regard this as the most serious problem in front of the New Towns at the moment and it may well be that before very long we shall encounter an inability to pay the rent, however desirable the house" (*First, Second and Third Reports From the Committee of Public Accounts*, 1951–1952, p. 242). See also B. L. Richards, "Some Practical Aspects of New Town Development," address given at the General Meeting of the Royal Institution of Chartered Surveyors, February 11, 1952 (unpublished manuscript).

21. Lord Beveridge, *New Towns and the Case for Them* (London: University of London Press, 1952), pp. 10–11.

22. Hart, p. 70.

23. The rent ranges differ with the corporation and the locality. Probably a spread of about 6s. is the average (*First, Second and Third Reports From the Committee of Public Accounts*, 1951–1952, p. 242).

24. For a recent critical but somewhat one-sided appraisal of the notion of balance by a social anthropologist, see H. Orlans, *Utopia Ltd.* (New Haven: Yale University Press, 1953; published in the United Kingdom under the title *Stevenage: A Study of a New Town* by Routledge & Kegan Paul, Limited), pp. 81–95.

25. *First, Second, Third and Fourth Reports From the Committee of Public Accounts* (1950–1951), p. lxxii, para. 104. See also Chap. 5, note 1.

26. *RDC* (March 31, 1950), p. 100. However, intervention of the minister helped somewhat in 1951 (*RDC*, March 31, 1952, pp. 181–182).

27. Hart, p. 69.

28. Block, p. 43. See also White, *New Towns: Their Challenge and Opportunity*, pp. 51–56; and "Housing — Illusion and Reality," *The Economist*, vol. XLXXII, no. 5789 (August 7, 1954), pp. 426–429.

29. *RDC* (March 31, 1952), p. 11; and Bennett, "Residential Neighbourhood Development," *Housing Centre Review* (November–December 1952), p. 20; D. Chapman, "Social Aspects of Town Planning," *Report of Proceedings, Town and Country Planning Summer School, Cambridge University, 1948*, p. 89. See also *RDC* (March 31, 1954), pp. 166–167.

30. R. J. Allerton, "Industrial Selection Scheme," *Town and Country Planning*, vol. XXIII, no. 124 (August 1954), pp. 406–407.

31. White, pp. 28, 51–55; see also Bennett, *Housing Centre Review* (November–December, 1952).

32. L. Wolfe, *The Reilly Plan* (London: Nicholson and Watson, 1945).

33. Cf. Chap. 7, also Chapman, pp. 76–80.

34. Professor Lynch makes this observation in an unpublished memorandum on urban design.

35. J. M. Richards, "Failure of the New Towns," *Architectural Review*, vol. 114, no. 679 (July 1953), pp. 31–32.

36. G. Cullen, "Prairie Planning in the New Towns," *Architectural Review*, vol. 114, no. 679 (July 1953), pp. 34–35.

37. J. M. Richards, p. 32.

38. J. M. Richards, *The Castles on the Ground* (London: The Architectural Press, 1946), pp. 58–59.

39. L. Brett, "Failure of the New Towns," *Architectural Review*, vol. 114, no. 680 (August 1953), p. 119.

40. Tom Mellor, "The Persistent Suburb," *The Town Planning Review*, vol. XXV, no. 4 (January 1955), pp. 251–254.

41. Osborn, *Town and Country Planning*, vol. XXII, no. 117 (January 1954), p. 120.

42. Osborn, *Town and Country Planning*, vol. XXIII, no. 119 (March 1954), p. 153.

43. L. Mumford, "Old Forms for New Towns," *The New Yorker*, vol. 29 (October 17, 1953), pp. 131–132.

44. Osborn, *Report of Proceedings, Town and Country Planning Summer School, Oxford University, 1951*, pp. 71–82. Osborn also suggests in this very thoughtful article that "central planning policy must be the resultant of two streams of force: the prevailing philosophy of the responsible directors in certain ministries . . . and the pressures of the few minority interests that are well organized, determined and affluent. And there must be a parallel resultant at the local levels. In any public administration there is a certain tendency to consistency, a viscosity of policy, due to the past evolution of an outlook, an administrative tradition, a respect for the printed record on White Papers, Regulations, Minutes, answers in Parliament and precedents generally. Modifications in the policy are, however, continuously brought about, not only by the contagion of ideas within the directorate, which may come from anywhere . . . but also by the sensing of an outside pressure liable to start a chain reaction in a party or an influential parliamentary group or council group.

"The numerical demand for housing is such a pressure, so strong that it overrides powerful pressures for economy or the diversion of resources to other purposes, and can be an obstacle to planned dispersal. The defence of farm land . . . is another . . . strong enough to depreciate the hard won housing density standard. The widespread hatred of development charges is a third . . . Yet another pressure . . . is that of the great municipalities to retain their full quotas of housing sanctions: this forces the central planning directorate to choose between allowing cities to build further into their green

225

belts or to increase the density and height of buildings; and as we see in London the die has been cast for multi-story flats in defiance of known popular opinion.

"There are no comparably strong outside pressures for the accepted policy of lower density redevelopment, dispersal of industry, greenbelts and new towns. The besieged stronghold of this policy is simply the intelligence or common-sense of informed inner circle opinion and its regard for the record. Lacking the reinforcement of current pressures, any citadel thus harried must weaken. The new towns already started, having had much money spent on them, will go on; they are small outcrops of rock in an erosive flood. But if the present balance of effective influences had existed in 1946–1947 I don't think anything like a dozen new towns would have been started even by the extraordinary personal dynamism of Lord Silkin" (pp. 79–80).

In a later editorial on the eve of the general election in May 1955, Osborn noted "that neither the [town and country planning] function itself, nor any policy or feature of it has become a party issue. . . But," he added, "let us be under no illusions. The immunity of planning from party controversy is due to the absence of passionate interest in it in any party; and this in turn is due to the indifference of public opinion to the vital social issues with which planning is and still more ought to be, concerned.

"By contrast, the related function of housing has long been a highly contentious issue; and though, in office, both major parties pursue much the same housing policy, the policy would have been very different if it were not for the intense public feeling housing arouses, party cultivation of this feeling, and the necessity this forces on ministers to respond to overt pressures, and if they are clever, to forestall latent ones" ("Parliament and Planning," *Town and Country Planning*, vol. XXIII, no. 133, May 1955, p. 213).

45. In a debate on Wednesday, June 29, 1955, the Earl of Selkirk, replying for the government, indicated that to stop the merry-go-round the government was prepared to pay 50 per cent of the loss involved in purchasing vacated factories (*Town and Country Planning*, vol. XXIII, no. 136, August 1955, p. 363).

CHAPTER 7

New Towns: Personal History

1. T. S. Eliot, "London Letter," *The Dial*, vol. 73 (September 1922), p. 331.

2. This section leans heavily on Orlans' study cited earlier. It is easily the most authoritative examination of the history of Stevenage. Orlans' materials have been supplemented by other studies and personal discussions with the leading personalities associated with the town.

3. Orlans, p. 52.

4. *Ibid.*, p. 59.

5. *Ibid.*, p. 65. The rules were later changed in favor of owner occupiers getting the economic value of their homes.

6. Cited in Orlans, p. 71.

7. *Ibid.*, p. 75; also *RDC* (March 31, 1953), p. 342.

8. G. Santayana, "Normal Madness," in *Dialogues in Limbo* (New York: Scribner's Sons, 1926), p. 56.

9. E. M. Forster, "The Challenge of Our Time," *Two Cheers for Democracy* (London: Edward Arnold and Co., 1951), p. 70.

10. Orlans, p. 76.

11. *RDC* (March 31, 1953), p. 342.

12. *Ibid.*

13. *RDC* (March 31, 1952), p. 341.

14. *RDC* (March 31, 1953), p. 341; *ibid.* (March 31, 1954), pp. 375–377.

15. H. Rankin, *New Towns For Old*, London, The Bureau of Current Affairs, Bulletin No. 75, 5th March 1949, p. 8. See also Peterlee Development Corporation, "Social Survey in Easington Rural District," (mimeographed; July 1948); *Further Tabulation* (1949); "History of Housing in Easington Rural District" (mimeographed; April 1950).

16. *RDC* (March 31, 1949), pp. 111–112.

17. *Ibid.*, pp. 112–113.

18. *Ibid.*, p. 11.

19. Report of the Architect Planner, "Analysis of Planning Problems, Peterlee" (mimeographed; January 16, 1950).

20. *RDC* (March 31, 1949), p. 111.

21. Report of the Architect Planner.

22. *RDC* (March 31, 1950), pp. 157–158, 160; *ibid.* (March 31, 1951), pp. 225–226. See also Report of the Architect Planner.

23. *RDC* (March 31, 1949), pp. 115–116.

24. *Ibid.* (March 31, 1951), pp. 227–228.

25. *Ibid.* (March 31, 1952), p. 307.

26. *Ibid.*, pp. 307–308.

27. *Ibid.*

28. *Ibid.*, p. 310.

29. *RDC* (March 31, 1953), p. 317.

30. *Manchester Guardian*, September 22, 1951, p. 7.

31. *Ibid.*; see also *RDC* (March 31, 1951), p. 229.

32. *Ibid.* (March 31, 1953), p. 319.

33. S. Pollock, "Modernising the Mines," *The Listener*, vol. L, no. 1273 (July 23, 1953), pp. 125–126.

34. "Report of the County Planning Officer on Future Development in Easington Rural District" (mimeographed; Durham, April 21, 1952).

35. Rankin, p. 17.

36. *RDC* (March 31, 1952), pp. 314–315.

37. Two thoughtful unpublished papers on this subject were prepared by M. H. Verrender, formerly Research and Social Development Officer at Peterlee. They are titled "Factors in the Social Development of Peterlee" and "The Occupational Middle Class and Peterlee."

38. *RDC* (March 31, 1953), p. 317; *ibid.* (March 31, 1954), p. 344.

39. Brigadier W. G. D. Knapton, "Basildon's Special Problems," *Town and Country Planning*, vol. XXI, no. 114 (October 1953), p. 511.

40. *RDC* (March 31, 1951), pp. 44–45; *ibid.* (March 31, 1952), pp. 54–55; *ibid.* (March 31, 1953), p. 53.

41. *Ibid.* (March 31, 1952), pp. 47–50; and Knapton, pp. 511–512.

42. *Ibid.*

43. *RDC* (March 31, 1951), p. 43; *ibid.* (March 31, 1953), pp. 50–51.

44. *Ibid.* (March 31, 1952), p. 57.

45. *Ibid.*, pp. 47–48; *ibid.* (March 31, 1953), p. 50.

46. *RDC* (March 31, 1953), p. 52. See also *ibid.* (March 31, 1954), pp. 46, 51.

47. *Ibid.*, p. 54.

48. *RDC* (March 31, 1953), p. 234. See also "Harlow New Town," *The Architectural Times* (no date or place; reprints available from the Harlow Development Corporation); F. Gibberd, *Harlow New Town — Master Plan* (Harlow Development Corporation, 1947; reprinted 1952).

49. *RDC* (March 31, 1952), pp. 240–241. For a brief review of public works problems in new towns, see J. W. Henderson, "A Public Works Review," *Town and Country Planning*, vol. XXI, no. 105 (January 1953), pp. 33–37.

50. Orlans, Appendix A, p. 293.

51. *Ibid.*, p. 296.

52. *Ibid.* The ministry now expects the scheme to cost £5 or £6 million. Cf. *First, Second and Third Reports From the Committee of Public Accounts* (1951–1952), p. 236.

53. *Ibid.*, pp. 297–299.

54. *Ibid.* See also *RDC* (March 31, 1951), p. 301; *ibid.* (March 31, 1952, p. 341; also *First, Second and Third Reports From the Committee of Public Accounts* (1951–1952), p. 236.

55. *RDC* (March 31, 1953), p. 243.

56. *Ibid.*

57. *Ibid.*, p. 231.

58. *Ibid.*, p. 239.

59. *Ibid.*, p. 235.

60. *Ibid.*, p. 243; *RDC* (March 31, 1954), pp. 259–260.

61. Osborn, *New Towns After the War*, pp. 7–8.

62. Ministry of Local Government and Planning, *Town and Country Planning 1943–1951*, p. 127.

63. Sir Theodore Chambers, the Chairman of Second Garden City Limited (Welwyn), dubbed the decision "an injustice of a high order." For a detailed discussion of these issues, see Purdom, *The Building of Satellite Towns*, pp. 347–360.

64. "The estate of Welwyn Garden City Ltd. was acquired by the New Town Corporation in 1948–9. Its successor company, Howardsgate Trust Ltd., continued to hold certain leasehold properties and a number of businesses including Welwyn Stores. The claim for £770,000 under the Town and Country Planning Acts, 1947 and 1954 is expected to be paid shortly . . . The Trust's . . . interests (were) . . . sold to a financial and investment group. The sum of £1,700,000 is to be distributed to the shareholders. Added to the £663,000 distributed on the liquidation of Welwyn Garden City Ltd., the total cash they

will have received is £2,363,000. The total original investments were £1,017,121. . .

"By the working out of events, some holders now get back 88s. for each 20s. invested. Even the unlucky ordinary shareholder will retrieve 8s.6d. for each £1 share reduced to 2s. in 1934. It is a romance, an adventure story or a tragi-comedy, according to the way you look at it" ("Values in a New Town," *Town and Country Planning*, vol. XXIII, no. 129, January 1955, pp. 35–36). See also Purdom, *The Building of Satellite Towns*, pp. 355–360.

65. *First, Second, Third and Fourth Reports From the Committee of Public Accounts* (1950–1951), pp. 503–504.

66. *Ibid.*

67. *Ibid.*; note Appendix 14, which discusses the acquisition of land and buildings by Welwyn Garden City Development Corporation (pp. 627–628).

68. *Ibid.*, pp. 504–507; and *RDC* (March 31, 1954), pp. 431–432.

69. *Ibid.* (March 31, 1953).

70. *Ibid.*, p. 424.

71. *Ibid.*; *RDC* (March 31, 1954), pp. 468–471.

72. *Town and Country Planning 1943–1951*, p. 126.

73. Hart, pp. 62–63.

74. *Ibid.*

75. *Ibid.*, p. 61.

76. *RDC* (March 31, 1953), p. 274; *ibid.* (March 31, 1954), pp. 299, 303.

77. *Ibid.*, p. 283.

78. *RDC* (March 31, 1951), pp. 63, 68; *ibid.* (March 31, 1954), p. 97.

79. *Ibid.* (March 31, 1953), p. 88.

80. *Ibid.*, p. 78.

81. *Town and Country Planning 1943–1951*, p. 126.

82. *RDC* (March 31, 1953), p. 141.

83. "New Towns in 1954," *Town and Country Planning*, vol. XXIII, no. 129 (January 1955), p. 8.

84. For further discussion of these problems, see A. C. Hobson, "The Great Industrial Belt," *Economic Journal*, vol. 61 (September 1951), pp. 562–576; J. Sykes, "The Great Industrial Belt," *ibid.*, vol. 62 (June 1952), pp. 431–436; Hobson, "A Rejoinder," *ibid.*, pp. 436–440.

85. R. Grieve, "The Clyde Valley — A Review," *Report of Proceedings, Town and Country Planning Summer School, St. Andrews University*, 1954, p. 22.

86. See Tables I–III.

87. *Reports of the East Kilbride and Glenrothes Development Corporations for the year ended 31st March, 1950–1953* (henceforth referred to as *RDC Scotland*; Edinburgh: HMSO).

88. *Ibid.* For a good brief discussion of Scotland's housing, subsidies, and rents, see "Housing in Scotland," *Town and Country Planning*, vol. XXIII, no. 125 (September 1954), pp. 448–450. See also *RDC Scotland* (March 31, 1953), pp. 18–19.

89. *Ibid.*

90. *Ibid.*, p. 10. See also *RDC Scotland* (March 31, 1954), pp. 20, 22, 56–57.

91. *RDC Scotland* (March 31, 1952), p. 13.

92. Self, *The Planning of Industrial Location*, pp. 43–44.

93. *RDC Scotland* (March 31, 1953), pp. 201–221.

94. Grieve, "The Clyde Valley," *Town and Country Planning*, vol. XXII, no. 125 (September 1954), p. 459. With the appointment of a new chief architect for Glasgow in 1952, the Glasgow development possibilities are being reevaluated as well as the possibility of more new towns and expanded towns, aided by the resources of Glasgow's building organization. Cf. E. B. Mitchell, "Scotland and the New Towns," *Town and Country Planning*, vol. XXI, no. 105 (January 1953); Osborn, "Skyscraper Housing – Glasgow's Redevelopment Dilemma," *ibid.*, vol. XXII, no. 122 (June 1954), pp. 277–280; *Town and Country Planning*, vol. XXIII, no. 134 (June 1955), p. 280; *ibid.*, vol. XXIII, no. 135 (July 1955), pp. 344–345.

95. Grieve, *Town and Country Planning*, p. 459.

96. Cf. Chap. 9, p. 156, and Chap. 9, n. 37.

97. Glenrothes Development Corporation, *Glenrothes* (pamphlet; 1952), p. 1.

98. See Tables I–III.

99. *RDC Scotland* (March 31, 1953), p. 54. See also *ibid.* (March 31, 1954), pp. 47–48.

100. This point was called to my attention by responsible administrative officials.

101. *RDC Scotland* (March 31, 1953), pp. 50–51.

102. *Ibid.* (March 31, 1951), p. 29.

103. *Ibid.* See also *ibid.* (March 31, 1954), pp. 45–46.

104. Minoprio, Spenceley, and Macfarlane, *A Master Plan for Cwmbran New Town* (London: The Cwmbran Corporation, March 1951), p. 7.

105. *Ibid.*, p. 8.

106. *RDC* (March 31, 1953), p. 204. A general reduction of 10 per cent on all house rents was authorized in August 1953 (*RDC*, March 31, 1954, p. 217).

107. *Town and Country Planning 1943–1951*, p. 127; *RDC* (March 31, 1948), pp. 7–8.

108. This point was called to my attention in discussion with responsible officials. It has actually been suggested that "the new town should be increased in size to accommodate a population of 23,000" considering the employment capacity of the trading estate (*RDC*, March 31, 1950), p. 7.

109. *Ibid.* Mr. Dalton was the Chancellor of the Exchequer and later the Minister of Town and Country Planning in the Labour government under Clement Attlee.

110. *RDC* (March 31, 1953), p. 19.

111. See Tables I–III.

112. *RDC* (March 31, 1953), p. 19.

113. Holford and Wright, *Corby New Town: A Report to Accompany the Master Plan of the Corby Development Corporation* (December 1952), p. 5.

114. *Ibid.*

115. *Ibid.*, p. 6.

116. *Ibid.*, p. 7.

117. *Ibid.*, p. 38.

118. *Ibid.* This point was made on p. 14 in the draft version of this report, published in November 1951. See also *RDC* (March 31, 1952), p. 126.

119. Holford and Wright. The quotation is from the draft version of the report on pp. 12–15.

120. *Ibid.* The quotation is from the draft master plan, p. ii.

121. RDC (March 31, 1953), pp. 113–118; *ibid.* (March 31, 1952), pp. 125–130.

122. K. H. Turner, "Corby's Major Problem," *Town and Country Planning,* vol. XXII, no. 117 (January 1954), p. 58.

123. *Ibid.*, pp. 58–59.

124. Holford and Wright, p. 38. This proposal, however, is not without difficulties. For instance, "The bus company is not prepared to put on extra services until it is sure they will pay since more than one route from Corby is now running at a loss. The employees, on the other hand, are not prepared to take jobs in places which they cannot reach within thirty or forty minutes. In addition, a certain portion of married women are ready to take jobs in Corby but are very unwilling to travel to other towns" (*Town and Country Planning*, vol. XXI, no. 111, July 1953, p. 331).

125. Holford and Wright, p. 12 of the draft version of the report.

CHAPTER **8**

The Background of the Town Development Act

1. For a review of some of the evidence indicating the interest of the Labour government in the town expansion policy, see Block, pp. 46–47; *Hansard*, vol. 496, no. 41, February 25, 1952, p. 743. During the second reading, Dalton observed "I am the father of this bill. The right hon. Gentleman discovered a likely infant at some stage of development and he completed the clothing of it. I am not committed to all the details of the clothing as embodied in this Bill . . . but I am committed to the principle that this is a sound infant whose life should be encouraged and preserved" (*ibid.*).

2. The Conservatives proposed to build 300,000 dwelling units a year, despite materials and labor shortages, in contrast to the Labour Party's objective of 200,000.

3. *Hansard*, Standing Committee C, March 18, 1952, column 42.

4. Block, p. 22, cites the following overspill population within the next twenty years as estimated by development plans:

AREA	OVERSPILL POPULATION
West Midlands "Conurbation"	276,000
The County of London	316,000
The County of Middlesex	30,000

The County Boroughs of Cheshire	33,200
The County Boroughs of Lancashire	333,000
The County Boroughs of Staffordshire	137,000

5. Block, p. 27. See also London County Council, *Postwar Housing: A Survey of the Postwar Housing Work of the L.C.C. 1945–49* (London, 1949).

6. Stamp, *Town and Country Planning*, vol. XXI, no. 108 (April 1953), p. 160.

7. White, *Community or Chaos*. See chap. 2, note 23.

8. *Report of Hertfordshire County Council Education Committee*, August 25, 1951, cited in Block, pp. 27–28.

9. *Ibid.*

10. *Hansard*, vol. 496, no. 41, February 25, 1952, columns 725–767.

11. *Hansard*, March 26, 1952, column 180.

12. G. Sutton Brown, *A Preliminary Plan for Lancashire* (Lancashire County Council, 1951), p. 37. Cf. *Evidence of County Planning Officer, Lancashire, on Liverpool Boundary Extension Bill* (1951), pp. 2–7; Brown, "Population Movement From South Lancashire in Theory and Practice," *Twenty-Sxith Annual Country Meeting, Town Planning Institute* (May 16, 1952); "Problems in County Planning," *Manchester Statistical Society* (read March 8, 1950), p. 16.

13. F. J. McCulloch, "The Lancashire Development Plan," *National Housing and Town Planning Council* (available in Lancashire County Planning Office — no date); Brown, "Population Movement From South Lancashire in Theory and Practice," pp. 19–20. Since the passage of the Town Development Act, the county council has asked Salford to pay the £8 18s. rate subsidy for ten years on each house built at Ainsley. This request was in conformity with the proposed procedure under the new legislation. Salford has acceded to this under protest, claiming that the minister should pay part of this subsidy. The county has also asked the minister to defray a substantial part of the £300,000 trunk drainage system required for the expansion of Worsley.

14. Brown, "Population Movement From South Lancashire in Theory and Practice," pp. 20–21.

15. McCulloch, *National Housing and Town Planning Council*, p. 6. See also Lancashire County Council, Planning and Development Committee, *Report on the Industrial and Employment Position in Lancashire* (June 27, 1952).

16. Brown, "Population Movement From South Lancashire in Theory and Practice," pp. 25–28.

17. *Ibid.*, p. 29.

18. The services that involved significant financial outlay under the Worsley scheme were education, health, police, and library for the county; and sewerage, parks, recreation, and public hall for the district council.

19. Wythenshawe, a planned satellite of Manchester, was designed on the neighborhood principle to provide 20,000 local authority houses and 5,000 privately built houses, serving an estimated population of 100,000 persons. (The Manchester Plan has reduced the ultimate population to 80,000.) Three industrial areas are planned nearby. Wythenshawe was begun in 1927 and is

practically completed. Bowlee in Middleton is scheduled as Manchester's next large development. Plans also were made for a new town in Mobberly, but an adverse local decision against annexation forestalled such action, at least temporarily. See *Town and Country Planning 1943–1951*, p. 64; "Manchester's Dispersal Schemes," *Town and Country Planning*, vol. XXIII, no. 118 (February 1954), pp. 91–94; R. Nicholas, *City of Manchester Plan* (London: Jarrow & Sons, 1945); Sir Ernest and Lady Simon, "Wythenshawe," chap. vi in *The Rebuilding of Manchester*, edited by D. Simon and J. Innan (London: Longmans Green and Co., 1935). Speke was started by Liverpool in 1936 with a planned population of approximately 22,000 persons. It was to be a satellite town designed to increase and diversify job opportunities for Liverpool's residents. Liverpool's industries were too dependent on fluctuating and export activities; and Liverpudlians had suffered severely from unemployment. To date, however, the industries on Speke's trading estate have come principally from Liverpool, though some outside activities were attracted. An even larger industrial and residential development has been planned at Kirkby, providing for 47,000 persons in residential areas designed along neighborhood lines. Cf. Mercer, *The Town Planning Review*, vol. XXIV, no. 3 (October 1953), pp. 215–238; *Evidence of County Planning Officer, Lancashire, on Liverpool Boundary Extension Bill* (1951), pp. 11–12.

20. Brown, "Population Movement from South Lancashire in Theory and Practice," p. 18.

21. *Ibid*. Another town was proposed for Lancashire's overspill in Skelmersdale, but if it materializes it is more likely to proceed under the Town Development Act. The proposal was opposed by Liverpool's Postwar Redevelopment Committee, which preferred building closer to Liverpool.

22. Brown, *A Preliminary Plan for Lancashire*, pp. 5–8, chap. iv.

23. *Ibid.*, pp. 16–17.

24. Brown, "Population Movement from South Lancashire in Theory and Practice," p. 18. For a brief description of some of the subsequent discouraging developments in Lancashire since the passage of the Town Development Act, see D. Senior, "The Town Development Act in Lancashire and Cheshire," *Town and Country Planning*, vol. XXIII, no. 124 (August 1954), pp. 424–428.

25. Overspill is expected in Staffordshire from within and outside the county (mainly Birmingham). About 171,000 persons have to be accommodated. It was arranged for the county council "to pay about a half (six elevenths) of the statutory rate fund contribution for each overspill house provided in an expanded town" plus a contingent commitment accepted by the county "so that no receiving authority shall incur a rate burden of more than 1/- in pound." Like Lancashire, technical assistance is also available from the county (cited in Block, pp. 52–53). See also D. W. Riley, "Overspill Plans in Staffordshire," *Town and Country Planning*, vol. XXIII, no. 126 (October 1954), pp. 537–538.

26. *Town Development Act*, 1952, 15 & 16 Geo. 6 and 1 Eliz. 2, Ch. 54.

27. Ministry of Housing and Local Government, *Memorandum on the Town Development Act* (London: HMSO, 1952), p. 3. The congested cities may be either a county borough, the administrative county of London, a county district in an area of continuous urban development adjacent to the administrative

county of London, a similar area adjacent to another big center of population, or a county district outside the county in which the development is to be carried out. The new powers for land acquisition, development, and contributions for costs of development apply generally to town development for the relief of congestion. But financial assistance from the Exchequer is provided only if the program is on a substantial scale in relation to the size and resources of the receiving district and if the program relieves congestion or overpopulation, as defined above. Cf. A. E. Telling, "The Act in Brief," *Town and Country Planning*, vol. XXIII, no. 124 (August 1954), pp. 379–380.

28. *Ibid.*, pp. 4–10.

29. Ministry of Housing and Local Government, *Movement of Population to New and Expanded Towns*, Circular No. 29 (May 6, 1953), p. 4. For brief discussions of details of these town expansion schemes, see J. F. Smithee, "Bletchley: As Pioneer," *Town and Country Planning*, vol. XXIII, no. 124 (August 1954), pp. 412–414; W. C. Blake, "Needs of a Country Town," *ibid.*, pp. 415–417; W. Ellis Clarke, "Thetford's Expansion: Finance," *ibid.*, pp. 418–419; N. G. Liddiad, "The Expansion of Swindon," *ibid.*, pp. 420–422; Senior, *ibid.*, pp. 424–428.

30. W. A. Wood, "What the Town Development Act Can Do For Country Towns," *Summary of Address, Country Towns Conference, Leamington Spa, February 26–27, 1953* (London: Country Towns Committee, Town and Country Planning Association), p. 3. "No help is given for county services, nor for expenditure falling on the district councils in improving roads leading to the site of town development or providing playing fields, community centres and other incidentals" (*ibid.*).

31. *Ibid.*

32. W. A. Wood, p. 2.

33. *Memorandum on the Town Development Act*, pp. 4–8.

34. W. A. Wood, p. 1.

35. In the *Memorandum on the Town Development Act*, p. 4, it is reiterated that "The Minister regards adequate provision for industry . . . as an essential part of a sound development scheme," and also that "The Minister will arrange for consultation as appropriate with the Board of Trade and for putting the development authority in touch with the Board. There are no powers to direct industry to particular areas, but the Board of Trade will do their best to steer suitable industries from exporting areas to the expanded towns consistently with their general obligations to unemployment areas. Developing authorities can also help themselves by coordinating their efforts with action taken by the local planning authorities of the exporting areas to move non-conforming industry."

CHAPTER **9**

The Town Development Act: Problems and Implications

1. The Labour Party's opposition did criticize the bill quite carefully during the second-reading and committee stages, and they made it somewhat more

satisfactory from their point of view. They always favored the legislation in principle, and in fact violently attacked a Conservative "backbencher's" proposal that the legislation should be temporary, i.e., become inoperative after five years.

2. The cost of Lancashire's assistance to Worsley, based on 1950 prices and grants, excluding industrial development, has been estimated as follows:

County Council Services	£	£
Education	498,452	
Health	169,300	
Police	65,000	
Library	20,000	752,752
District Council Services		
Sewerage	250,000	
Parks, Recreation	23,800	
Public Hall	90,000	363,800
Shops, Houses, etc., excluding roads and services		5,000,000
Roads, Sewers, Land		756,742
		6,873,294

On an annual basis these outlays are:

1. County Council Services Net Annual expend, minus specific grants	58,716	
Minus Proportion of Equalization Grant	17,514	
County Rate Burden		41,202
Estimated Rate Income at '50/'51 rate		33,892
DEFICIENCY PER ANNUM		7,310
2. District Council Services (Sewerage and sewage disposal, public hall, refuse collection, lighting, highways, parks, etc.)	45,126	
Minus Capitation Grants	9,395	
To be borne by local rates		35,731
Est. Local Rate Income		21,457
DEFICIENCY		14,274
3. Housing Rate Fund Contributions (at time of calculations) @ £5 10s.0d. per annum met by County Council on 4,000 houses		22,000

SUMMARY

		Per House		
	Deficiency	£	s.	d.
County Council Services	7,310	1	16	7
District Council Services	14,274	3	11	5
Housing Rate Fund Contribution	22,000	5	10	0
	43,584	10	18	0

Source: G. Sutton Brown, "Population Movement from South Lancashire in Theory and Practice," *Twenty-sixth Annual Country Meeting, Town Planning Institute* (May 16, 1952).

3. W. L. Abernethy, "TDA: The Financial Effects," *Town and Country Planning*, vol. XXII, no. 124 (August 1954), pp. 399–402. See also *ibid.*, vol. XXIII, no. 135, p. 329.

4. *Hansard*, vol. 496, no. 41, February 25, 1952, col. 762.

5. *Hansard*, Standing Committee C, March 18, 1952, col. 41.

6. *Hansard*, Standing Committee C, March 18, 1952, col. 766. See also *Town and Country Planning*, vol. XXIII, no. 124 (August 1954), pp. 376–378. Note that Reginald Stamp, Chairman of the LCC Housing Committee, is now emphasizing that under this legislation the LCC will proceed with development subject to the following conditions: that discussions disclose a prima-facie case for development; that good agricultural land should generally be avoided; that the amount and rate of expansion should be in accordance with local desires; that jobs should be available for families moving from London; that segregation of newcomers should be avoided; that the LCC will provide the local subsidy for every family exported from London; that the LCC will act as an agent for expanding a local community, provide the money for the whole development, do the work and assume the costs up to the point that the houses earn revenue; and that joint consultative and advisory committees representing the two authorities should be established during the period of expansion (Stamp, "Planned Expansion of Country Towns," *Town and Country Planning*, vol. XXII, no. 124, August 1954, pp. 383–384).

7. W. A. Wood, *Summary of Address, Country Towns Conference*, p. 4.

8. T. B. Oxenbury, "Country Towns Conference," *Town and Country Planning*, vol. XXI, no. 108 (April 1953), p. 166.

9. Stamp, *Town and Country Planning*, vol. XXII, no. 124 (August 1954), p. 384.

10. "Town Expansion," *The Manchester Guardian Weekly*, vol. 71, no. 8, August 19, 1954, p. 9. See also *The Economist*, August 19, 1953, cited in *News Sheet of the International Federation For Housing and Town Planning*, no. XXXI (February 1954), p. 30; "Dispersal: A New Phase," *Town and Country Planning*, vol. XXI, no. 106 (February 1953), pp. 63–64.

11. Executive of the Town and Country Planning Association, "Dispersal: A Call For Action," *Town and Country Planning*, vol. XXIII, no. 132 (April 1955), p. 167.

12. *Hansard*, vol. 496, no. 41, February 25, 1952, col. 737.

13. *Movement of Population to New and Expanded Towns*, p. 3.

14. Stamp, *Town and Country Planning*, vol. XXI, no. 108 (April 1953), p. 161.

15. *Ibid.*, pp. 162–163.

16. *Ibid.*

17. *The Economist*, December 19, 1953. See also P. Abercrombie, "Old Towns for New," *Town and Country Planning*, vol. XXI, no. 110 (June 1953), pp. 262–264; Stamp, "A Planner Outplanned," *ibid.*, vol. XXI, no. 111 (July 1953), pp. 303–305.

18. Stamp, *Town and Country Planning*, vol. XXI, no. 108, p. 161. Local authorities must pay compensation under Section 27 of the Town and Country Planning Act if they "order the discontinuance of any use of the land and

the removals of any buildings" which render the property "incapable of reasonably beneficial use." For a more detailed discussion in relation to a specific area, see Munby, *Industry and Planning in Stepney*, pp. 347–348 et seq.

19. Self, "Industrial Development From Cities," *Town and Country Planning*, vol. XXIII, no. 124 (August 1954), p. 398. See also *The Manchester Guardian Weekly*, vol. 71, no. 8, August 19, 1954, p. 9, for further evidence of the slow progress during the first two years; and Chap. 6, note 45.

20. A. Beacham, "Industry in Country Towns," *Country Towns Conference* (mimeographed), p. 4.

21. Self, *The Planning of Industrial Location*, p. 29. See also *First, Second, Third and Fourth Reports From The Committee of Public Accounts* (1950–1951), Appendix 16 "Distribution of New Industries Between Development Areas and New Towns," pp. 630–631.

22. Self, *The Planning of Industrial Location*, p. 29.

23. Self, "Is the Barlow Policy Failing," *Town and Country Planning*, vol. XXIII, no. 138 (October 1955), p. 457. New factory space authorized for the London region as a per cent of the national total has sharply increased in 1953 and 1954.

24. C. Clark, *The Conditions of Economic Progress* (London: Macmillan and Company, Limited, 1951, second edition), chap. 9. G. D. H. Cole and B. Postgate, *The British People 1746–1946* (New York: A. A. Knopf, 1947), pp. 526–527. Objections have already been raised to schemes in London involving more office space for the City, for South Bank and for Berkeley Square (see Chap. 5, note 23). A similar trend on a vaster scale has occurred and is in fact still being encouraged by some groups in New York City. Mr. Zeckendorff indicated in a talk before the American Society of Civil Engineers that New York City, by substituting office for industrial space, had "recaptured at $5 a square foot what it had lost at 50 cents a square foot." Since 1947, he announced, more office buildings were completed or started in New York City than existed in all of Chicago (*The New York Times*, Oct. 27, 1955, p. 26).

25. Stamp, *Town and Country Planning*, vol. XXI, no. 108 (April 1953), p. 162.

26. *Report of the London Planning Administration Committee*, pp. 13, 16–17.

27. *Report of the London Planning Administration Committee*, pp. 3, 9. A similar opinion is voiced by L. B. Keeble about Manchester, in "The New Act and Manchester," *Town and Country Planning*, vol. XXI, no. 106 (February 1953), pp. 72–74; and by D. N. Chester, *Central and Local Government* (London: Macmillan & Co., 1951), p. 332. See also Self, "How To Make Regional Planning Effective," *Town and Country Planning*, vol. XX, no. 27 (May 1952). Self claims that "Whitehall regionalism is the least democratic of all institutions, since it is well beyond the attention of Parliament yet it has no responsibility whatever to the local electorate. For this reason alone it is bound to be ineffective if it attempts more than the functions of liaison." He also points out that the Town and Country Planning Act reduced the number of planning authorities from 136 to 10, but that they "have refused to form themselves into an advisory committee. . . There is a London regional plan without the machinery to enforce it — a situation which is paralleled in other

regions" (p. 213). Self has proposed local authority representation on regional panels, a joint board, an advisory committee and the formation of a regional housing association (*Town and Country Planning*, vol. XX, no. 27, May 1952, p. 214). See also Appendix B, Tables IV and V; Self, *The Planning of Industrial Location*, pp. 36–37; and Munby, *Industry and Planning in Stepney*, pp. 351–353.

28. *Ibid.* See also Fogarty, *Plan Your Own Industries* (Oxford: Basil Blackwell, 1947), chaps. i, ii, vi, xii; Self, *Town and Country Planning*, vol. XX, no. 27 (May 1952), p. 214.

29. *Movement of Population to New and Expanded Towns*, p. 2.

30. *Ibid.*

31. The exceptions applied to persons in requisitioned premises or on housing lists of exporting authorities "who could move directly to a New Town without changing their job, e.g., people who already work in or near the New Town area, self employed people, retired people and so forth" (*ibid.*, p. 3).

32. *Ibid.*

33. *Ibid.*, Appendix I. Thus far these efforts have had limited success. While some families on housing lists have been helped, the procedures are somewhat cumbersome and expensive both for the employee and employer. Aside from the usual problem of red tape, housing is not assigned to the employee until he has been with the firm for a sufficiently long period to be sure that he will stay employed. However justifiable this may be, increased expenses, uncertainty, and irritation are entailed. This is one of the reasons why many eligible workers have changed their minds when they received offers of employment and why most of those eligible to move are not expected to do so.

Another serious difficulty arises because the demand is only for certain kinds of workers. At present, for instance, the need is for employment in light engineering, rather than in transport, although transport workers constitute the largest number of workers now eligible for housing on the LCC's lists. Perfect synchronization, however, could hardly have been expected, and it would be difficult to substitute a fairer system. See Allerton, *Town and Country Planning*, vol. XXII, no. 124 (August 1954), pp. 405–407.

34. *Ibid.*, pp. 3–4. An exception, previously noted, applies to housing provided for key workers not nominated by the exporting authorities because they were not in need of a house.

35. As Circular 29 puts it, "It appears to the Minister only fair that the same arrangement should apply where nominees of local authorities obtain houses in new towns. Otherwise authorities whose nominees find houses mainly in new towns will have an advantage over those whose nominees find them mainly in expanded towns" (*Movement of Population to New and Expanded Towns*, p. 4).

36. Mr. Macmillan observed, in a phrase now widely quoted that "if towns are not allowed to swell, they must be encouraged to hop" (*Hansard*, vol. 496, no. 41, February 25, 1952, col. 725). The new minister, Mr. Duncan Sandys, has expressed the same views even more forcefully. He said it was necessary

to define the limits of towns and to make it "damned difficult" to go past these limits (*Town and Country Planning*, vol. XXIII, no. 134, June 1955, p. 276).

37. It may be technically possible for a local authority to build a new town under the Town Development Act of 1952. But to date such an approach has not been encouraged in England and Wales. In Scotland, however, one of the issues between Glasgow and the Secretary of State for Scotland is whether New Cumbernauld, the additional new town for Glasgow, should be built by a development corporation or by Glasgow. In this situation Glasgow has argued in favor of a development corporation. The chief advantage would be the subsidy for housing that would be provided by the Secretary of State. There is no town development act for Scotland. But the Secretary of State has suggested that if a second new town is built to serve Glasgow's overflow population, Glasgow should provide the normal local housing subsidy.

38. Hart, *Report of Proceedings, Town and Country Planning Summer School, Bangor, 1952*, p. 66.

39. For a provocative world outlook, see E. A. A. Rowse, "World Economic Trends in Urban Development," *Report of Proceedings, Town and Country Planning Summer School, Bangor, 1952*, pp. 79–94. See also "Dispersal: A Call for Action," Statement By the Executive of the Town and Country Planning Association, *Town and Country Planning*, vol. XXIII, no. 132 (April 1955), pp. 167–169.

CHAPTER 10

Reflections on Newtopia

1. Cf. Appendix A: The Achilles Heel of British Town Planning.

2. This view has some unfortunate aspects. Hart has protested that "There are many theories in search of a laboratory in which to be tested: for the sake of the people who will inhabit them we must protect the new towns from being regarded as the natural place for this to be done" (p. 71).

3. Cf. Appendix A.

4. Metropolitan decentralization may refer to (a) the deconcentration of activities or population from the central city to peripheral areas of the same region; (b) the relative decline in the concentration of activities or population in the central city compared to peripheral areas of the same region; (c) an absolute or relative shift from older more concentrated metropolitan regions to other less developed regions. The British new towns policy was originally intended to decongest London and to reduce its excess or overspill population. There was also some hope of arresting the movement of population from other regions to London and the home counties. This policy presupposed at least redistribution of population from the central areas to the periphery, and possibly some transfer of population and activities to other regions of Britain.

5. For some suggestive theoretical observations, see A. Lösch, *The Economics of Location* (New Haven: Yale University Press, 1954), pp. 75–84, 345–359; J. Isaac, *Economics of Migration* (London: Kegan Paul, Trench, Trubner and Co., Limited), pp. 70–78. See also W. Isard, "Some Empirical Results and Problems of Regional Input-Output Analyses" in W. Leontief and

others, *Studies In the Structure of the American Economy* (New York: Oxford University Press, 1953), chap. v. For a simpler exposition with further references, see Isard and R. A. Kavesh, "Economic Structural Interrelations of Metropolitan Regions," *The American Journal of Sociology*, vol. LX, no. 2 (September 1954), pp. 152–162.

6. W. H. Ludlow, "Urban Densities and Their Costs" in *Urban Development: Problems and Practices*, edited by Coleman Woodbury (Chicago: University of Chicago Press, 1953), pp. 101–214.

7. Accessibility is intended to be defined broadly in this context. It is not physical access. If possible, it should include the physical characteristics of the site, the kind of access, and its propinquity to various physical and nonphysical features of the environment required by households and firms. If the concept of accessibility is to serve as an adequate tool, distinctions should be made between time, cost, and physical and social distance. Indeed, accessibility requirements may vary in any one or more of these ways for technical needs such as adequate space for port facilities; for functional linkages to employment areas, markets, ancillary activities, the labor force, suppliers of materials or services; and for social influences such as prestige or preference patterns. Stated otherwise, the spatial distribution of activities may be interpreted as the interaction of accessibility requirements and other forces, such as the supply and accessibility characteristics of existing structures, technological possibilities, geography, and the like. If this view seems to deserve exploration, then one of the highest-priority areas of research is to devise an adequate technique for identifying, classifying, and weighting these accessibility requirements and characteristics.

A more detailed outline of this approach may be found in the writer's unpublished report entitled "Suggestions for Research on the Spatial Distribution of Activities in Metropolitan Regions," submitted to the Bureau of Business and Economic Research Real Estate Research Program, University of California, Berkeley, 1952.

8. Bowley, *Housing and the State: 1919–1944.*

9. H. T. Hough, "The Liverpool Corporate Estate," *The Town Planning Review*, vol. XXI, no. 3 (October 1950), pp. 246–250.

10. J. M. Richards, *The Castles on the Ground*, p. 76.

11. *Ibid.*, p. 15.

12. *Ibid.*, p. 76.

13. Holford, for example, has warned that "in a world of official departments, councils and committees, the risk is that design is controlled by accountants, administrative decisions are left to architects and social doctrines are preached by everyone except sociologists" (*Report of Proceedings, Town and Country Planning Summer School, University of Bristol, 1953*, p. 12). On the other hand, J. M. Richards has counselled that "To inculcate restraint and refinement — which are admirable qualities to set off a life lived at full stretch in the bustle of the busy world — in the depth of the suburban jungle is only to put a brake on the creative instinct and therefore on the proper exercise of some of its most valuable functions . . . By careful planning and controlled good taste they have eliminated the very qualities of romance and rhetoric on

which the suburban style flourishes . . . The suburban style is not a type of architecture but the setting of suburban life itself, and its taste is but the local colour the inhabitants gather round themselves in accordance with their peculiar instincts and aspirations. If you take this colour away by teaching them that there are other tastes they ought to prefer, or by means of any other improvements imposed from without you take away suburbia itself" (*The Castles on the Ground*, pp. 58–59).

14. F. C. J. Iklè, "The Social Versus the Physical Effects from Nuclear Bombing," *The Scientific Monthly*, vol. LXXVIII, no. 3 (March 1954), pp. 186–187.

15. Cf. Los Alamos Scientific Laboratory, *The Effects of Atomic Weapons*, (Washington: Government Printing Office, 1950); Associated Universities Inc., *Project East River*, Interim Report (New York, June 23, 1952); Iklè, "The Impact of War Upon the Spacing of Urban Population," Ph.D. Dissertation, Department of Sociology, University of Chicago, September 1950; "Project East River — The Strategy of Civil Defense," *Bulletin of the Atomic Scientists*, vol. IX, no. 7 (September 1953); W. L. C. Wheaton, C. Woodbury, L. S. Hamilton, M. J. Schussheim, *Reports on Metropolitan Dispersal for Project East River*, Parts I and II (Cambridge: Department of Regional Planning, Harvard University, 1952); B. Kelly, "The Necessity for Dispersion," *Proceedings of the Conference on Building in the Atomic Age*, June 16 and 17, 1952, sponsored by the Department of Civil and Sanitary Engineering, Massachusetts Institute of Technology; *The Need for Industrial Dispersal, Materials prepared for the Joint Committee on the Economic Report*, 82nd Congress, 1st Session (Washington, D. C.: Government Printing Office, 1951).

16. Kelly, p. 110.

17. *Ibid.*, p. 111. Professor Kelly emphasizes that the central government should furnish the lead, especially for those things "it builds or finances itself. If the danger is serious, public funds should not be expended in such a way as to increase it."

18. M. F. Millikan, "The Economist's View of the Role of Housing," *Housing and Economic Development* (Cambridge: School of Architecture and Planning, Massachusetts Institute of Technology), Mimeographed and Bound Report of a Conference Sponsored at the Massachusetts Institute of Technology by the A. F. Bemis Foundation on April 30 and May 22, 1953, edited by Burnham Kelly, pp. 22–23. Other papers presented at this conference may be of interest to the reader. See also R. Gardner-Medwin, "United Nations and Resettlement in the Far East," *The Town Planning Review*, vol. XXII, no. 4 (January 1952), pp. 288–298; O. H. Koenigsberger, *ibid.*, vol. XXIII, no. 2 (July 1952); L. Rodwin, "Measuring Housing Needs in Underdeveloped Areas," *Newssheet of the International Federation for Housing and Town Planning*, no. 34 (August 1954), pp. 8–11; *Survey of Problems of Low Cost Housing in Tropical Areas; A Preliminary Report with Special Reference to the Caribbean Area* (ST/SOA/Z), United Nations, Department of Social Affairs (New York: United Nations, 1950); *Low Cost Housing in South and Southeast Asia; Report of Mission of Experts on Tropical Housing* (ST/SOA/3/Rev. 1), United Nations Department of Social Affairs; *Workers Housing Problems in Asian Countries*, Inter-

national Labor Organization (Geneva: ILO, 1953); Colonial Office, *Housing in British African Territories,* Colonial No. 303 (London: HMSO, 1954).

19. Cf. Appendix A: The Achilles Heel of British Town Planning.

20. The Ministry of Housing and Local Government is now making a major effort to deal with the existing stock of housing. See for example the White Paper, *Housing: the Next Step,* Cmd. 8996 (London: HMSO, 1953). See also *Newssheet of the International Federation for Housing and Town Planning,* no. XXXI (February 1954), pp. 4–9, 31–32.

21. Source unidentified, cited in J. Schumpeter, "Keynes the Economist" in *The New Economics,* edited by Seymour Harris (London: Dennis Dobson, Limited, 1949), p. 100.

22. *Ibid.*

APPENDIX A

The Achilles Heel of British Town Planning

1. *The Report of the Committee on Qualifications of Planners* (hereinafter cited as the Schuster Report) gives the following description and definition of the present function of British town planning and the planning process: "The function is to create a well balanced synthesis of what might otherwise be a mere collection of separate policies and claims, to combine them into one consistent policy for the use and development of land within the area in question, to devise the means of translating this policy in the physical conditions of that area into a plan that is practical, economic and aesthetically pleasing, and to organize the carrying through to realization of the development for which the plan has made provision" (Cmd. 8059, London: Ministry of Town and Country Planning, HMSO, 1950, pp. 12–21). Similarly, Professor F. J. Adams has emphasized that "City and Regional planning deals with ways of guiding or controlling the use and development of land in such a way that the maximum social and economic benefits may accrue to the people of the community or region being planned through the improvement of the physical environment. . . The professional planner makes his contribution through the analysis of existing conditions and trends, the interpretation of long range needs and potentialities as a basis for programs of physical development, and the translation of abstract and technical considerations to specific designs and programs which can be understood by and exert an influence upon the people, in whom the power of decision rests. It follows that the planners' most important role is the part he plays in the interacting processes by which long range socio-economic needs and goals are determined and by which these goals are achieved through a program of physical development" (*Urban Planning Education in the United States,* Cincinnati: The Alfred Bettman Foundation, 1954, pp. 1–4).

2. *Ibid.*, p. 25.

3. This fact was reported to me by several important officials in the ministry.

4. When the author raised his eyebrows at the absence of social scientists on the staff, one of his informants remarked that the members of the council

really represented the social side of things. See also Munby, *Industry and Planning in Stepney*, p. 392.

5. There is impressive evidence of this in the Lancashire Plan. Cf. Brown, *A Preliminary Plan for Lancashire*. See also the thoughtful articles of McCulloch: "Physical Planning and Industry," *Town Planning Review*, vol. XX, no. 1 (April 1949); and "Research and Planning," vol. XXIII, no. 1 (April 1952).

6. At the time that this view was expressed, this obviously able officer was not yet a qualified member of the Town Planning Institute.

7. In fact, the more discerning planning leaders recognized this much earlier than the social scientists.

8. A few pioneers like Geddes were far in advance in their recognition of the role of the social survey.

9. The surveyors' training and examination have been in the following fields: land agency, urban estate management, valuation, building, quantities, mining, land survey. In 1952 a successful effort was made to introduce courses in economics. Cf. *Rules and Syllabus for the Professional Examination*, by the Royal Institution of Chartered Surveyors (May 1949), pp. 12–26 (May 1952), pp. 6–7.

10. Such views were expressed to the writer personally by several high-ranking officials.

11. There are some exceptions. One example is the daylighting control methods incorporated in the handbook *The Redevelopment of Central Areas* (London: HMSO, 1947).

12. Schuster Report, p. 81.

13. *Yearbook of the Town Planning Institute* (1949–1950), p. 38.

14. Fogarty, *Town and Country Planning*, p. vii. Examples of social science studies are Munby's appraisal of industrial decentralization in Stepney; P. Sargant Florence's investigations of Hertfordshire, the Black Country, and Worcester; Luttrell's studies of the cost of industrial movement; Bowley's and Jarmain's books on housing policy; R. Glass's investigations of housing estates and the neighborhood concept; Robson's administrative studies of London.

15. Schuster Report, pp. 70–73.

16. J. Hudnut, "What a Planner Has to Know", *Planning 1946: Proceedings of the Annual Meeting of the American Society of Planning Officials* (Chicago, 1946), pp. 157–163.

17. For example, the Schuster Committee emphasized that it "received from the Universities a strong preponderance of evidence to the effect that town and country planning does not itself offer a field of study suitable for a first degree course, and that the man who is to engage in it should undergo a basic educational discipline in one of the normal university faculties, and that this should be followed by a post-graduate university course in subjects related to planning" (Schuster Report, p. 39). Most planning courses in the United States are also graduate courses. Cf. Adams, chap. iii.

18. For example, he should understand that he exceeds his responsibility and trenches on the architects' domain if he attempts to design houses or the precise street pattern.

19. Some of these subjects, like the scientific ones, are ultimately far more than "tools."

20. Fogarty, *Town and Country Planning*, pp. 194–195. See also PEP, *Land Use Planning*, vol. 18, no. 333 (September 10, 1951); PEP, *Government Aid for the Social Sciences*, vol. 17, no. 323 (February 5, 1951), especially pp. 146–147.

21. Local and central authorities, too, may sooner or later be obliged to expand their own research activities. More applied rather than basic research can be anticipated. The ministry will want to develop techniques of analysis to perform its operating functions well, to improve its data collection, and to guide and check basic decisions. Less immediate problems might be assigned by contract to the universities or to research stations where more specialized staff may be available to deal with these tasks. Precedents for this already exist in the Board of Trade's financing of industrial location studies by the National Institute of Economic and Social Research. Local authorities and development corporations may not be able to maintain even small research staffs. But they might enlist the aid of nearby universities in analyzing and helping to solve some of their special problems.

ACKNOWLEDGMENTS

I was helped in many ways in writing this book. The initial inspiration for the study reaches back to the provocative seminar I attended at the University of Wisconsin in 1945 with Professor John M. Gaus, generally recognized as one of the great teachers, regionalists, and authorities on public administration in the United States. Since then, aided by two trips to Britain, I have been studying the evolution and administration of the British new towns policy. I have discussed aspects of this policy with responsible British civil servants in the various ministries, with the officials of the local authorities, with directors and staff of most of the new town development corporations, and with leading planners and specialists in fields related to planning in the British universities. I have also benefited from discussions with economists, political scientists, and sociologists on both sides of the Atlantic. I am grateful for their assistance and regret only that I do not have a more adequate token of my appreciation. I also take pleasure in thanking once again the United States Educational Commission in the United Kingdom for making possible a year in Britain as a senior lecturer at the University of Liverpool, coupled with favorable arrangements for research and travel.

I am especially obliged to Mr. Frederick Gibberd for providing and obtaining permission to reproduce photographs of aerial views and town details of Harlow. All of these photographs are under copyright either by Mr. Gibberd or the Harlow Development Corporation.

For prints of the other towns, I am indebted to a number of persons, especially Mr. A. C. Turner, General Manager, Crawley Development Corporation, Mr. H. Kellett Ablett, Chief Architect, Hemel Hempstead Development Corporation, Mr. Donald Reay, formerly Chief Architect and Planning Officer of the East Kilbride and later the Stevenage development corporations, Mr. D. M. H. Evans, Basildon Development Corporation (Chief Architect: N. Tweddell), Mr. G. A. Goldstraw, Chief Architect, Aycliffe Development Corporation, Mr. W. J. Scott, Chief Architect, Peterlee Development Corporation, Mr. P. Pinto, Chief Architect and Planning Officer, Glenrothes Development Corporation, Mr. L. G. Vincent, Chief Architect, Stevenage Development Corporation, Mr. Lionel Brett, formerly Chief Architect of the Hatfield Development Corporation, and Dame Evelyn Sharp, Permanent Undersecretary, Ministry of Housing and Local Government. I am also grateful to the above-mentioned development corporations for the cooperation of their staffs and for permission to reproduce photographs from their files. In addition, I owe thanks to Mr. Gordon Cullen, Miss W. G. Constable, and the *Architectural Review* for copies of photographs used in the July 1953 issue of the *Architectural Review*. The maps and plans of the various towns were drawn by Miss Ellen Dirba under my direction, following useful suggestions by Professor Kevin Lynch and Miss Muriel Cooper.

ACKNOWLEDGMENTS

Tables IV and V, prepared by Mr. J. J. Clarke, and used in his book *Local Government of the United Kingdom,* are reproduced with his kind permission and that of his publisher, Sir Isaac Pitman & Sons, Limited.

The text of the book has been peppered with the incisive criticisms of friends and associates, especially Professors Kevin Lynch, John T. Howard, and Burnham Kelly of the Massachusetts Institute of Technology Department of City and Regional Planning; Professor Leo Grebler, Institute of Urban Land Use and Housing Studies, Columbia University; Professor John M. Gaus, Department of Government, Harvard University; and two dissenting British students, David E. Crinion and Ivan D. Owen. Dean Pietro Belluschi and Professor Frederick J. Adams provided friendly encouragement and made available strategic stenographic assistance at critical periods. Catherine Bauer Wurster, Lewis Mumford, Frederick J. Osborn, and Professor Gordon Stephenson, by their brilliant advocacy of the new towns policy, furnished often unwittingly a constant challenge and foil for my thinking; and I acknowledge my debt to them, however much they may deplore my conclusions. Professor Reginald Isaacs, Chairman of the Department of City Planning and Landscape Architecture, Harvard University, who gave unforgettable encouragement in a difficult period, is responsible for the publication of this volume in the Harvard City Planning Series. I also owe an extraordinary debt to the unfailing friendship, counsel, and shrewd practical insights of Mr. Charles Abrams.

Miss Katherine MacNamara and Miss Caroline Shillaber were always helpful and gracious in tracking down references. The manuscript has also been substantially improved by the editorial suggestions and efficient technical assistance of the Harvard University Press. Miss Marjorie Bruchner and Miss Dulcie Jones bore well the burden of typing and retyping the manuscript.

It is impossible to record adequately the obligation to my wife for typing, editorial revisions, analysis of ideas, and sheer patience, sympathy, and fortitude.

The nature of the conclusions are such that probably no one but the author will want to accept full responsibility for them. This lugubrious responsibility I cheerfully assume in deference to the ancient rituals of the world of scholarship.

The editors of the following journals have kindly granted permission to incorporate here articles of my own that first appeared in their periodicals. Most of these articles have been substantially revised for use in this book. Chapter 3 first appeared as "Garden Cities and the Metropolis" in the *Journal of Land and Public Utility Economics* (now *Land Economics*), August 1945; Chapter 5 as "British New Town Development: Some Administrative Weaknesses" in the *Public Administration Review,* Summer 1953; Chapter 6 as "Some Problems of British New Towns" in *Land Economics,* November 1953; Chapter 8 as "England's Town Development Act, 1952; Part I: Background of the Act"; and Chapter 9 as "England's Town Development Act, 1952; Part II: Problems and Implications" in the *Journal of the American Institute of Planners,* Fall 1952 and Winter 1953, respectively; Appendix A under its present title, "The Achilles Heel of British Town Planning," in the *Town Planning Review,* April 1953.

ACKNOWLEDGMENTS

Finally, I wish to express my appreciation to the following authors and/or publishers for permission to quote from the books and publications listed below:

S. Anderson, *Winesburg, Ohio* (New York: The Modern Library, 1919). Used by permission of The Viking Press, copyright holder.

G. Cullen, "Prairie Planning in the New Towns," *Architectural Review*, vol. 114, no. 679 (July 1953).

M. P. Fogarty, *Town and Country Planning* (Hutchinson's University Library, 1948). Longmans, Green and Co., Inc., 55 Fifth Avenue, New York City 3, sole agent in the United States.

R. Grieve, "The Clyde Valley," *Town and Country Planning*, vol. XXIII, no. 125 (September 1954).

E. Howard, *Garden Cities of Tomorrow* (London: Faber and Faber, Limited, 1945).

W. G. Holford and M. Wright, *Corby New Town* (Corby: Corby Development Corp., 1952).

L. Mumford, "Old Forms for New Towns," *The New Yorker* (October 17, 1953).

H. Orlans, *Utopia Ltd.* (New Haven: Yale University Press, 1953). Published in Canada and the United Kingdom as *Stevenage, A Study of a New Town* (London: Routledge and Kegan Paul, Limited).

F. J. Osborn, *Town and Country Planning*, vol. XXIII, no. 119 (March 1954); and "Public Influences on Planning," *Town and Country Planning*, vol. XXIII, no. 133 (May 1955).

J. M. Richards, "Failure of the New Towns," *Architectural Review*, vol. 114, no. 679.

—— *The Castles on the Ground* (The Architectural Press, 1946).

P. Self, *The Planning of Industrial Location* (The University of London Press, 1953).

R. Stamp, "Old Towns for New," *Town and Country Planning*, vol. XXIII, no. 108 (April 1953).

LLOYD RODWIN

Cambridge, December 1955

Index

Abercrombie, Sir Patrick, 118, 131, 187
Abernethy, W. L., 146
Adams, F. J., 242
Adshead, Stanley D., 187
Agriculture, 16, 41, 91, 214
Agriculture and Fisheries, Ministry of, 58, 108, 166
Anderson, Sherwood, 35–36
Architectural Review, 109, 204
Aycliffe, *see* Newton Aycliffe

Barlow, Sir Montague, 17
Barlow Commission, 17–19, 23, 30, 65, 178, 211
Basildon, Essex, 44, 51, 77, 83, 107–10
Beacham, A., 152–153
Bellamy, Edward, 11
Bennett, Sir Thomas, 44, 98, 217, 224
Bevan, Aneurin, 146, 147, 158
Beveridge, Lord William, 44, 81
Birmingham, 27, 67, 153, 186, 233
Bishop Auckland, Durham, 124
Black, Robert B., 64
Bletchley, Buckinghamshire, 147
Block, G. D. M., 62, 83
Board of Trade, *see* Trade, Board of
Bogue, Donald J., 172
Bootle, Lancashire, 138
Borsodi, Ralph, 35
Bourneville, 39, 69
Bowlee, Lancashire, 138
Bracknell, Berkshire, 41, 44, 90, 116–17
Brett, Lionel, 88
Bronowski, J., 221
Brown, G. Sutton, 232, 233
Buckingham, J. S., 11

Carter, Sir Edgar Bonham, 30
Central Land Board, 44, 108
Chamberlain, Neville, 17, 19
Chamberlin, Edward, 172

Chambers, Theodore, 30
Churchill, Winston, 20, 23
Clarke, J. J., 203
Coal Board, *see* National Coal Board
Committee on Land Utilization in Rural Areas, *see* Scott Committee
Committee on the Qualifications of Planners, *see* Schuster Committee
Compensation and Betterment, Expert Committee on, 18–19
Compensation for property, 18–19, 20, 21, 25, 95–96, 107–108
Conservative Party government, 19–20, 21, 131
Corby, Northamptonshire, 41, 47, 51, 73, 85, 125–28
Costain, Richard R., 44, 112
Costs of new towns, *see* New towns
Crawley, Sussex, 40, 41, 44, 73, 77, 79, 82, 116–17; Report of Corporation, 73–75
Cripps, Sir Stafford, 97
Cullen, Gordon, 86–87
Cwmbran, Wales, 47, 51, 122–23

Dalton, Hugh, 124, 132, 231
Darlington, Durham, 124
Decentralization of industry and population, 3, 4, 18, 20, 21, 29–30, 65–68, 169–73, 176–78, 239. *See also* Industry; Population
Design of new towns, *see* New towns
Development Areas, 20, 59–60 (map), 82
Development corporations, 40–41, 47; administrative staffs of, 43–44; powers of, 42–43, 73; relations with other ministries and with local authorities, 40, 58–61, 63–66, 72–76, 89–92, 96, 112, 115, 126
Durham, University of, 190, 191

249